Werner Oswald
&
Jeremy Walton

BMW – The Complete Story
from 1928

BMW
The Complete Story
from 1928

Werner Oswald

&

Jeremy Walton

Foulis

Haynes

ISBN 0 85429 315 9

This edition first published in 1982, original edition in German "Alle BMW Automobile" first published in 1978 by Motorbuch Verlag, Stuttgart.

© Motorbuch Verlag & Haynes Publishing Group

A FOULIS Motoring Book

Published by:
Haynes Publishing Group
Sparkford, Yeovil, Somerset BA22 7JJ, England

Distributed in North America by:
Haynes Publications Inc.
861 Lawrence Drive, Newbury Park, California 91320 USA

Update & revision: Jeremy Walton
Translation: Virginia Hinke & Jeremy Walton
Editor: Rod Grainger
Jacket design: Carlo Demand
Photographs & line illustrations: Werner Oswald archives (223), BMW archives (72), Hans Jurgen Mertink archives (11), Erik Eckermann archives (5), Wolfgang Schmarbeck archive (3), Federal Archive (2). Photographs: Dr Paul Simsa (7), Max Hahn (3), Friedrich R. Wolf (2), Peter de Crousaz (1), Wolfgang Hecht (1), Joachim Wolfer (1), Joseph Herink (1), Erhard Zhorzel (1). Additional pictures from research by Jeremy Walton with the co-operation of BMW Munich and BMW (GB) Ltd.
Printed, in England, by: J.H. Haynes & Co. Ltd.

Contents

Dear readers,

There were over 200 individual car marques in the earlier German Republic, but only seven survive today in the Federal Republic. All seven marques give pleasure all over the world. Each one is an individual and is in harmony with the needs of a particular section of the car buying public.

BMW certainly has a strong identity. Enthusiasts speak highly of the marque's sporting image, but always with understanding. The BMW specialist likes to qualify such knowledge, but the layman can misunderstand. Either way, of course, the marketing of the 'sporty' car with the famous white and blue insignia is extraordinarily effective — that was how it was in the thirties and again in the sixties and seventies, bringing much prestige to the BMW name.

BMW began to build cars in 1928. From pre-Dixi days to the present, there are many interesting models that are worthy of reminiscence and which still live up to the legends they created in their own time.

The changing fortunes experienced by BMW over the years are recorded accurately and impartially by this book. For this purpose worthy support and assistance came to the author from Hans Fleischmann (BMW Archives), Peter Schneider (BMW Museum) and Klaus Bandow (BMW Press Department). Important supplementary information regarding Eisenach production, for this story was delivered by Klaus-Jurgen Mertink (Berlin) and Wolfgang Roediger (Erfurt). Some especially welcome pictures were forwarded by Erik Eckermann, Wolfgang Schmarbeck and Dr Paul Simsa. Everybody who sent their private photographs receives my heartful thanks. I have accepted, with pleasure, much useful advice and further photographic material for the pages of this book from other sources.

Ing. Werner Oswald
Postfach 126
8024 Deisenhofen bei Munchen.

It has been my pleasure to work on such a primarily factual work. I have tried — together with my Stuttgart-born co-translator Virginia Hinke and the *Collins German Dictionary* — to keep the spirit of the original 1978 book *Alle BMW Automobile 1928-1978* by Werner Oswald. Occasionally the sheer length of counterpart German expressions, or easier reading requirements, have meant departures from the literal translation. Introduction dates are for Germany, unless otherwise stated.

The addition of some material, particularly post August 1978 information; a look at what the Americans have been offered, and some additional photographic material from (mainly) British or German sources have been my contribution.

My compliments to Werner Oswald on his fine work, the account of BMW's diverse beginnings is the most detailed I have read: fascinating! Congratulations to BMW also for making such an interesting history possible. I hope we have maintained their standards ....

Jeremy Walton
Henley on Thames
Oxon

Dixi and still earlier:
The forerunners of the BMW

Bayerischen Motoren Werke (Bavarian Motor Works) was founded in 1916 and began building cars in 1928. Yet this tale goes much further back: as a special date one must memorise December 3, 1896, when a Bank consortium under the Chairmanship of Privy Councillor Heinrich Ehrhardt formed the *Fahrzeugfabrik Eisenach AG* (vehicle makers Eisenach) with a capital expenditure of 1.25 million Gold Marks. General Director of the newly formed Company Dr Ing e.h. Heinrich Ehrhardt (1840-1928) was a man full of ideas and a multi-talented inventor who previously when with the *Rhinemetall Konzern* (Rhine Metal Combine), had built up the second largest (after Krupp) armaments manufacture capacity in the German Empire. His factories in the Rhineland, Westphalia and Thuringia produced guns, armour plating, lots of other military requirements, plus some machine tools and various consumer goods.

Wartburg motor cars (1898-1903)

At the start, the new Eisenach company, under the management of Ehrhardt, obtained through the *Kaiserliche Militarverwaltung* (Imperial military administration) orders for over 1000 military vehicles of several kinds (munitions carriers, ambulances, field kitchens and gun carriages). These were reliably delivered, thus further orders were forthcoming, and the chance to branch out into other activities.

Other than the foregoing, they took up bicycle manufacture, namely of the "Mountain Bike" which had shaft transmission and two gear ratios. At this stage a motor vehicle was a pipe dream rather than a practical project because the military had not used them. Yet, unobserved, they began their own series of experiments with three and four-wheeled motor cars. Working from the ground up, little apparent success was promised. Therefore, on September 12, 1898, Privy Councillor

Ehrhardt formed the alliance for Germany with the French firm Decauville, who in 1897 had announced a very good and saleable *Voiturette* (small car). The next move for the Eisenach manufacturers saw them complete their chassis in France before they could become the fifth German manufacturers, following Daimler in Cannstatt, Benz in Mannheim, Durkopp in Bielefeld and Opel at Russelsheim, all of whom had already begun series production of motor cars. The "Wartburg-Kutchierwagen" (Wartburg coach-car), as it was nicknamed, provided for Eisenach until 1901 with its air-cooled, 500cc, motor of 3.5HP. Alternatively they offered 5HP with a water-cooled twin-cylinder engine of 750cc. The car had an entirely open, and unprotected, chain transmission (which lay under the driver's seat!), a rigid front axle, transverse, half-elliptic, springing and a handwheel control for the engine. Then 'bodywork' in the style of a high-sided wagon was the requirement, but one wouldn't like to use it today!

By 1899 the Company had already won 22 gold medals and first prizes for automotive achievements including racing the Wartburg car up to 60km/h and exhibiting at the first International Berlin Motor Show where they were the centre of attention having gained a considerable reputation. This reputation was especially good for overseas sales and, under the name "Cosmobile", the cars from Eisenach reached as far as America. Today there are still five of these pioneering Wartburgs in existence. They can be found in the Eisenach works museum, Prague's technical museum, and also in Oslo.

From 1901 to 1903 the Wartburg cars were built in various two cylinder, open transmission, forms. They were still made with a Decauville licensing agreement, but now with a front-mounted engine, shaft transmission, and an angled steering column, complete with steering links and steering wheel.

8

One of the first of the Wartburg "Coach Cars", or 'jalopies' as they have been nicknamed. This one is from 1889 and has the air-cooled, 500cc, 3.5HP, twin-cylinder engine. Throughout BMW history two cylinder engines have played an important role: it is the flat twin born in the twenties, that lives on today in the motorcycles ...

Rear view of the "Coach Car" displays the water-cooled twin-cylinder engine of 750cc and 5.0HP. The engine could be controlled, from the driver's seat, by the handwheel on the right-hand side of the car.

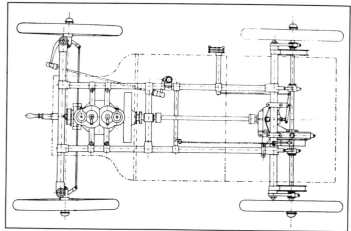

Top plan view of the Wartburg 1903 car shows the inline twin-cylinder engine, front mounted and using a shaft drive to power the rear wheels. Also shown is the simple steel frame, a basic ladder design, the links for the steering, and a dotted outline for coachwork.

Wartburg Tonneau dates back to 1902 and has a front mounted engine, starting handle and 'proper' steering system, with slightly angled column, in place of the vertical tiller-types seen elsewhere on the page. The 1.4 litre, twin-cylinder engine gave 8.5HP and was mated to a three speed gearbox. Wheelbase was 1758mm/69.2in, the weight 850kg/1870lb and the maximum speed between 35 and 40km/h (22 to 25mph).

The first big Wartburg appeared in 1902 with a 3.1-litre, 15HP, four cylinder engine. In racing car form it offered the sophistication of 22HP, a five-speed gearbox, 650kg/1430lbs kerb weight and a 120km/h (75mph) top speed. Frankfurt am Main, August 31, 1902, saw the car victorious at the International car race meeting.

Privy Councillor Heinrich Ehrhardt, with other shareholder colleagues, resigned his Chairmanship in 1903 and his position on the supervisory board. Taking with him the Decauville licensing agreement, he founded and ran, in Zella St. Blasien, his own marque "Ehrhardt" – which existed until 1924. *Fahrzeugfabrik Eisenach AG* were divorced from the *Rhinemetall-Konzern*, but construction of their own design of motor vehicles continued. About 250 Wartburg cars should have been delivered in the period 1889 to 1903.

Dixi: 1903 to 1925

The first Dixi, a name chosen for the Eisenach car a long time previously, was at the 1904 Frankfurt Motor Show. This initial Dixi was available first of all as a touring car, then as a coupe. It was also offered as a delivery wagon with a carrying capacity up to 12cwt. The car possessed a water-cooled, 2.8-litre, four-cylinder engine — the cylinders paired together and in double rows — and shaft drive. The gearchange mechanism was built into part of the back axle, the footbrake operated on the propshaft, and the handbrake on the wooden spoke rear wheels. By contemporary standards, engineer Willy Seck (1868-1955) had developed a really progressive car in the Dixi S 12. The Dixi's manufacturers were regarded as one of the most talented German car constructors; Seck already having made a name for Cudell and Scheibler. In

Dixi passenger car specification: 1904 to 1927

Type	Built	Total made	Cyls.	Bore x stroke	Capacity (cc)	Horsepower	Remarks
J 24	1904 – 1905	9	4	110 x 130 mm	4920	24	Chain drive
COS	1904 – 1906	120	1		1380	8,4	
S 6	1904 – 1905	18	2	95 x 100 mm	1408	10	Sidevalve
S 12, S 13, S 14	1904 – 1907	110	4	95 x 100 mm	2815	12 – 22	Sidevalve
S 15	1907 – 1910	75	4	100 x 110 mm	3430	28 – 32	Sidevalve
S 16	1911 – 1925	710	4	95 x 120 mm	3378	32 – 39	11550-15700 Marks
T 7	1904 – 1906	60	1	110 x 130 mm	1234	7,7	
T 12, T 13, T 14	1904 – 1907	60	2	110 x 130 mm	2468	12 – 17	
T 20	1911 – 1920	77	4	194 x 130 mm	4380	40 – 45	
T 24	1904 – 1905	5	4	110 x 130 mm	4920	24	Chaindrive
T 25	1906 – 1910	86	4	110 x 130 mm	4920	36 – 38	
					6502	45	Chaindrive
U 30, U 35	1907 – 1910	50	4	{ 117,5 x 150 mm			
				120 x 150 mm	6782	55	
				125 x 150 mm	7320	65	
UR 35	1908	2	4	125 x 150 mm	7320	75	Racing car?
R 8	1908 – 1916	650	4	74,5 x 90 mm	1558	14 – 16	
R 9	1912 – 1915	175	4	74,5 x 110 mm	1905	21	
R 10	1914 – 1923	500	4	74,5 x 120 mm	2078	22 – 24	8100-11200 Marks
R 12	1910 – 1921	553	4	87 x 110 mm	2598	22 – 30	10300-14300 Marks
R 16	1905 – 1908	3	4	105 x 130 mm	4470	20	
D 1(R 5)	1915 – 1923	404	4	65 x 98 mm	1292	5/14	
U 1(20)	1914 – 1924	78	4	100 x 165 mm	5148	55	17600-22000 Marks
G 1 – G 7	1921 – 1927	2300	4	70 x 102 mm	1559	18 – 30	G5 = Sports car
H 1	1925 – 1926	6	4	54 x 84 mm	763	12 – 15	Experimental
P 1	1925	4	6	70 x 102 mm	2341	36	Experimental
P 2	1926	4	6	80 x 118 mm	3518	60	Experimental
PP 3	1926 – 1927	16	4	70 x 102 mm	1559	24	6/24 PS with Puls gbx.
P 4 (Cyklon)	1927 – 1928	75	6	70 x 102 mm	2350	9/40	

Top left: the short but elevated roofline of the Dixi T 7 coupe came with an approximate 4200 Mark price in 1905.

Top right: even more civilised accommodation under an elegant roofline was promised by the Dixi S 14 Landaulet, which had a four-cylinder engine of 2.8-litres by 1907.

A touring car in 1910 meant just that, rather than the saloon car application of today. Here the open and spacious accommodation, with an air of gracious living, is offered within the 32HP Dixi S 15. Its four-cylinder, 3.4-litre, engine was said to allow 75km/h (47mph)

Again the air of a drawing room on wheels is apparent in the Dixi R 10 tourer. Built in 1914 this four door had a four-cylinder engine of 2.1-litres and a minimum 22HP rating.

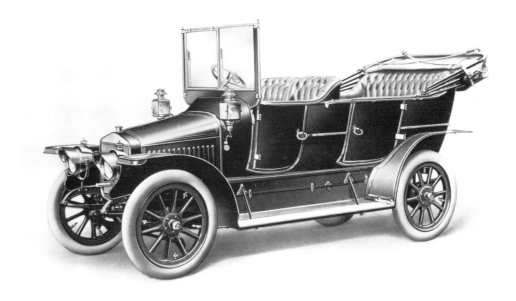

fact Seck stayed on only for a short time as Technical Director of the Eisenach factory. After him, the works were led by Obering. Out of the S 12 Schwarz made a succession of further derivatives, one of which continued until 1925.

In 1904, *Eisenach Fahrzeugfabrik* brought out the Ing. Trumann-designed small car as the Dixi T 7. This model had a one cylinder engine of 7.7HP and a two-speed gearbox. The price was 38,000 Marks and, from this basic concept, an extensive model series developed in the ensuing years.

One model developed from the T-range was the 1905 Type U 30, a very big luxury car with 6.5-litre, four-cylinder, engine. It still had chain drive which could not be replaced by shaft drive, as this form of transmission could not be trusted to take the extra power of the higher output engine. The U 30 was followed in 1908 by the Type U 35, which had an even larger 26/65 HP four-cylinder engine of 7.3-litres and, by now, shaft drive transmission was sufficiently trustworthy to be used. This offering was to be the biggest Dixi ever.

The first Dixi with a small four-cylinder engine, the 1.5-litre Type R 8 with 6/14HP, was brought to the market by the Eisenach factory in 1908. With this and the following R-types, the works first reached impressive production levels. This increased production allowed the construction of fabrication facilities containing manufacturing plant, so that by 1914 they had raised their potential production capacity from 300 vehicles per year to 400. Also, for the first time in their short history as an independent firm, they produced a commercial vehicle, the Eisenach lorry. From 1910 onwards, production was strengthened by building, as a priority, the four to five ton military models which had chain drive, derived from the system of the Type 30 luxury car. The Dixi lorry was to be available for over 16 years.

Dixi passenger car production: 1904 to 1929

	1899 – 1903	1904	1905	1906	1907	1908	1909	1910	1911	1912	1913	1914
Wartburg	c.265	c.250	1	1	2	9	2					
Dixi												
J 24	9	6	2	–	–	1						
COS	120	30	49	37	3	1						
S 6	18	6	12									
S 12, S 13, S 14	110	25	32	30	23							
S 15	75				8	22	20	25		7	37	32
S 16	710											
T 7	60	13	36	6	2	2	1					
T 12, T 13, T 14	60	1	24	18	10	1	–	2	12	14	14	19
T 20	77											
T 24	5	1	4									
T 25	86			17	30	24	12	3				
U 30, 35	50				16	16	7	11				
UR 35	2					2						
R 8	650					57	149	116	121	100	49	43
R 9	175									55	83	33
R 10	500											34
R 12	553							51	69	83	57	69
R 16	3		2	–	–	1						2
R 5 (D 1)	404											
U 1 (20)	78											
G 1-G 7	2300											
H 1	6											
P 1	4											
P 2	4											
PP 3	16											
P 4 (Cyklon)	75											
3/15 HP	9407											
	15822	c.250 83	162	110	101	129	189	208	206	259	240	232

In 1909 more potential production avenues had opened up. The company began building boat engines and, in the same year, development of an aeroplane engine was finalised. Other research projects in these early years included an electric Landau in 1905 and a steam-engined car, designed in 1910, but nothing came of these projects.

After the first World War, production of cars as opposed to military vehicles could be increased. In this period, as a marque mascot, they depicted, over the word "Dixi", a running, winged Centaur with a mane.

Of course, the company's main work, the production of the military vehicles simply stopped after the war creating serious financial problems. Rescue came in June 1921 in the form of a takeover by *Gothaer Waggonfabrik AG.* The Dixi Eisenach works continued to manufacture vehicles but, unfortunately, the *Gothaer Waggonfabrik* was not very much healthier than Eisenach as they too had manufactured for the military, but aeroplanes of various types rather than wheeled vehicles. Therefore, it was not long before control of the Dixi works passed into the hands of the notorious stock exchange speculator Jacob Schapiro (born Odessa, 1885) who was involved with NSU, Cyklon, Schebera, Hansa and Benz, bringing with him some of their influence and standards.

For a time, under the control of Schapiro, the Dixi works was fully employed. Yet, by 1926, they saw the beginnings of the standard market reaction to hard times – a subsidence in sales. In 1927 they gave up the manufacture of bicycles so that they could dedicate themselves to building small cars. This may have been the wrong policy for, despite extensive modernisation by Schapiro (by October 1, 1928, when BMW became involved), there were mounting debts for the Dixi works (who had some 1,200 employees) and BMW had to take all this on.

1915	1916	1917	1918	1919	1920	1921	1922	1923	1924	1925	1926	1927	1928/29
21	–	–	3	64	75	112	126	106	93	34			
–	–	–	–	12	6								
9	6												
4													
6	26	–	–	40	93	125	99	77					
7	–	–	–	77	80	60							
2	1	–	–	53	99	110	92	47					
–	–	–	–	2	4	8	8	25	29				
						10	132	232	498	823	520	85	
										6			
										4			
											4		
											1	15	
													75
												142	9265
49	33	–	3	248	357	425	457	487	620	867	525	242	9340

The biggest Dixi that had existed until this time was the Type U 35. Here we see it as a luxury touring limousine, complete with splendid bulb horn (to clear the peasantry?), and ornate coach lamps that used acetylene and candle lighting. Built in 1910, the top speed was 85km/h (53mph).

A much beloved middle class car of the period, the Dixi R 12 is seen here as a double Phaeton with four door bodywork. The chassis alone cost 7500 Marks.

14

FAHRZEUGFABRIK EISENACH

This Eisenach factory advertisement comes from January 1919. This postwar period saw the earlier Dixi models characterised by the pointed radiator and flattened nose.

The Dixi S 16 was a heavy touring car with a 3.4-litre engine of four-cylinders. This 1922 flat radiator example was built with the owner who hated to be in the dark as a priority, judging by the installation of five lamps at various locations!

Dixi 6/18 and 6/24HP (1921 to 1928)

Until 1924/25 the Dixi works built even more of the original pre-World War 1 types. These included the difficult to sell 5/14HP (D 1); the 8/24HP (R 10); the 13/39HP (S 16) and finally the 20/55HP (U 1), which shared the engine of the lorries being built at the time. These vehicles were tried with various fashionable body styles to increase their appeal, but outdated mechanical specification and moderate performance limited their sales. Thus it was necessary to produce a successor — the G type.

Type G 1 appeared in 1921 with a 1.6-litre engine and 6/18HP, however it was not long before the 1923 Type G 2 of 6/24HP was originated from this forebear. Considerable and lavish planning went into this car (from Technical Director Leonhard C. Grass), and it acquitted itself well in terms of sportiness, reliability and economy during everyday use. For these reasons, in spite of relatively high prices, the Dixi found excellent approval from customers. For motor sport the G 5 held many possibilities with 30 to 36HP available: two of these cars were constructed as single-seater racers! The popularity, appearance and sporting results of the Dixis were all very useful when the time came to sell 'standard' cars: in fact, there was almost no other choice for the sporting motorist ...

At Frankfurt Motor Show in Autumn 1923, the Dixi works exhibited a streamlined G 1 designed by Paul Jaray. Of the progress shown in "Walfisch" (Whale), special emphasis was laid upon the self-changing planetary gear gearbox, installed as a credit to the work and invention of engineer Erich Friedrich Puls. This polished light blue car was greatly admired and nearly every newspaper printed its picture but, unfortunately, no one wanted to buy it, so only the one prototype was made.

The six-cylinder Type P 1 originated from the addition of two more cylinders to the G engine, giving a capacity of 2341cc but, because the performance of this unit was not satisfactory the factory then developed a 13/60HP six-cylinder engine. This 3.5-litre unit, with seven crankshaft bearings, reached peak output at 2500rpm. Prototypes, four of them, were built to this specification and from these one car was constructed as a luxury six-seater limousine. The factory had hoped for acclaim of

The Dixi 6/24HP had the earlier 1568cc engine of the then usual long stroke bias (70 by 102mm), but this was persuaded to yield 24 bhp at 2200rpm rather than 18 horsepower of Dixi 6/18. This is a taxicab Landaulet model of the kind made between 1923 and 1928.

	Dixi 6/18 HP Type G 1 1921-23	Dixi 6/24 HP Type G 2 1923-28
Motor		
Cylinders	4 inline	4 inline
Bore x stroke	70 x 102mm	70 x 102mm
Capacity	1568cc	1568cc
Power	18bhp @ 2000rpm	24bhp @ 2200rpm
Compression	–	5.2:1
Carburettor	1 Dixi spray type	1 sidedraught Zenith
Valves	Side standing	Side standing
Crankshaft bearings	Side camshaft with chain drive	Side camshaft with chain drive
Cooling	3	3
Lubrication	Thermosyphon	Thermosyphon
Battery	Pressure fed	Pressure fed
	12 volt	12 volt
Transmission		
Clutch	Rear wheel drive	Rear wheel drive
Gear selection	Cone	Cone
Gearbox	Lever, outside right	Lever, inside right
Gear ratios	4-speed	4-speed
	1st, 4.37	1st, 4.305
	2nd, 2.64	2nd, 2.706
	3rd, 1.59	3rd, 1.631
	4th, 1.00	4th, 1.00
	Optional: semi-automatic	Optional: semi-automatic
	Puls planetary box, pre-selection	Puls planetary box, pre-selection
	from column linkage. 1st, 3.55;	from column linkage. 1st, 3.55;
	2nd, 2.16; 3rd, 1.00	2nd, 2.16; 3rd, 1.00
Final drive ratio	4.50	4.50
Chassis		
Front suspension	Pressed steel frame	Pressed steel frame
Rear suspension	Rigid axle, half springs	Rigid axle, half springs
Steering	Rigid axle, outrigger half springs	Rigid axle, outrigger half springs
Foot brakes	Tiller	Tiller
	Mechanical, driveshaft outside shoes	Mechanical, driveshaft outside shoes
		From 1925:
		Four wheel mechanical, internal
		brake shoes
Handbrake	Mechanical, rear wheels	Mechanical, rear wheels
General data		
Wheelbase	2840mm	2840mm
Track front/rear	1150mm both	To 1925: 1150mm F & R. From
		1925: 1240mm/1226mm
Overall dimensions (Length x width x		
height)	–	4200 x 1500 x 1780mm
Wheels	Wire, spoked	Wire spoked
Tyres	710 x 100mm	To: 1925:760 x 100mm. From
		1925: 30.5.25 low pressure
Chassis weight	630kg	860kg
Kerb weight	Phaeton, 900kg	Phaeton, 1150kg
		Limousine, 1280kg
Max permissible, total weight	Phaeton, 1380kg	Phaeton, 1450kg
		Limousine, 1580kg
Top speed	40mph	47mph
Litres per 100km	9 (31.3mpg)	10 (28.1mpg)
Fuel tank	? (in engine bay)	45 litres (in back)

this model at the 1926 Berlin Motor Show, but there was little serious interest from the public. This heavy (1700kg) vehicle was not very convincing in its guise of a good quality machine and offered a maximum speed of only 85km/h (53mph). Also not destined to reach serious production was an even larger 5.8-litre prototype of 23/70HP.

Despite these problems, some 2300 G Types *were* built *and* sold between 1921 and 1928.

From the original G 1 series of 1921, this Dixi 6/18HP poses in the snow, displaying wire wheels and rear doors designed with decent clearance for formal headgear.

From the 1924 G 2 series, a 24HP Dixi 6/24 Phaeton. Here in a sedate summer parkland setting. The G 2's maximum speed, slightly under 50mph, would almost allow the young lady's open air headgear to remain firmly in place!

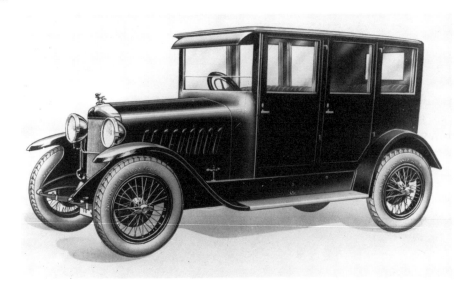

A few years on, but still from the five year Dixi G 2 production run, a Dixi 6/24 in four door limousine coachwork that dates from 1926.

Conceived by Paul Jaray this extraordinary streamliner attracted plenty of publicity, but no buyers. Underneath this Glaser-executed two door body was the mechanical running gear of a 1923 Dixi 6/18 of the G 1 series. Detailed even down to the use of wheel trims for reduced drag at speed (a feature to be found in the 1981 BMW 5-series, so they had the right idea), the streamliner remained in prototype form only.

Another prototype, but this time from 1926, was the technically interesting Dixi Type P 2. This utilised a 3½-litre engine (13/60HP) which added two cylinders on to the well proven G-series four: only four examples were constructed.

Dixi 9/40HP (1928)

The Cyklon motor factory in Mylau-Vogtland was well known for its early work in Berlin, where they manufactured the Cyklonette three wheel saloon. Cyklon was taken over, in 1922, by Jacob Schapiro and an immediate arrangement was made so that control passed, through him, to the *Gothaer Waggonfabrik AG:* a company that had acquired Schapiro's interests at Dixi in 1921.

Cyklon had made the chassis frames for the small Schebera cars for years, but these models were selling badly. So Cyklon decided to bring out an entirely new car, manufactured under their own name. It arrived in

the autumn of 1927 as the Cyklon 9/40HP. Designed by Director, Dr Eisner, the car made a favourable impression in both style and technical content.

The Dixi factory urgently needed a modern follow-up to the 6/24 model and this was achieved by adopting a suitable sales programme using the Cyklon 9/40HP. The assembled final result of this amalgamation was primarily manufactured by *Gothaer Waggonfabrik,* but some small parts came from Eisenach. Even though this, the cheapest Six on the German market, was a good car, it found only a moderate sales success. Altogether, despite the original optimistic estimates, not even 1000 such cars were delivered. Like the Adler Standard 6, these 'Cyklon' cars had bodies from Ambi-Budd in

An Ambi-Budd body again, but this time a six window, four door, limousine of 1928 clothes the Dixi 9/40 series.

The chunky appearance of the Dixi 9/40HP series was supplied, in the case of this 1928 model, by Ambi-Budd's open tourer, four door, coachwork.

Also in 1928, Karmann supplied this two door, two window cabriolet for the Dixi 9/40.

saloon and open tourer form. There was also a cabriolet and a roadster by Karmann.

After the sale of the Dixi factory to BMW in 1928, these six-cylinder cars were still offered by the Cyklon factory. However, there was really little point in this because of the deficiences of the dealer organisation. At the end of 1929 Cyklon announced another, smaller, 1.8-litre six-cylinder, but no more than two were built. In 1931 the Cyklon firm expired.

Dixi 3/15HP (1927-1929)

During the middle twenties it was not only the three large cars developed by Dixi which did not make production. There was also a small one, the 1925/6 Type H 1 "Diana" which had three seats and a 3/13HP engine of 763cc. Because of its complicated specification this model was not suitable for manufacture as an attractive and price-conscious production series.

This development work was carried out while there was a shortage of time and money — a bank credit for the necessary production changes involved large sums of money: cash that had to be found quickly. Therefore they decided not to handle the development of a small car themselves. Schapiro purchased secondhand, from the largest car manufacturers in England, a licence to build the Austin Seven. Manufactured in UK since 1922, it had proved the best and most popular small car of that period.

At the beginning of 1927 the Dixi works were allowed 100 original Austins, which came to Germany by rail. From April these cars, with some detail changes (but retaining right-hand drive) were sold as Dixi models. For the German production version all the drawings and final production documents had to be translated to metric measurement very quickly. Important modifications were necessary like left-hand drive and a battery-powered starter instead of magneto ignition. Main features retained included the robust, water-cooled,

	Cyklon 9/40HP Dixi 9/40HP 1927–29	Dixi 3/15HP Type DA1 1927–29
Motor		
Cylinders	6 inline	4 inline
Bore x stroke	70 x 102mm	56 x 76mm
Capacity	2350 (Steuer, 2339)cc	748.5 (Steuer, 743) cc
Power	40bhp @ 3200rpm	15bhp @ 3000rpm
Compression	5:1	5.6:1
Carburation	1, sidedraught Zenith 26 K	1, sidedraught Zenith 22K or Solex
Valves	Sidevalve Camshaft drive, Novotext spur gears	Sidevalve Camshaft drive, cast spur gear wheels
Crankshaft bearings	3	2
Cooling	Thermosyphon	Thermosyphon, 5-litres water
Lubrication	Combination: pressure and submerged, 8-litres oil	Pressure, 2.5-litres of oil
Battery	6v. 125 ah	6v. 45 ah
Generator	Underfloor, left rear	Under right front seat 60 Watt
Transmission		
Clutch	Rear wheel drive	Rear wheel drive
Gearchange	Single disc, dry	Single disc, dry
Gearbox	Lever, floor mounted	Lever, floor mounted
Synchromesh	3-speed	3-speed
Ratios	None	None
	1st, 3.55	1st, 3.25
	2nd, 1.87	2nd, 1.82
	3rd, 1.00	3rd, 1.00
Final drive ratio	5.50	4.90
Chassis		
Front suspension	U-profile pressed steel frame	U-profile frame
Rear suspension	Rigid, half springs	Rigid, 1 transverse spring
Steering	Rigid, underslung half springs	Rigid, outrigger quarter springs
Foot brakes	Worm, LHD	Worm, LHD
	Mechanical (linkage), drums, 4 wheel. Diam. 350mm; width, 40mm	Mechanical (cable), to rear wheels only
Handbrake	Mechanical linkage, rear wheels	Mechanical, cable, front wheels
General data		
Wheelbase	2950mm	1905mm
Track (front/rear)	1376mm, both	1000/1030mm
Overall dimensions (Length, width, height)	4350 x 1650 x 1780mm	2800 x 1170 x 1625mm
Wheels	Disc	Wire, spoke
Rims	For beaded edge tyres	Straight edge for low pressure tyres
Tyres	Initially 30 x 5.77in balloon then 775 x 145 low pressure	26 x 3.50in low pressure
Chassis weight	900kg	280kg
Vehicle weight	Tourer, 1200kg Saloon, 1300kg	Tourer, 440kg
Max permissible total weight	Tourer, 1650kg Saloon, 1750kg	Tourer, 700kg
Top speed	56mph	47mph
Litres per 100km	15 (18.79mpg)	6 (46.99mpg)
Fuel tank	50 litre, rear	20 litre, engine bay

engine of 750cc with its quiet running characteristics, the gearbox and the split propshaft, the really adventurous brakes, the refined but simple chassis and a top speed that did not exceed 75km/h (47mph).

Eisenach production of the Dixi 3/15HP Type DA 1 (Dixi Austin or *Deutsche Ausfuhrung,* standing for German Workmanship) began in December 1927, sales starting in January 1928. The original bodywork was also made in Eisenach. After the BMW takeover, production of the 3/15HP Dixi Type DA 1 was allowed to continue for approximately half a year. Then, in July 1929, the 3/15HP BMW Type DA 2 was announced.

Altogether 9307 examples of the Type DA 1 were made – more than all the earlier Dixi models put together! Though the small Dixi 3/15 was the last to carry the Dixi insignia, it was also their most famous model. Still, after more than 50 years, there are numerous examples running.

A Dixi 3/15 of 1928-29, Type DA 1 series, in two-seater open body form.

A two-seater coupe Dixi 3/15 (Type DA 1) of the same period.

A 3/4-seater tourer of 1927-29 built on Type DA 1 Dixi 3/15HP running gear.

Owner Klaus-Jurgen Mertink's Dixi 3/15 (DA 1 series) with 3/4-seater saloon coachwork could be found in Berlin-Kaulsdorf.

Cabriolet two-seater Dixi 3/15 (Type DA 1) from 1929 was specially built by a Gotha coachworks.

The story of the Bavarian Motor Works to 1945 and the BMW car from Eisenach

BMW, the Bavarian Motor Works *(Bayerischen Motoren Werke)* owed thanks for their existence, and their quickly acquired marque reputation, essentially to three men. Today their names are readily remembered only by older enthusiasts. There were two Austrians and one Swabian (the district including Stuttgart in West Germany) namely: Commercial Councillor Camillo Castiglioni; the General Director Franz Joseph Popp (1896-1954) and the Director Dr Engineer Max Friz (1883-1966).

As a young engineer graduate, the Viennese-born Popp went to work at the AEG-Union in his home town. At the outbreak of the 1914 war, they wanted to take on the building of aero engines but, before they could do this, they needed the authorization of Austro-Daimler. Therefore the firm sent Popp to study the building of such aero engines at Daimler, Benz and NAG. Their probe into such manufacture failed owing to deficiences in their machine tool capabilities.

Then Popp, now a reserve officer in the Austro-Hungarian Navy, disillusioned by the failure to find a suitable aero engine to build at AEG, grabbed the chance of a licence to build the 350HP Austro-Daimler at Rapp Motor Works in Munich.

This company had prepared and built aero engines since 1913, although not with the traditional quality of Prussian or Bavarian workmanship. Yet its standards sufficed for the Austrian military administration, so they were given work by the Austrian Navy. Therefore the management agreed with Popp's suggestion and sent him as Delivery Engineer of the Imperial Navy to Munich; there to supervise the building of 224 Austro-Daimler 350HP engines. On this assignment it was not long before Popp saw that neither the commercial or technical management of the factory, nor its workmanship, was really competent for the task in hand.

Popp's next step concerned his wish to provide employment for the experienced designer Max Friz. He founded, with help from Trieste banker Camillo Castiglioni, a new company to be controlled by Austro-Daimler from July 20, 1916. Out of the aeroplane factory *Gustav Rau GmbH* and the *Rapp Motorenwerken GmbH* came the *Bayerische Motorenwerke GmbH,* the factory managed by Popp as Rapp moved out.

It became obvious that the commission for engines for the Kaiser's Navy was not sufficient, because the Bavarian war ministry people had freely made available manpower, materials and precision tools. Therefore the Prussian military administration must be won as customers, to keep the extra equipment and manpower busy.

Before Max Friz came to Rapp he was very actively involved with the Daimler engine company. There he was primarily concerned with the design of the first serviceable military aeroplane engines. In much the same role, he had worked on the engine of the triumphant Mercedes racing cars, an example of which had won the French Grand Prix in 1914. Friz left the company because they showed no interest in his own high flying engine and ignored his request for a 50 Mark pay rise. Friz was able to realise his design in Munich; despite using mass production building techniques his unit considerably bettered the proven benchmark of the 160HP Mercedes engine. This was enough to ensure that in 1917, work began to come from the Prussian military administration – with a first order for over 200 engines!

Consider this: On May 20, 1917 they started design of the BMW 111a. By September 17, 1917, the first engine was readied and ran test bed trials without any incidents. Early in November flying trials started and were so satisfactory that an order for 2000 engines was raised.

Because the means of the existing company were not sufficient to carry out such an extensive piece of business, a new joint stock company was formed. This happened on August 13, 1918, with capitalisation of 12 Million Marks. The first board of directors for the subtly renamed *"Bayerischen Motoren Werke AG"* comprised the following: Director Dr H. Chr. Dietrich (Bayer. Vereinsbank, Munich), Chairman; Commercial Councillor Camillo Castiglioni (Vienna Bank organisation); General Director Fritz Neumeyer (Zundapp, Nurnberg); Dr Hjalmer Schacht (National German Bank, Berlin); General Director Wiedmann (Bayer. Mortgage & Change Bank, Munich); Commerce Councillor Josef Bohm (Bayer. Commercial-bank, Munich); Director Paul Goldstein (General Deposit Bank, Vienna); Captain Dr Joseph (Inspector, Flying Corps, Berlin). As General Director, Chief Engineer Franz Joseph Popp was appointed, while Chief Designer remained Max Friz. On the edge of Munich Airport's Oberweisenfeld, just outside the city, the completion and expansion of newly-built factories was taking place. These were already partly built when the aero-engine orders were received. Other sites built BMW aero engines under licence, including the Deutz gas engine factory and Opel at Russelsheim.

The end of war in 1918 abruptly curtailed the unprecedented expansion of the young firm. In just two years of war the previously unimportant, and vulnerable to bankruptcy, Rapp engine works had become one of the largest aero engine factories, employing 3,500. Most of these employees were building the production series of old engine designs, as only some 70 of the 2000 BWM 111a engines ordered were actually delivered. After the war, no aero engines were allowed to be made in Germany, so Max Friz designed engines for lorries, boats, stationary and auxiliary motors: all sold under the name of "Bayern Motor". A flat twin engine used the name "Victoria".

In their bid to diversify, it was not long before the most important business of the works became the fabrication of the Knorr air brakes for railway carriages. Soon the Kunze-Knorr brake company took over all the factories of BMW at Moosacher Street, calling their new offspring the "South German Brake Company" *(Suddeutsche Bremsen AG)*. Castiglioni bought the *"Bayerischen Motoren Werke"* company name which included the engine building rights, personnel, designs and material. All of this was acquired by Castiglioni fairly easily because it was of little use to Knorr AG.

Castiglioni next purchased the Lerchenauer Street site and one right next door to the closed Bavarian Aeroplane Works — founded in 1915 with an entry in the companies register on March 7, 1916. This date also counted as that of the official foundation of *Bayerischen Motoren Werke AG*. The re-purchased engine building operation took the factory space previously used in the manufacture of aero engines. One of the prime objectives of the 'new' Bavarian Motor Works was to initiate construction of one of the Max Friz-designed motorcycles. This plan owed much to the fact that the designer was unhappy about the use of his Boxer engines in the rather nasty Helios bikes! In 1923 the exciting BMW R 32 motorcycle with double tube frame, shaft transmission and the air-cooled Boxer engine design of two cylinders and 500cc was launched. Thus began the glorious story of the BMW motorcycle ...

In 1924, the factory resumed rebuilding aero engines.

The next goal of General Director Popp was to undertake building a complete small car, so BMW participated in the development of an unconventional car that the *Schwabischen Hutte Werke AG*, of Boblingen, had

BMW turnover & workforce: 1926 to 1942		
	Turnover	Workforce
1926	9 Mill. RM	1 000
1927	17 Mill. RM	1 500
1928	27 Mill. RM	2 600
1929	34 Mill. RM	3 800
1930	36 Mill. RM	3 100
1931	27 Mill. RM	2 900
1932	19 Mill. RM	2 800
1933	32 Mill. RM	4 700
1934	82 Mill. RM	12 500
1935	128 Mill. RM	11 100
1936		
1937	143 Mill. RM	14 000
1938	180 Mill. RM	18 600
1939	275 Mill. RM	26 900
1940	287 Mill. RM	30 000
1941	385 Mill. RM	35 400
1942	560 Mill. RM	47 300

originally built to the design of Dipl-Eng Wunibald Kamm. This car wore the "SHW" insignia and had a Boxer engine layout for its two cylinders and a capacity of 1020cc. Rated at 4/20HP, this advanced baby car also featured front-wheel-drive, self supporting (unitary style) bodywork and coil springs for each individually sprung wheel. This project used up much of Popp's time, but remained full of problems. Three prototype SHW cars ran, but they never developed into serious production models. Finally, the men from Munich disentangled themselves from such a risky design — a decision that was certainly to prove to their advantage.

The BMW company was highly in debt when the opportunity — which they wanted very much indeed — arose to acquire the Dixi works. Faster commercial success was promised if they could start to build their own car. After the level of share capital in the Bavarian Motor Works had been raised from 10 million Reich Marks to 16 million, BMW was able to buy the Dixi works on November 16, 1928. The sale price of 10 million RM was a massive over-valuation of the Dixi works because, on takeover, it was found that Dixi's debts amounted to 7.8 million RM. Nevertheless with effect from October 1, 1928, the Dixi factory, Eisenach, became a subsidiary of *Bayerische Motoren Werke AG,* Munich.

Essentially the transaction was carried out by Camillo Castiglioni. However, his influence dwindled rapidly in the new organisation. His effective rival was Dr h.c. Emil Georg von Stauss, director of the German Bank (Berlin). Stauss had already been with Daimler-Benz since 1927, and was also on the board of directors at Bavarian Motor Works. Therefore Stauss looked at Castiglioni's participation in BMW with more than just passing interest. Stauss formed a consortium under the leadership of the German and Danat Banks to acquire Castiglioni's 5 million RM shareholding in BMW, and his 3.4 million holding in Daimler-Benz. Castiglioni abdicated his shares in October 1929 and resigned from the BMW board of directors. His relinquishment of responsibility meant that the Eisenach works limited itself entirely to BMW's interests.

After the takeover in Eisenach, production and further development of the 3/15HP cars became their rather limited programme. The Munich board of directors made the Eisenach works their responsibility, though director Leonard Grass stayed on as factory manager. (Grass had already been responsible for drawing the design of the 6/24 Dixi, and the company's drawing office continued to carry out much of 'his' work). Obviously the directors felt that the competence of director Max Friz was diminishing. For a couple of years Friz sat it out in the Munich design office, working solely for the Eisenach car factory.

By March 1, 1932, BMW had, prematurely, got out of the licence contract with Austin and brought out their own 3/20 model, the bodywork of which was completed in Sindelfingen's Daimler-Benz AG factory. Unfortunately this car re-inforced the view that Max Friz possessed no feeling for car techniques (as also already shown by the unlucky modifications to the 3/15HP) — even though he was a qualified car and motorcycle designer. So it proved a genuine blessing for BMW that the Eisenach design office had worked on other designs, under their own initiative in the absence of Friz. In 1933, the small Eisenach-designed BMW 303, a 1.2-litre, 30HP, six-cylinder car was launched. This smartly designed small car immediately won everyone's appreciation.

Production of the BMW 303 was already underway in the summer of 1933, when Dipl Eng Fritz Fiedler (previously with Stoewer and then Horch), came to the Eisenach car building works as head designer. He was to strongly influence the styling and technical content of BMW cars until 1964.

In September 1937 Georg Ostermayer (formerly at Auto Union and Röhr) succeeded director Leonard Grass as manager of the Eisenach factories.

The new six-cylinder design may have been small but nevertheless it was a most prestigious saloon car model in direct competition with those of Daimler-Benz. BMW's collaboration with Daimler-Benz to build cars lasted only a short period because, owing to a swing in the market, Daimler-Benz were once more able to use fully the production facilities of their works. Anyway the 'Stuttgarters' and 'Muncheners' were to remain in friendly contact because, well before all others, they considered the interesting possibilities of effectively fencing off for themselves the construction of aero engines. In fact, Dr Wilhelm Kissel (Daimler-Benz AG) was to stay on the BMW board of directors until his death in 1942.

During the difficult crisis years of 1930-32, BMW was able to keep its head above water. Up-to-date market appeal came from their motorcycles and small cars, but losses were made at this time even if they were only a fraction of the debts discovered upon the takeover of Dixi. From 1933 onwards a quick production growth was once more provided by aero engines. In 1933, of the firm's 4,700 employees, only 2,400 worked building cars. By 1935 a new aero engine factory in Eisenach was ready to commence deliveries. Management of this enterprise was undertaken by Max Friz. As a further branch to BMW's manufacturing activities in Eisenach, from 1936, they began the manufacture of military apparatus: infantry and anti-tank guns, smoke cannister throwers and infantry carriers. In 1939 the *Brandenburgischen Motorenwerke GmbH* (Bramo) was purchased by BMW.

So, in the thirties, BMW's car building nearly became a subsidiary operation, but they still carried a substantial and good reputation for the high quality of the cars they produced. From the 1.2-litre, six-cylinder, BMW 303 there evolved a 1.5-litre and, in 1935, a 1.9-litre was born. Also the 2-litre BMW 326 and the 80HP BMW 328 came into being from the same origins, and were to become the most popular and successful sports cars of their time. Eventually, shortly before the second world war, a 3.5-litre model appeared, of which no more than 1000 could be completed before hostilities began.

In 1941 car constructors Stoewer, Hanomag and BMW were asked by the military weapons department to build an unproven 2-litre land car (to fulfil a Jeep role) for front line service. Until 1944 this armed forces heavy design stayed in production together with the BMW R 75 sidecar combination.

In September 1942 General Director Popp changed the Bavarian Motor Works board of directors. Dipl-Eng Fritz

Chassis numbers of Dixi & BMW cars: 1927 to 1941

Model	Year	Chassis numbers	Model	Year	Chassis numbers
Dixi 3/15 HP (DA 1)	1927	1001–1042	BMW 329	1936/37	86001–87179
	1928	1043–7785			
	1929	7786–10308	BMW 320 (1911cc)	1937	90001–90642
BMW 3/15 HP (DA 2)	1929	10309–15658	BMW 320 (1971cc)	1937	90643–91539
	1930	15659–19908		1938	91540–94185
	1930	20009–21008	BMW 321	1939	94186–97246
	1930	21059–22450		1940/41	97247–97882
	1931	22451–22597	BMW 326	1936	75001–77069
BMW Wartburg (DA 3)	1930	19909–20008		1937	77070–82099
	1930	21009–21058		1938	82100–85000
BMW 3/15 HP (DA 4)	1931	22598–25776		1938	110001–111867
	1932	25777–26256		1939	111868–114999
BMW 3/20 HP (AM1, AM3)	1932/33	30001–32500		1940/41	115000–115894
BMW 3/20 HP (AM4)	1933/34	32501–37215	BMW 327 (55 HP)	1937	73001–73014
BMW 303	1933	45000–46300		1938	73015–73761
	1934	46301–47300		1939	73762–74130
BMW 315 and 315/1	1934	47301–50690		1940	74131–74200
	1935	50691–52000		1940/41	87201–87376
	1935	66001–68395	BMW 327/28 (80 HP)	1938	74201–74339
	1936	68396–70785		1939	74340–74755
	1937	70786–71065		1940	74756–74770
BMW 309	1934	60001–63658	BMW 328	1937	85001–85173
	1935	63659–65538		1938	85174–85329
	1936	65539–66000		1939	85330–85464
BMW 319 and 319/1	1935	53001–56095	BMW 335	1936	100001
	1935	56201–56423		1938	100002–100004
	1936	56424–59466		1939	100005–100305
	1937	59467–59703		1940	100306–100390
				1941	100391–100410

Hille, who transferred in 1935 from Bramo to BMW, became the new chairman of the board. Popp died during 1954 at the age of 68, in Stuttgart.

The Eisenach factory remained undamaged by war and when the fighting action ceased, the Americans were in occupation of Thuringen. In June 1945 they handed over the Eisenach land and works to the Soviets, by which time the plundering and devastation of the Red Army had already ceased. For years the BMW works remained under the control of the Russian occupiers. The parent organisation became the Soviet AG, later a state organisation called *"Awtovelo"* (commonly called "Autovelo" in the West) materialised. Because they enjoyed a priority in the allocation of materials, considerable production levels were achieved again very quickly. But it would be June 1952 before these factories came into German possession again, and then as a declared "People's Works".

From October 1945 automobile building began again. They started with the BMW 321 which they supplied for some years, followed by a modest number of BMW 327s. The 321 was finally supplanted by the Type 326, from which came the EMW *(Eisenacher Motoren Werke)* 340. Production of this and 327 carried on until 1955, when the authorities wanted to use the full production facilities at the works for the construction of the DKW derivative, the IFA F9. This had first been transferred to Eisenach production in July 1953.

Even in 1978 the *Eisenacher Motoren Werke* were the second largest automobile makers of the *DDR* (East Germany), their Wartburg saloon cars having three-cylinder, two-stroke, engines and front wheel drive. But the best of the popular BMW tradition died with the BMW/EMW 340 when production ceased in 1955. These later Eisenach designs were based on BMW running gear, but often sported rather crude imitations of American-styled bodies!

As *Bayerische Motoren Werke AG* struggled to get back into production in the American-occupied Munich zone, they were displeased at the Eastern attempts to sell their designs as genuine BMWs. On October 11, 1949, their official subsidiary in Eisenach was declared dissolved. Henceforth the name and insignia "BMW" should appear only on the Munich cars, but Autovelo still used both until the end of 1951 in a piece of curious manipulation aimed at Western export markets. For a period, pre-Wartburg, they used an adapted BMW symbol (the blue portions changed to red!): the problem was eased when they were renamed *Eisenacher Motoren Werke* during 1952.

BMW cars production: 1929 to 1941

	3/15 HP	3/20 HP	303	309	315	319	329
1929	5350						
1930	6792						
1931	3326						
1932	480	2406					
1933		4453	1386				
1934		356	914	3658	3390	4	
1935				1880	3705	3139	
1936				462	2390	3265	621
1937					280	238	558
Total	15948	7215	2300	6000	9765	6646	1179

	320	321	326	327	327/328	328	335
1936	7		2098			3	1
1937	1518		4939	14		171	
1938	2660	55	4705	746	132	164	3
1939		3073	3313	370	427	126	301
1940		490	776	140	10		85
1941		79	118	36			20
Total	4185	3697	15949	1306	569	464	410

BMW 3/15HP (1929-1932)

For a while longer after the purchase of the Eisenach factories, BMW built the small Dixi 3/15HP, Type DA 1. They simply replaced the oval radiator badge with three-edged Dixi insignia, though there are some surviving examples with BMW *and* three-edged badges. By mid-April 1929, prices of the ordinary touring cars were 2,200 RM, or 2,500 RM downward for the open two seaters. Alternatively it was possible to pay by hire purchase in 24 instalments from 93 to 107 RM. The last of the original Dixis were sold in 1930 for 1,750 RM.

In July 1929 the Dixi 3/15HP (Type DA 1) was superseded by the BMW 3/15HP (Type DA 2). Their publicity slogan? *"Inside larger than outside!"* It was different to the previous model, not only through its insignia and another radiator design but — more importantly — through the use of four effective brakes and the loss of running boards in favour of a wider body construction. A new, all-steel, saloon body was designed and made by Berlin-based Ambi-Budd, which was similar in looks to that made by licenced Austin Seven builders, Rosengart, in France. Other characteristics of the new saloon were winding, instead of sliding, door windows, larger rear windscreen, adjustable front seating, and windscreen visors upon the opening front screen. Further derivatives of Eisenach were the two open models, now built in lighter form with artificial leather trim and unframed, stuck-in, celluloid screens.

From 1930 the Type DA 2 became available also as a two window Cabriolet with 3/4-seats and coachwork of steel on a wood frame containing upholstery in artificial leather. A further development was a box-type delivery van which offered a 250kg/551lbs maximum load, a 1.75 square metre load area and 0.75 metre load height. From the published statistics, only a modest number of chassis with this special and inadequate coachwork were delivered: inherent faults presumably outweighed by usefulness to the German Army.

From 1931 BMW offered the 3/15HP front 'swing axle' for the Type DA 4, a rather primitive construction and design (without parallel control in the linked front wheels!) that made the handling characteristics worse, rather than better than they had been on the earlier rigid axle DA 2 models!

The body style of the DA 4 was modernised, the saloon, having renounced the small boot, was some 20 cm longer in the back. Now four adults could be found room, though even then it was hardly enough.

In 1930 the BMW Wartburg (Type DA 3) had come along. It had very good looks, the works-manufactured two-seater body having a boat tail, light metal coachwork and a splinter-free fixed windscreen. The model also boasted increased engine performance, Bosch shock absorbers and the purpose-built low-lying axle crammed into the front. Thus was the dubious swing axle saved for introduction on the 1931 model. This small sports car was a very successful racing car, in its class.

At this point it should be mentioned that, from about 1932, approximately until 1937, the bodywork manufacturers *Gebruder Jhle Karosseriebau* at Bruchsal made a couple of hundred Dixi conversions. They would

	Dixi (Austin) 1927	Dixi DA1 1927	1928-1929	BMW DA2 1929-1931	BMW Wartburg DA3 1930	BMW DA4 1931-1932	BMW AM1-4 1932-1934
Open 2-seater	5	–	1727	1387	150	475	405
Open Tourer	80	42	4831	1834	–	175	252
2 door Saloon	5	–	1879	6600	–	2575	5055
2 door Saloon + sunroof	–	–	–	120	–	–	800
2-seater Coupe	–	–	674	–	–	210	–
2-seater Cabriolet	–	–	–	300	–	–	11
4-seater Cabriolet	–	–	–	1374	–	–	471
Ambulance	10	–	19	435	–	–	53
Chassis	–	–	136	268	–	45	168
	100	42	9266	12318	150	3480	7215

take secondhand Dixi or BMW 3/15HPs and replace the production body with an attractive, two-seater sports superstructure. Such rebuilding cost some 1,200RM.

Up until early 1932, some 25,356 Dixi and BMW 3/15 HPs were delivered to customers. They divided up into model sales as shown in the accompanying chart.

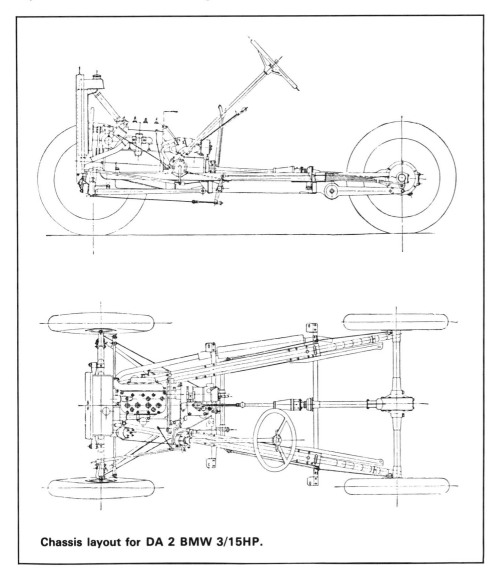

Chassis layout for DA 2 BMW 3/15HP.

Type DA 2 BMW 3/15HP Saloon, 3 to 4 seats: 1929-31.

Type DA 2 BMW 3/15HP Open Tourer, 3 or 4-seater: 1929-31

Type DA 2 BMW 3/15HP Open 2-seater: 1929-31.

Type DA 2 BMW 3/15 HP box-type Delivery Van: 1929-31.

Type DA 2 BMW 3/15HP, Cabriolet 2-seater: 1930-31.

Type DA 2 BMW 3/15HP Cabriolet 3 to 4-seater: 1930-31.

Type DA 4 BMW 3/15HP, 4-seater Saloon: 1931-32.

Type DA 4 BMW 3/15HP 2-seater Coupe from 1931-32 period.

Type DA 3 BMW Wartburg Sports 2-seater from 1930.

A Jhle rebodied sports BMW 2-seater from the 1933-37 era.

30

	BMW 3/15HP Type DA 2:1929-31 Type DA 4:1931-32	BMW Wartburg Type DA 3 1930-31	BMW 3/20HP AM 1&AM 3:1932-33 Type AM 4:1933-34	
Motor				
Cylinders	4 inline	4 inline	4 inline	
Bore x stroke	56 x 76mm	56 x 76mm	56 x 80mm	
Capacity	748.5 (Steuer 743)cc	As 3/15	782cc	
Power	15bhp @ 3000rpm	18bhp @ 3500rpm	20bhp @ 3500rpm	
Compression	5.6:1	7:1	5.6:1	
Carburation	1 sidedraught Solex	As 3/15	As 3/15	
Valves	Sidevalve	As 3/15	Overhead valves	
	Side camshaft driven	As 3/15	Rocker, tappet & spring	
	with spur gears	As 3/15	Side camshaft, duplex	
			chain-driven	
Crankshaft bearings	2	2	2	
Cooling	Thermosyphon, 5	As 3/15	Pump, 7.5 litres	
	litres of water		of oil	
Lubrication	Pressure, 2.5 litres	As 3/15	As 3/15	
	of oil			
Battery	6v 45ah	6v 45ah	6v 45ah	
	Under right F/seat	As 3/15	–	
Generator	60Watt	60Watt	60Watt	
Transmission	Rear wheel drive	As 3/15	As 3/15	
Clutch	Single disc, dry pressure	As 3/15	As 3/15	
	plate			
Gearchange	Lever, floor mounted	As 3/15	As 3/15	
Gearbox	3-speed	As 3/15	3-speed (1932/33)	4-speed (1933/34)
Synchromesh	None	None	None	None
Ratios	1st, 3.25	1st, 3.25	1st, 4.0	1st, 4.3
	2nd, 1.82	2nd, 1.82	2nd, 1.82	2nd, 2.64
	3rd, 1.00	3rd, 1.00	3rd, 1.00	3rd, 1.62
				4th, 1.00
Final drive	5.35	5.35	5.90	5.85
Chassis	U-profile frame	As 3/15	Unitary lower frame	
Front suspension	Rigid axle, 1 transverse	Rigid axle, 1 transverse	No axle, 1 transverse	
	spring. DA 4:no axle,	spring (revised F/axle)	spring	
	1 transverse spring			
Rear suspension	Rigid, outrigged $\frac{1}{4}$ springs	As 3/15	Swing axle, 1 transverse	
			leaf spring	
Steering	Worm	Worm	Worm	
Foot brake	4 wheel, cable	As 3/15	As 3/15	
Handbrake	Front wheels, cable	As 3/15	Rear wheels, cable	
Lubrication	Grease points	As 3/15	As 3/15	
General data				
Wheelbase	1905mm	1905mm	2150mm	
Track, front/rear	1000/1030mm	1000/1030mm	1100mm (F & R)	
Length x width x height	3000 x 1275 x 1625mm	3100 x 1150 x 1300mm	3200 x 1420 x 1550mm	
Wheels	Wire, spoke	As 3/15	Disc	
	Saloon, disc covers			
Rims	Half flattened	As 3/15	Low shelf, 2.75 x 17	
Tyres	27 x 4in Balloon	26 x 3.50 in Balloon	17 x 4.50in	
	Type DA 4:4.0 x 18in	or 4.0 x 18in		
Turning circle	–	–	10 metres	
Chassis weight	300kg	300kg	475kg	
Vehicle weight	Two & three-seater	Sports car, 410kg	Saloon, 650kg	
	open:485kg			
	Saloon & Cabriolet:			
	535kg, (DA 4) 550kg			
Max permissible weight	800kg	–	940kg	
Top speed	47mph	53mph	50mph	
Litres/100 km	6 (46.9mpg)	6.5 (43.36mpg)	7.5 (37.58mpg)	
Fuel tank	20 litres (in engine bay)	As 3/15	25 litres (in engine bay)	

BMW 3/20HP (1932-34)

By March 1, 1932, BMW had prematurely cancelled their licencing agreement with Austin. From that point onward, director Max Friz wanted a car built to their own design. BMW worked on a car which had front drive and a two-cylinder, two-stroke, engine but this did not bring them the performance they were looking for. Pressure of time and internal discussion finally took them to a radical modernisation of the existing engines. The result was an excellent new design. Ignoring contemporary fashion they made the engine of still longer stroke for the extra performance required. The crankshaft ran in two roller bearings, the cylinder head featured two overhead valves per cylinder and the side-mounted camshaft was driven by a Duplex chain, instead of the previous cast iron gear train.

At the close of March 1932 the BMW 3/20HP Type AM 1 ("AM 1" for 1 *Auto Munchen)* appeared with this new engine. An unfortunate amateurish touch was the retention of the previous DA 4 type of swing axle at the front of the car. Other notable features included the front frame to accommodate the engine; a centre 'spine' to the box frame chassis; one piece propshaft; a rear swing axle with transverse leaf springs, and complete bodywork from the Daimler-Benz AG factories in Sindelfingen. The BMW 3/20HP looked a little plump, but inspired confidence with its solid finish and relatively roomy body. However this body was really too heavy for the engine – and the quality of both braking and steering was best described as 'tricky'.

Altogether 7,215 BMW 3/20HP models were built. All four series production derivatives had coachwork out of

Opposite page: Daimler Benz works at Sindelfingen produced the bodies for all the cars shown on these two pages. This is the fabric roof option for BMW 3/20HP of the 1932-34 production span, as are all the examples on this spread.

Right: The two window BMW 3/20HP Cabriolet with the pressed steel wheels that had become more popular since the demise of the DA series

Middle right: The two-seater with two further occasional seats (provided under rear hood) again based on BMW 3/20HP.

Below: Details of BMW 3/20 soft top, four-seater, manufactured at Sindelfingen during the 1932-34 production run

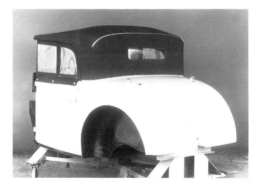

Sindelfingen. Only a modest number of these chassis were seen with specialist bodywork — some very attractive two-seater sports cabriolets, or open two-seater sports cars, which contrasted with the roadsters by having only slight side cutouts for entry — instead of doors — and no folding seat offered in the back. Suppliers of such special bodies included primarily TRS Reutter at Stuttgart and Ludwig Weinberger of Munich. Typical prices:

Roadster 2 (2) seats	2,650 RM
Touring Saloon 4-seater	2,650 RM
Saloon 4-seater	2,650 RM
Roll-up fabric roof Saloon, 4-seater	2,785 RM
Cabriolet, 2 window, 4-seater	3,260 RM
Chassis	2,050 RM

BMW Three-wheeler Delivery Vans (1932-34)

In the Autumn of 1932 BMW brought out a typical product of the thirties depression years: a three-wheeler delivery van. Inside was the motorcycle engine in blower-cooled form. Initially the engines were of 200cc and 6HP, then 400cc and 14HP was also offered. Other features included a three-speed gearbox and shaft drive to the single rear wheel, which had swinging arm suspension.

A front axle of the rigid type, a trapeze-type tubular frame and a weight of just 350kg/772lb, were amongst other basic features of these machines, which could

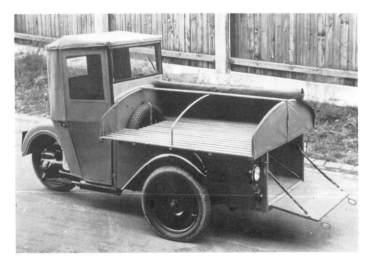

Rakish Special Sport Cabriolet body for BMW's 3/20.

carry 650kg/1433lb and two passengers. The loading area measured 1600 x 1900mm and fuel consumption was given as 6 litre/100km (approximately 47mpg). BMW were especially proud of the locking driver's cabin on this version, but elsewhere the course of events and the evolutionary progress made by leading marques such

Which way are they going? BMW experimented with three-wheelers and produced the tri-wheeler delivery van shown on this page.

as Tempo and Goliath were rapidly making the work of the Munich designers obsolete. The February 1933 Berlin Motor Show saw Tempo and Goliath go from front loader (the style BMW followed in our picture) to rear loading bay, with a locking compartment cover.

Production of the three-wheeler BMW transporter began as the recession began to lessen. Altogether only 600 of these BMW three-wheelers in van form were completed.

34

Atmospheric Berlin show picture dates back to 1933 when Bayerische Motoren Werke AG offered an exciting variety of exhibits from the multi-cylinder vee aero motor in the foreground to the new 1.2-litre small sixes (above). The design of the three specimen saloons was all worked out, but largely unfinished. Less than a month later series production began, so at least the body style was right!

They were:
1932: 40 BMW Type F 76 (200cc/1350 Reich Marks)
1933: 210 BMW Type F 76
297 BMW Type F 79 (400cc/1500 Reich Marks)
1934: 53 BMW Type F79

Retaining the basic two wheels at the front, one at the rear and the philosophy of using as many motorcycle parts as possible, BMW also experimented with a two-seater passenger prototype. As can be seen in our pictures they were a long way from production which was possibly a pity for BMW. Both three-wheeler prototypes were run in Munich, not Eisenach.

BMW 303, 309, 315, 319 and 329 (1933-37)

BMW 303 (Type 3) introduced a completely new product line. The Eisenach-designed chassis had deep frames made from 90mm tubular steel, a much safer, transversely-sprung, front axle, rigid rear axle with underslung half springs, and exceptionally direct (two turns lock-to-lock) rack and pinion steering. Also included were 16in diameter Aero tyres to match the outstanding choice of shock absorbers aand springs. Derived from the 3/20 four-cylinder, the twin carburettor, 1.12-litre six gave lively performance in a relatively small car.

At the February 1933 Berlin show three prototypes showed the model's body style clearly but were otherwise not totally complete. The original limousine coachwork was supplied by Daimler-Benz AG works at Sindelfingen. Production bodies of April 1933 onward came from Ambi Budd, Berlin. Introduction was by a 'Baptism of fire' for the new cars, via an immensely popular and well-advertised 2000km journey throughout Germany.

The 303 was produced until the BMW 315 appeared in April 1934. By 1934 both BMW 303 and 315 looked very similar. Prices for 303 range were:

BMW 303 Limousine (2 doors) 3600 RM
BMW 303 Cabriolet (4 window) 4400 RM
BMW 303 Sport Cabriolet (2-seater) 4600 RM

The 309 Type 3 made sense of BMW numbers with an 0.9-litre four-cylinder engine. (Today the numbering system survives with a 3-series, 2-litre being a "320" and a 3.5-litre 7-series a "735", and so on). From February 1934 the 309 succeeded the 3/20, its larger engine offsetting increased weight and offering a little more performance. The diagonal rubber mountings of the engine allowed from the four a similar standard of silent running to that of the previous six.

With a chassis and body as for the new six-cylinder model, production of the BMW 309 was dropped in 1936 to allow for the growing need to cover six-cylinder manufacture. Prices of the 309 series were as follows:

BMW 309 Limousine (2 doors) 3200 RM
BMW 309 Cabrio-Limousine (2 doors) 3400 RM
BMW 309 Touring Car (2 doors) 3700 RM
BMW 309 Cabriolet (4 windows) 4000 RM
BMW 309 Sport Cabriolet (2-seater) 4200 RM

Logically named too was the Type 3, 1.5-litre 315 of six-cylinders. It followed the 303 from April 1934 and differed only in its larger capacity engine. Capable of nearly 70mph the 315 set a new high point in Type 3 performance. In the Summer of 1934 a very pleasing two-seater sporting version materialised (315/1) which had a triple carburettor engine with raised compression. Straight away this exciting machine scored sensational sporting success in the 1.5-litre classes. Later on came a detachable coupe roof: just as with the standard folding roof version, the attractive lines of the car were ruined. Prices of the 315 were as follows:

BMW 315 Limousine (2 door) 3750 RM
BMW 315 Cabrio-Limousine (2 door) 3950 RM
BMW 315 Touring Car (2 door) 4100 RM
BMW 315 Cabriolet (4 windows) 4800 RM
BMW 315 Sport Cabriolet (2-seater) 4750 RM
BMW 315/1 Sports Car (2-seater) 5200 RM

	BMW 303 1933-1934	BMW 309 1934-1936	BMW 315 1934-1937	BMW 319 1935-1937	BMW 329 1936-1937
Saloon, 2-door	1503	2859	4881	3029	–
Saloon, 2-door & sunroof	150	1	1	–	–
Cabrio-Saloon, 2-door	2	1456	1378	569	–
Cabriolet, 4 window	542	284	2281	2066	1011
Sport Cabriolet, 2-seater	27	–	20	238	42
Open tourer	2	179	137	75	–
Open sports, 2-seater	–	–	230	178	–
Chassis	74	1221	837	491	126
Total	**2300**	**6000**	**9765**	**6646**	**1179**

This BMW 303 of 1933 has the six-cylinder/1.2-litre engine and Ambi-Budd 2-door coachwork. The 303 series introduced the distinctive BMW *nierenformig* (kidney-shaped) grille.

A 1933 Cabriolet with the 1.2-litre six and four window body. As with all 303s and many subsequent BMWs it had a tubular steel chassis and a six-cylinder engine developed from a four-cylinder (that of the 3/20) sharing the same bore and stroke. The gain in capacity over 3/20 (to 1173cc) came only from the additional cylinders.

BMW 303 in Glaser coachwork, two-seater Cabriolet sports style. The 303's rack and pinion steering was unusually direct and contemporary reports speak well of 303's ability to quickly reach 62mph with fuel mpg averaging out somewhere in the middle twenties.

From 1934-36 this two door saloon (formally known as Limousine) was available with Ambi-Budd coachwork clothing the 845cc four-cylinder engine common to all BMW 309s.

Above is another BMW 309 body by Ambi-Budd, this the compromise Cabrio-Limousine with two doors and the usual 0.9-litre engine of four-cylinders. As with all 309s on this page it dates from the 1934-36 range.

Above is the smart four window Cabriolet body made available for the BMW 309. All models had a four-speed gearbox, mechanical brakes and 50mph capability.

The two door touring body covers the usual 22HP four-cylinder of BMW 309. This model saw the introduction of some logic to the BMW numbering system (Type 3 and 0.9-litre) but, alas, there were many more illogically named models before the rigid system used today was applied throughout the range.

Ambi-Budd would supply this two door Limousine coachwork for either 1.2-litre 303 or 1.5-litre 315, both six-cylinder models of 1934.

BMW 315 chassis ready for its bodywork.

Complete with rear spare wheel, BMW 315 Tourer of 1934.

Above is the 315 six-cylinder with Sport Cabriolet two-seater coachwork from Reutter. This 1934 design continued numbering logic and offered 34HP from its 1.5-litre motor.

This 4 window Cabriolet style was available for either 303 or 315 with six-cylinders in 1934.

Between 1935-37 the BMW 315 was sold with this two door Ambi-Budd Limousine bodywork and the normal production 1½-litre six.

Below: Ludwig Weinberger of Munich was a thirties BMW agent and coachwork bespoke tailor. By the time war broke out he had produced 300 BMW chassis with special coachwork. Below we show a two-seater in the English style – complete with wire wheels, based on a 1935 BMW 315. Weinberger also built typically portly German-styled Cabriolets, particularly in the late thirties.

Above, another 315 with special two-seater Sport Cabriolet body. This example dates from 1934 and is the work of Wendler. The 34HP BMW six was particularly attractive to both body specialists and enthusiastic drivers, providing just over 60mph in production form.

At first it was thought the 1.9-litre version of the BMW six would just be for sporting use, but the 45HP twin carburettor version was also utilised for staid BMW 319 saloons, like this two door saloon from Ambi-Budd and BMW's 1935-37 run.

Catalogue pictures on this page all show variations on the 1935-37 production run of BMW 319. This is the two door Cabrio-Limousine from Ambi-Budd.

Open comfort is promised by the four window Cabriolet BMW 319 powered by the 1.9-litre six.

Again, 1.9-litres powers this sleek BMW 319 Sport-Cabriolet two-seater.

A two door open tourer that offered accommodation for at least four, another derivative of BMW's versatile 319 design.

Another Sport-Cabriolet 319 with two seats and a rakish air, but the normal twin carburettor engine from 1935-37.

This is it! A clearly defined beginning to BMW's sports car tradition with uprated running gear matching the sporting looks provided by the coachwork specialists. BMW 315/1 Sport was made between 1934-36 and had the triple carburettor 6.8:1 compression version of the 1490cc six. BMW promised 120kph (74.5mph) as the maximum speed, and quite a few were tuned to comfortably exceed 75mph. From its 1933 show debut the 303-based sports two-seater had the faired-in rear wheels that are beginning to make a comeback in eighties "design cars of the future"!

Another step closer to the immortal 328, the 319/1 Sport was manufactured from 1934-36 and had the triple Solex carburettor version of the 1911cc six that was also used in 319. This two-seater sports car had a maximum speed in the region of 81mph.

Artist's impression of the coupe hardtop in place on the sporting 315/1 six-cylinder model.

A soft top BMW 315/1 sports car with its racy bonnet strap on display. Notice the tail light arrangement compared with lack of rear lights on (prototype?) opposite!

Also without visible rear lighting is this specially-bodied Sport Cabriolet two-seater from Drauz during 1935.

Same 319 under-pinnings and running gear, new bodies. BMW 329 in four window, two door, Cabriolet style of 1936-37.

Wendler coachworks provided this Sport Cabriolet body for the BMW 329 of the same period.

Autenrieth bodied this 1936-37 BMW 329 in their two door Sport Cabriolet style.

	BMW 309 1934-36	BMW 303 1933-34
Motor		
Cylinders	4 inline	6 inline
Bore x stroke	58x80mm	56x80mm
Capacity	845cc	1173cc
Power	22bhp @ 4000rpm	30bhp @ 4000rpm
Compression	5.6:1	5.6:1
Carburation	1, sidedraught	2, sidedraught
	Solex 26 BFLV	Solex 26 BFLV
Valves	Overhead	Overhead
	Rocker tappet and spring	As 309
	Side camshaft, duplex	As 309
	chain-driven	As 309
Crankshaft bearings	2	4
Cooling	Pump, water, 6 litres	Pump, water, 7.5 litres
Lubrication	Pressure, 2.5 litres	Pressure, 4.0 litres
Battery	6v 45ah	6v 75ah
Generator	60 Watt	60 Watt
Transmission	Rear drive	Rear drive
Clutch	Single, dry pressure plate	As 309
Gearchange	Lever, floor mounted	As 309
Gearbox	4-speed	4-speed
Synchromesh	3rd-4th	3rd-4th
Ratios	1st, 4.42	1st, 4.42
	2nd, 2.54	2nd, 2.54
	3rd, 1.65	3rd, 1.65
	4th, 1.00	4th, 1.00
Final drive	5.85	5.15 (7.36)
Chassis	Tubular frame, box section	
	cross beams	As 309
Front suspension	Under, linking cross-spring 1,	
	transverse spring above	As 309
R/suspension	Rigid axle, half springs	As 309
Steering	Rack & pinion (11.2:1)	As 309
Footbrakes	Mechanical 4, wheel integral	Mechanical 4 wheel, integ
Handbrake	Cable, rear wheels	As 309
Lubrication	1 central grease point	As 309
General data		
Wheelbase	2400mm	2400mm
Track (front/rear)	1153/1220mm	1153/1220mm
Length, width and height	3750x1440x1550mm	3900x1440x1550mm
Rims/Wheels	Disc, Tiefbett 3.25 D x 16	As 309
Tyres	5.25x16in	As 309
Turning circle	10.6 metres	10.6 metres
Chassis weight	500kg	550kg
Vehicle weight	750kg	820kg
Max permissible weight	1200kg	1270kg
Top speed	50mph	56mph
Litres/100km	8.5 (33.15mpg)	10 (28.18mpg)
Fuel tank	35 litres (engine bay)	As 309
Price		
Saloon, 2 doors	RM 3200	RM 3600
Cabrio-Saloon, 2 doors	RM 3400	–
Tourer, 4-seats	RM 3700	–
Cabriolet, 2 doors, 4 window	RM 4000	RM 4400
Sport Cabriolet, 2 seats	RM 4200	RM4600
Sports car, 2 seats	–	–

	BMW 315 1934-37	BMW 315/1 Sport 1934-36	BMW 319/1 Sport 1934-36	BMW 319 1935-37	BMW 329 1936-37
	6 inline	6 inline	6 inline	6 inline	
	58x94mm	58x94mm	65x96mm	65x96mm	
	1490cc	1490cc	1911 (Steuer 1898)cc	1911 (Steuer 1898) cc	
	34bhp @ 4000rpm	40bhp @ 4300rpm	55bhp @ 4000rpm	45bhp @ 3750rpm	
	5.6:1	6.8:1	6.8:1	5.6:1	
	2, sidedraught	3, sidedraught	3, sidedraught	2, sidedraught	
	Solex 26 BFLV	Solex 26 BFRV	Solex 30 BFRH	Solex 26 BFLV	
	Overhead	Overhead	Overhead	Overhead	
	As 309	As 309	As 309	As 309	
	As 309	As 309	As 309	As 309	
	As 309	As 309	As 309	As 309	
	4	4.5	4	4	
	Pump, water, 7.5 litres	Pump, 7 litres	Pump, 7.5 litres	Pump, 7.5 litres	
	Pressure, 4 litres	Pressure, 4.0 litres	Pressure, 4.5 litres	Pressure, 4.5 litres	
	6v 75ah	6v 75ah	6v 75ah	6v 75ah	
	90 Watt	90 Watt	90 Watt	90 Watt	
	Rear drive	Rear drive	Rear drive	Rear drive	
	As 309	As 309	As 309	As 309	
	As 309	As 309	As 309	As 309	
	4-speed (Hurth)	4-speed (Hurth)	4-speed (Hurth)	4-speed (Hurth)	
	3rd-4th	3rd-4th	3rd-4th	3rd-4th	
	1st, 4.08	1st, 4.08	1st, 3.63	1st, 3.63	
	2nd, 2.35	2nd, 2.35	2nd, 2.07	2nd, 2.07	
	3rd, 1.52	3rd, 1.52	3rd, 1.38	3rd, 1.51	
	4th, 1.00	4th, 1.00	4th, 1.00	4th, 1.00	
	5.15 (7.36)	4.50 or 5.15	4.50 or 5.15	4.38	
	As 309	As 309	As 309	As 309	
	As 309	As 309	As 309	As 309	
	As 309	As 309	As 309	As 309	
	As 309	Mechanical 4 wheel,	Mechanical 4 wheel,	Mechanical 4 wheel,	
	Mechanical 4 wheel, integral	integral	integral	integral	
	As 309	As 309	As 309	As 309	
	As 309	As 309	As 309	As 309	
	2400mm	2400mm	2400mm	2400mm	2400mm
	1153/1220mm	1153/1220mm	1153/1220mm	1153/1220mm	1153/1220mm
	3900x1440x1550mm	3800x1440x1350mm	3800x1440x1350mm	3900x1440x1550mm	4000x1440x1550mm
	As 309	As 309	As 309	As 309	As 309
	As 309	As 309	As 309	As 309	As 309
	10.6 metres	10.6 metres	10.6 metres	10.6 metres	10.6 metres
	550kg	550kg	550kg	550kg	550kg
	830kg	750kg	780kg	850kg	880kg
	1270kg	1100kg	1140kg	1300kg	1300kg
	62mph	75mph	81mph	72mph	68mph
	10.5 (26.84mpg)	11.5 (24.51mpg)	12 (23.48mpg)	11 (25.62mpg)	11.5 (24.51mpg)
	As 309	50 litres (engine bay)	As 315/1	40 litres (engine bay)	As 319
	RM 3750	–	–	RM 4150	–
	RM 3950	–	–	RM 4350	–
	RM4100	–	–	RM 4500	–
	RM 4400	–	–	RM 4800	RM 4950
	RM4750	–	–	RM 5150	RM 5800
	–	RM5200	RM5800	–	–

The Type 3, six of 1.9-litres was logically named 319. Originally the 1.9-litre was planned and developed for the 2-litre sports car class. The first example of BMW 319/1, completed at the end of 1934, did not resemble the 315/1 in appearance. The inevitable happened to the 1911cc engine: it was developed not only for unrestrained competition power, but also went from triple to twin carburettor layout to power the five other body styles offered in the BMW 319 range, these generally being similar to 315.

BMW 319 Limousine (2 door) 4150 RM
BMW 319 Cabrio-Limousine (2 door) 4350 RM
BMW 319 Touring Car (2 doors) 4500 RM
BMW 319 Cabriolet (4 window) 4800 RM
BMW 319 Sport Cabriolet (2-seater) 5150 RM
BMW 319/1 Sports Car (2-seater) 5800 RM

The logical numbering disappeared for a while with BMW 329, which was a special version of 319. It used the same engine and chassis, but had a slightly updated general styling with a reminder in its lines of the 326. Offered as a four-seater Cabriolet with ungainly, roomier rear section, or as a sporting Cabriolet with two seats and rather more agreeable proportions. Some 1179 of these transitional models, prior to 320, were made.

BMW 329 Cabriolet (4 window) 4950 RM
BMW 329 Sport Cabriolet (2-seater) 5800 RM

Inner dimensions of BMW 320 Saloon

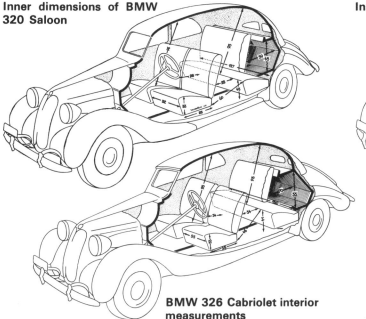

BMW 326 Cabriolet interior measurements

BMW 326 (1936-1941)

These were the first large cars from BMW. Announced at the Berlin Show of February 1936, the 326 went into series production by the middle of that year. Early examples were notable for comfort and solid value, which made them the most popular pre-war BMWs while later models emphasised sporting performance. The saloons got their bodies from Ambi-Budd, Cabriolets were by Autenrieth and other companies. The 326 price range ...

BMW 326 Chassis, 4450 RM
BMW 326 Limousine, 4 doors, 6 windows, 5500 RM
BMW 326, as above with sliding sunroof, 5810 RM
BMW 326 Cabriolet, 2 doors, 4 windows, 6650 RM
BMW 326, with Autenrieth sliding doors, 7300 RM
BMW 326 Cabriolet, 4 windows, 4 doors, 7300 RM

BMW 320 and 321 (1937-41)

The BMW 320 appeared in July 1937, after the company's 319 and 329. Produced only with two doors it was smaller, lighter and cheaper than 326 which preceded it. The first 640 BMW 320s had the well proven twin carburettor 1911cc engine of the 319 and 329. Then the single carburettor 1971cc engine of similar power and 1mm larger bore was installed. The BMW 321 came in January 1939, distinguished by its

Inside the BMW 326 Saloon

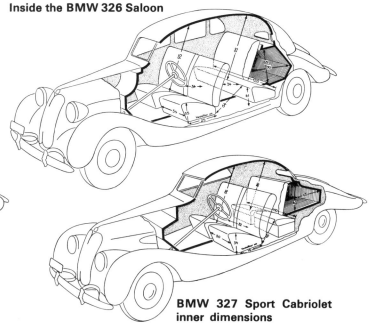

BMW 327 Sport Cabriolet inner dimensions

use of rear-hinged doors and the front suspension of the BMW 326. Saloons, or Limousines as they were known in Germany, came from Ambi-Budd and Cabriolets from various concerns.

	BMW 320	BMW 321
Chassis	3980 RM	4150 RM
Limousine, 2 doors	4500 RM	4800 RM
Golde sliding roof	–	5100 RM
Cabriolet, 2 doors, 4 windows	5250 RM	5650 RM

BMW 327 and 327/28 (1937–41)

When the 327 was first displayed, in November 1937, there was immediate enthusiastic approval for the obvious beauty of the car. Incidentally, the first cars had Hurth quick-change gearboxes and 4.55 final drive. From April 1938 the 327 was optionally available with the 80BHP engine of the BMW 328. The coachwork was by Ambi-Budd.

BMW 327 Cabriolet	(from November 1937)	7500 RM
BMW 327 Coupe	(from October 1938)	7450 RM
BMW 327/28 Cabriolet	(from April 1938)	8130 RM
BMW 327/28 Coupe	(from October 1938)	8100 RM

BMW 328 (1937–39)

Announced by its victorious 2-litre class performance in the *Eifelrennen* of June 1936, driven by Ernst Henne, the BMW 328 went on sale from February 1937. It immediately turned out to be one of the most successful and popular sports cars of the pre-war years–and was also modfied for Britain after the war, courtesy of Bristol Cars.

Some 462 such cars were built, from which half are reckoned to have survived as much prized examples of a truly classic sports car. Most of the 328s that were delivered had the Eisenach body: open two-seaters with light canvas hoods. However, to special order, there were also wonderful two-seaters available from Glaser, Wendler, Drauz and Ludwig Weinberger.

BMW 328 chassis, 5900 RM
BMW 328 Sports Car, 7400 RM

BMW 335 (1939–41)

Biggest and most luxurious of the pre-war BMWs, the 335 had its introduction in the Autumn of 1938. With BMW 326 coachwork, this model was built for longer and marked a temporary return to logical numerals (Type 3, 3.5-litres). Because of the war only 410 such cars were made: 233 Saloons, 118 Cabriolet 2 doors, 40 Cabriolet 4 doors and 19 chassis destined for special bodies.

BMW 335 chassis, 6700 RM
BMW 335 Limousine, 4 doors, 6 windows, 7850 RM
BMW 335 Cabriolet 2 door, 4 windows, 9050 RM
BMW 335 Cabriolet, 4 door, 4 windows, 9600 RM

Coachwork types	BMW 320 1937 – 1938	BMW 321 1939 – 1941	BMW 326 1936 – 1941	BMW 327 1937 – 1941	BMW 327/28 1938 – 1940	BMW 328 1937 – 1939
Saloon, 2, door	2416	2078	–	–	–	–
Saloon, 4 door	–	–	10142	–	–	–
Cabriolet, 4 window	1635	1551	4060	–	–	–
Cabriolet, 4 door	–	–	1093	–	–	–
Open Sports, 2-seater	–	–	–	–	–	403
Sports Cabriolet	–	–	–	1124	482	–
Sports Coupe	–	–	–	179	86	–
Chassis	189	8	641	1	1	59
Total	4240	3637	15936	1304	569	462

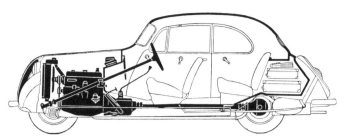

BMW 320, 1937-38

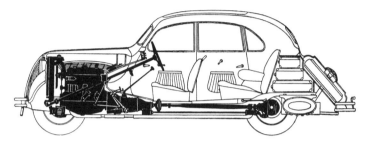

BMW 326, 1936-41

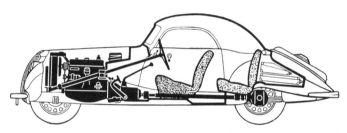

BMW 327, 1937-41

BMW 328, 1938-40

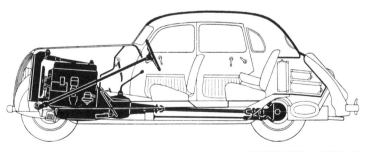

BMW 335, 1939-41

	BMW 320 1937 – 38	BMW 321 1939 – 41
Motor		
Cylinders	6 inline	
Bore x stroke	66 x 96mm	
Capacity	1971cc	
Power	45bhp @ 3750rpm	
Compression	6:1	
Carburation	1, sidedraught Solex 30 BFLVS	
Valves	Overhead Rocker, tappet & spring Side camshaft, duplex chain driven	
Crankshaft bearings	4	
Cooling	Pump, 7.5 litres water	
Lubrication	Pressure, 4 litres oil	
Battery	6v 75ah	
Generator	90 or 130 Watt	
Transmission		
	Rear wheel drive	
Clutch	Single dry plate	
Gearchange	Lever, floor mounted	
Gearbox	4-speed (Hurth)	
Synchromesh	3rd-4th	
Ratios	1st, 3.66 2nd, 2.22 3rd, 1.51 4th, 1.00	
Final drive ratio	4.38, (from 1938) 4.55	
Chassis		
	Box section frame	
Front suspension	Under, transverse wishbones Over, 1 transverse spring	Over, transverse wishbones Under, 1 transverse spring
Rear suspension	Rigid, axle half spring	
Steering	Rack and pinion	
Footbrakes	Hydraulic 4 wheel, integral	
Handbrake	Cable, rear wheels	
Lubrication	1 central point	
General data		
Wheelbase	2750mm	2750mm
Track (Front/Rear)	1160/1300mm	1300/1300mm
Length, width, height	4500/1540/1500mm	4500/1670/1500mm
Wheels	Five hole fixing, steel disc 3.25 D x 16	As 320. 3.50 D x 1
Tyres	5.25 x 16	5.50 x 16
Turning circle	13 metres	11 metres
Chassis weight	750kg	
Vehicle weight	Saloon, 1000kg	
Max permissible weight	1600kg	
Top speed	68mph	
0-100kph (0.62mph)	35 seconds	
Litres/100km	11 (25.62mpg)	
Fuel tank	50 litres (in back)	

BMW 326 1936 – 41	BMW 327 1937 – 41	BMW 327/28 1938 – 40	BMW 328 1937 – 39	BMW 335 1939 – 41
6 inline	6 inline	6 inline	6 inline	6 inline
66 x 96mm	66 x 96mm	66 x 96mm	66 x 96mm	82 x 110mm
1971cc	1971cc	1971cc	1971cc	3485cc
50bhp @ 3750rpm	55bhp @ 4500rpm	80bhp @ 5000rpm	90bhp @ 3500rpm
6:1	6.3:1	7.5:1	5.8:1
2, sidedraught Solex 26 BFLV	2 sidedraught Solex 26BFLV	3, downdraught Solex 30 JF	1, twin choke Solex 35 VMNOVS
Overhead	Overhead	Overhead, V-pattern	Overhead
Rocker, tappet & spring	Rocker, tappet & spring	Rocker, tappet & spring	Rocker, tappet & spring
Side camshaft, duplex chain driven	Side camshaft, duplex chain driven	Side camshaft, duplex chain driven	Side camshaft, driven by spur gears
4	4	4	4
Pump, 7.5 litres water	Pump, 7.5 litres water	Pump, 7.5 litres water	Pump, 14 litres water
Pressure, 4 litres oil	Pressure 4 litres oil	Pressure, 4 litres oil + oil cooler	Pressure, 7 litres oil
6v 75ah	6v 75ah	6v 75ah	12v 62.5ah
90 or 130 Watt	90 or 130 Watt	90 or 130 Watt	150 Watt
Rear wheel drive	Rear wheel drive	Rear wheel drive	Rear wheel drive
Single dry plate	Single, dry plate	Single, dry plate	Single, dry plate
Lever, floor mounted	Lever, floor mounted	Lever, floor mounted	Lever, floor mounted
4-speed (Hurth)	4-speed / 4-speed (ZF) (Hurth)	4-speed (ZF) / 4-speed (Hurth) (ZF)	4-speed (ZF)
3rd-4th	3rd-4th / 1st-4th	1st-4th / 3rd-4th / 3rd-4th	1st-4th
Freewheel in 1st & 2nd	Freewheel, 1st 2nd
1st, 3.85	1st, 3.85 / 1st, 3.75	1st. 3.75 / 1st,3.63 / 1st, 3.07	1st, 3.89
2nd, 2.38	2nd, 2.38 / 2nd, 2.28	2nd, 2.28 / 2nd, 2.07 / 2nd, 1.82	2nd, 2.165
3rd, 1.54	3rd, 1.54 / 3rd, 1.48	3rd, 1.48 / 3rd, 1.50 / 3rd, 1.25	3rd, 1.355
4th, 1.00	4th, 1.00 / 4th, 1.00	4th, 1.00 / 4th, 1.00 / 4th, 1.00	4th,' 1.00
4.875	3.90	3.90 / 3.88 / 3.70	3.90
Box section frame	Box section frame	Tubular frame, fabricated cross beams	Box section frame
Over, transverse wishbones	Over, transverse wishbones	Under, transverse wishbones	Over, transverse wishbones
Under, 1, transverse spring	Under, 1 transverse spring	Over, 1 transverse spring	Under, 1 transverse spring
Rigid axle, 2 longitudinal torsion bars	Rigid axle, half springs	Rigid axle, half springs	Rigid axle, 2 longitudinal torsion bars
Rack and pinion	Rack and pinion	Rack and pinion	Rack and pinion
Hydraulic 4 wheel, integral	Hydraulic 4 wheel integral	Hydraulic 4 wheel, integral	Hydraulic 4 wheel, integral
Cable, rear wheels	Cable, rear wheels	Cable, rear wheels	Cable, rear wheels
1 central point	1 central point	1 central point	1 central point
2870mm	2750mm	2400mm	2984mm
1300/1400mm	1300/1300mm	1153/1220mm	1306/1404mm
4600/1600/1500mm	4500 x 1600 x 1420mm	3900 x 1550 x 1400mm	4840 x 1700 x 1665mm
As 320. 1936: 3.25 E x 17	As 320. 3.50D x 16	As 320. Optional: centre nut knock-off 3.25 or 3.50 D x 16	As 320. 4.00 E x 16
From 1937: 3/50 D x 16
1936: 5.25 x 17
From 1937: 5.50 x 16			5.25 or 5.50 x 16	6.00 x 16 extra
12 metres	5.50 x 16		10.6 metres	12.5 metres
800kg	11 metres		500kg	1020kg
Saloon, 1125kg	750kg	750kg	830kg	Saloon, 1300kg
Saloon, 1700kg	1100kg	1100kg	1220kg	1750kg
72mph	1600kg	1450kg	93mph	96mph
35 seconds	78mph	87mph	—	—
12.5 (22.55mpg)	—	—	14.5 (19.44mpg)	16 (17.61mpg)
65 litres (in back)	12 (23.48mpg)	14.5 (19.44mpg)	50 litres (in back)	65 litres (in back)
	50 litres (in back)	50 litres (in back)	Optional: 100 litres	

49

BMW 320 saloon of 1937-38 run, displaying forward hinge arrangement for two door bodywork with divided front bumpers. The 320 was based on shortened 326 box frame chassis but used 319 transverse leaf front suspension.

BMW 320 Cabriolet from the same period, this two door also sharing the forward hinged doors and divided bumpers. From Autumn 1937 all 320s went up in engine size from the 1911cc to 1971cc via a larger bore for the same inline six-cylinder layout. As usual Solex carburettors were utilised, a single carb for this 45bhp unit.

Typical of the 1939-41 BMW 321 production output, this two door Cabriolet has rear-hinged doors and single blade bumpers and 329-style bonnet louvres. The 320s were capable of 68mph and were reckoned to take 35 seconds to reach 62mph . Some 40 years later *Autocar* reported the then-new 1977 BMW 320/6 as capable of 111mph and 0-60mph in 9.8s. Interesting to note that the 1937 BMW 2-litre is credited with 25.6mpg, while *Autocar's* demanding test produced 24.6mpg: subsequent widespread fitment of five speed gearboxes had tipped the mpg balance back in favour of the modern 320s by the eighties.

Smooth contours of the 1936-38 BMW 326 four door saloon properly complement the engineering beneath. The live rear axle utilised torsion bars and was located by a transverse rod, the chassis was of box section instead of tubular construction and the braking system became hydraulic instead of mechanical. At the rear the spare wheel is neatly accommodated above the twin blade, divided, bumpers.

Inside the BMW 326, the company's first four door executed by Ambi-Budd. Comprehensive instrumentation included an eight day clock. Note windscreen panes can still be opened individually and that the seating looks more accommodating than many cars of the eighties!

Front view of 1939-41 BMW 326 saloon with 4 doors and centre B-pillar hinges, plus continuous front bumper. The 326 was BMW's most popular thirties design. Weighing some 3740lb, acceleration of the 50bhp 2-litre was similar to the less powerful 320 and 321, but top speed was slightly over 70mph.

Autenrieth used to offer this safety-orientated sliding door BMW 326 Cabriolet in 1938. There was only space for two doors, but rear seating was quite generous, despite the neatly furled convertible top.

An unusual four door BMW 320 Cabriolet, again from Autenrieth in 1938, displays rather more ornate double bumpers in two sections.

From the 1936-39 output, Glaser used to produced this tidy two seater Sport Cabriolet. Based once more on the double carburettor 1971cc engine and utilising the 326's advanced running gear, it included a four-speed gearbox with synchromesh on the upper two ratios only.

Hood up or down, this two window 326 (belonging to Heinrich R. Wolf, Gutersloh) is a credit to the attractive lines offered by Autenrieth for this Cabriolet model

Showing off its naked spare wheel and posing in glorious touring country is this 1938 example of Drauz coachwork in Sport Cabriolet 2 ("2" for two-seater) style.

53

The Bavarian Motor Works displayed this streamlined saloon at the Berlin Motor Show of February 1938. It combined the coachwork of Wendler at Reutlingen and the patented work of Paul Jaray. It was built on the chassis of a BMW 326. In total Wendler made seven equivalent cars of similar style, five based on BMW 326 and two on the BMW 328.

Again the cowled rear wheels are in evidence, but perhaps the biggest problem in actually driving such streamliners was the restricted vision resulting from diminished areas of glass.

Here is the BMW 327 with special coachwork by Autenreith of Darmstadt. While the Autenreith coachwork achieves no more chic and elegance than the series production body, its beauty comes from the welcome harmony of balanced proportions. Werner Oswald knows of no superior special coachwork to that of this black convertible.

The rakish BMW 327/28 Sport Cabriolet of the 1937-41 era. Mechanically it was the same as the revered 328, sharing the triple Solex carburettor engine and the unique valve gear for the aluminium cylinder head. However the 327 was first introduced in 55bhp form (the 328 engine allowed another 35 horsepower) as a sportier, short wheelbase, alternative to the BMW 326.

The two door Sport Coupe version of BMW 327/28 of the 1938-41 era emphasises the BMW 'kidney' grille and has a simple sporting line. Note absence of rear wheel spats on lower example.

Claimed to be capable of 87mph, the 327.28's coupe shape (but not the powerplant in three carburettor form), was reborn along with other 327 derivatives under the then communist management of the Eisenach factory. The final 327 left the Eisenach lines, complete with one piece rear window, but still recognisable as the same sleek basic shape, in 1955!

The BMW everyone seems to have heard about from the pre-war years: the 328. Produced between 1937 and 1939 following its 1936 debut Nurburgring victory, the production 328 shown was such a good basis for competition that it swiftly inspired even more sporting offspring, an evolutionary process only interrupted by the war,

Middle: A definitive production 328, wheel cowls and bonnet straps in position and screen raised. This astonishing sports car is, in a sense, with us to the present day through the Sbarro replica. The original found wide acceptance in postwar Britain in modified Bristol guise. Although Bristols grew away from the 328 concept the basic power unit (giving 125bhp in one roadgoing form) continued until production was discontinued in 1959. Perhaps *the* company responsible for BMW's present powerful position in the UK was Frazer Nash (AFN) who brought BMWs into the UK from the 315 onward. The 315 was brought to Britain for under £300 in basic trim and sold as the Frazer Nash 34 in saloon as well as Cabriolet trim. There was also a wide variety of English sports bodies, and some of these influenced German coachwork.

A production 328 was capable of over 90mph. Writing in November 1981 *Motor* of a 1938 example owned by the Hon. Robin Finch-Hatton, Anthony Curtis commented: "the BMW 328 was 25-30 years ahead of its time." He also said that the example he drove was worth around £25,000 – the first examples to reach Britain sold for less than £700!

For the 1939 Le Mans 24 hours race, BMW ran the Carozzeria Touring (mainland) streamliner coupe in Superleggera trim. This car was fifth at Le Mans and won the 1940 Brescia-based substitute for the Mille Miglia.

Also for the 1940 'Mille Miglia' BMW entered three open racing two seaters, which took third, fifth and sixth places. These were the prototypes for the planned successors to the production BWM 328. The British firm Frazer Nash built their version of what was basically this car from 1946 to 1949.

Another BMW entry for the 1940 Mille Miglia-Brescia event was this racing saloon. This single car following the example of Professor Kamm's streamliner development.

BMW 328 racing car of 1942 was developed in co-operation with the Milan-based Italian coachwork specialists, Touring. This car was not actually ready to perform, but acted as a model for the postwar racing cars of Veritas. Such a Touring prototype was later acquired for the BMW museum in Munich.

Coupe coachwork by Wendler Reutlingen, offered a detachable hard top and half spats for the rear wheels, all based on the 1937-39 BMW 328.

Wendler also constructed this two-seater Sport Coupe version of the BMW 328, shown here with the roof off.

Sport Cabriolet BMW 328 of the same period in two seater trim from Ludwig Weinberger in Munich. Most of the 350 BMWs that Weinberger converted to his special bodies were based on the 328.

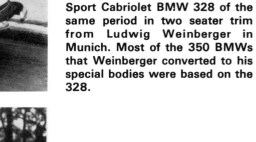

Opposite page: Glaser in Dresden were not prolific body manufacturers for BMWs, but when they turned their minds to such a project the results were quite striking. Here we show, hood up and down, the body they made for the BMW 328 of the 1937/39 era. Dubbed a Sport Cabriolet, this two-seater was notable for clean lines and a propensity for extra lighting, which is to be seen on the screen pillar, to the rear deck and offside front wing.

BMW 335 of 1938-40 marked a return to logical numbering, having a 3.5-litre six-cylinder engine to power this 2860lb saloon with its four door Ambi-Budd body. The 335 was based on the principles of the 326, but represented an all round stretch in engine and body, the wheelbase being some 4.5 inches longer.

Autenrieth supplied this two door Cabriolet based on the 1939-1941 BMW 335. The last production pre-war BMW had a 90bhp single Solex carburettor engine and a four-speed gearbox from ZF.

Autenrieth's four door Cabriolet BMW 335 of 1939-41 was capable of 90mph using the normal BMW six-cylinder development of the previous 2-litre engine. Official fuel consumption figure was 17.6mpg.

Opposite page, bottom picture: Officially this was a BMW 335-based research vehicle. It embodied the ideas of Professor Kamm in developing streamlined bodies. It was for driving on all the then-new state autobahns and had an alleged capability of 87mph and 28mpg. One other peculiarity of these research cars was that the seated driver could change tyre pressures while driving!

A sensational and beautiful car for any dealer today, that is what is represented by this BMW 335 bodied by Herman Graber, Wichtrach, Switzerland, in 1939. Although the original front section, wings, running board and bumpers were retained, the style of these Cabriolets was such a radical departure from the BMW theme, that the cars were reminiscent of earlier Alfa Romeos! For his coachwork Graber chose the colour black with green leather upholstery. This example belonged to Lucerne BMW dealer Max Hahn.

BMW Vehicles for the Armed Forces

In contrast to the BMW motorcycles, which played an important role in the German Army and throughout the other armed forces, BMW cars played very much the subordinate parts.

However the German Army already possessed an estimated 300 Dixi and BMW 3/15 cars, which were used as dispatch vehicles, often in stripped out bodies. There were also "MG-Wagen" versions of Dixi that were dressed up as dummy tanks! During the 1934-36 period the German Army purchased about 2000 chassis from BMW, including those of the 303, 309, 315 and 319. These were adapted as light vans or military staff cars, or used as telephone communication cars.

Most of these Type 3 vehicles survived the opening months in the Russian war zone, but even the longest-lived failed to survive the rigours of the real Russian Winter. Such comparatively dainty cars were not developed to meet such strains!

In the middle thirties the armed forces gave as guidance

their opinion that future vehicles for battle purposes should not have the traditional chassis. Therefore the 'standard' chassis for light, medium and heavy armed forces passenger vehicles were constructed under the auspices of the Military Arms Office. Production of these light standard vehicles was entrusted to three companies, each using their own 50bhp, 2-litre engine. From 1936-1943 Stoewer held the lion's share of the business, delivering 7500 vehicles. Hanomag managed about 2000 such cars between 1937 and 1940. BMW's record was: 1937-452; 1938-945; 1939-1093 and 734 for 1940. Therefore the total was 3225.

The light standard military passenger vehicles of all three companies, apart from engine differences, were completely identical externally, particularly as no manufacturer's insignia was allowed. At the battle front they all had this light standard military body, which was largely unproven. Overall, they were too complicated, too expensive, much too heavy, very sensitive to rough conditions and therefore prone to breakdown. Only an occasional specimen survived more than the first thousand Russian kilometres!

By 1942 the light standard military passenger car had already disappeared from the arms programme, and from use by the troops. Nobody cried about it! Yet, during the war the armed forces naturally conscripted various types of BMW cars for their use. Especially popular were the Saloon and Cabriolet bodied 320, 321, 326 and 335. Nearly all were destroyed, or simply worn out, which is why so few of these BMW models survive to the present day.

These extraordinary "sheep in wolves' clothing" are 1929 Dixi 3/15s dressed up to take their loads as dummy tanks. Both Dixi and equivalent BMW small car successor were pressed into all kinds of army duties, especially in the twenties, when the Treaty of Versailles prevented the German Army from using heavy vehicles. Then the 3/15 would be pressed into use with considerably lightened bodywork for manoeuvres.

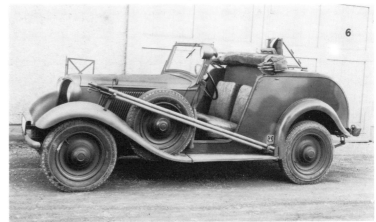

Above and alongside we show a vehicle based on BMW's 309 (four-cylinders, 0.9-litre, 22bhp) as a small 'phone communications car, complete with just two seats and able to carry the appropriate equipment along its flanks. The structure was by Magirus at Ulm, as was the development and manufacture.

Underneath this Kubelwagen design are the essentials of a BMW 315 (six-cylinder, 1.5-litre, 34bhp) as built from 1934 to 1936. It has four seats, weighs around 2,200lb and measures 4100mm by 1500mm by 1600mm. Four-seater accommodation may look bare by BMW standards today, but they certainly did not intend you to fall out of those high-sided perches.

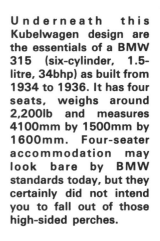

Hood up and hood down display from one of the BMW 325 light standard military passenger vehicles, produced by several manufacturers to a common specification for the Germany Army between 1937 and 1940. Unusual features included a five speed gearbox, four-wheel-steering, four locking differentials and a fuel consumption of just 11mpg in cross-country use! On the street things were a little better for this military use of the illustrious 1971cc six-cylinder engine, its top speed limited to only 31mph.

64

BMW 325 in lightweight telecommunications and radio vehicle role.

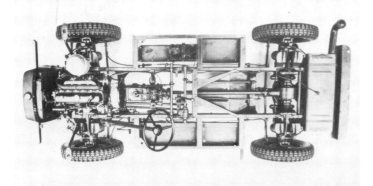

Chassis for 325 with four wheel steering displayed.

A conscript! The BMW 335 as a 'company car' for generals.

	Standard light military vehicle BMW 325 1937-1940
Motor	
Cylinders	6 inline
Bore x stroke	66x96mm
Capacity	1971cc
Power	50bhp @ 3750rpm
Compression	6:1
Carburation	2, sidedraught Solex 26 BFLV
Valves	Overhead
	Rocker, tappet & spring
	Side camshaft, duplex chain driven
Crankshaft bearings	4
Cooling	Pump.water
Lubrication	Dry sump, 6.5 litres of oil
Battery	12v 50ah
	(With radio equipment, 90ah)
Generator	190 Watt
Starter motor	1.4hp
Transmission	
Clutch	All wheels driven 4 locking differentials
Gearbox	Single pressure plate (dry)
Gearchange	5-speed
Ratios	Lever, floor mounted
	Cross country, 9.12 (ultra low 1st)
	1st, 5.01; 2nd, 2.86; 3rd, 1.89
	4th, 1.00
	2nd gearbox ratios: 1.358
Final drive ratio	4.84
Bodywork & chassis	Fabricated box & ladder frame.
	All steel bodywork
Front suspension	Double transverse wishbones
	2 coil spring for each wheel (2)
Rear suspension	Double transverse wishbones
	2 coil spring for each wheel (2)
Steering	Four wheel steering
Footbrakes	Mechanical, 4 wheels
Handbrake	Mechanical, 4 wheels
General Data	
Wheelbase	2400mm
Track (Front/Rear)	1400/1400mm
Length, width, height	3900/1690/1900mm
Tyres	6.00x18 Cross country
Body clearance	235mm
Water wading depth	500mm
Turning circle	With front wheel steer, 12.7 metres
	With 4-wheel steering, 6.5 metres
Vehicle weight	1775kg
Max permissible weight	2200kg
Max load	425kg
Top speed	50mph
Litres per 100km	Street: 17 (16.58mpg)
	Cross country: 25 (11.27mpg)
Fuel tank	50 litres + 10 litres (in back)
Driving range	Street: 217 miles (350kms)
	Cross country: 149 miles (240kms)

Autovelo BMW 321, 327 and 340 (1945-51)
EMW 327 and 340 (1952-56)

The Soviet joint shareholding company of Autovelo was born from the Communist occupation of Thuringia, including the former BMW factory at Eisenach. For a short period they made household items and handcarts, but it was not long before motorcycle manufacture began with the BMW R35. After Ambi-Budd's Berlin-Johannisthal pressing works were dismantled, the bodywork tools for BMW models 321, 326 and 327 were taken to Eisenach, where the building of cars recommenced in October 1945. The "Autovelo" name we use is a westernisation of *"Awtovelo"*, the name the company used formally.

For many years production was limited to the unchanged pre-war 321 model. It was made available almost exclusively to the Soviet occupying forces, or for export to Western Europe. The manufacturing record looked like this: 1945-68; 1946-1373; 1947-2053; 1948-2506; 1949-2750; 1950-250. Altogether exactly 9000 BMW 321 models.

The BMW 327 also reappeared; now with indicators and forward-hinged doors. The first 17 such cars were made in 1948. By 1956 some 505 had been constructed. These were mainly Cabriolets priced at 17,740 Eastern Deutschmarks, but a substantially smaller number of Coupes were sold at 18, 590 Eastern Dm.

Eisenach had a narrow escape from the initial Soviet inclination to dismantle the car building capability altogether. When they saw what they had won, they changed their minds – a decision which caused BMW some later problems when the resulting cars were exported for valued Western currency. A legal action in the fifties finally ensured that only Munich-made BMWs carried the company name and trademark.

The Autovelo BMW 340 of 1949-51 was succeeded by "EMW" branding for much the same car (EMW 340: 1952-55), which was derived from the thirties BMW 326. The 'BMW' 340 of Autovelo was exhibited at both the Brussels Show and the Leipzig Spring Exibition, 1949. Deliveries of the Limousine BMW 340-2 commenced in October 1949. Additionally an Estate Car derivative (340-7) came along in 1951, using the IFA Coachworks Halle superstructure based on their 340-4 ambulance and the box van design (340-3) which had a maximum load rating of 1100lb. From January 1952 the Soviet State company Autovelo handed over management to the East Germans, the concern described as *Eisenacher Motoren Werke*. Their insignia became a rendering of the famous BMW whirling propeller emblem, now red and white instead of blue and white, carrying the legend "EMW"!

Prices? In Eastern Dm they were: Autovelo BMW 340 (4 door saloon), 18,440 Dm; EMW 340 (4 door saloon), 15,000 Dm; Estate (2 doors), 14,835 Dm. By 1955 no successor to 340 had been planned and, amazingly, Eisenach reverted to its Wartburg origins, best known for two strokes of mediocre performance in the West. Altogether some 19,000 of the 321,327 and 340 were exported. In their homeland, the EMW 340 remained essentially a company car for management and industry. Other than that, they could be seen until the middle sixties in most *DDR* towns ... acting as taxis!

A 1949 advertisement by the Dutch importer of BMWs.

	Autovelo BMW 321 1945-1950	Autovelo BMW 327 1948-1951 EMW 327: 1952-1956	Autovelo BMW 340 1949-1951 EMW 340: 1952-1955	
Motor				
Cylinders	6 inline		6 inline	
Bore x stroke	66x96mm		66x96mm	
Capacity	1971cc		1971cc	
Power	45bhp @ 4000rpm		55bhp @ 3750rpm	
Torque	–		11.2mkg (81lb.ft) @ 2500rpm	
Compression	6:1		6.1:1	
Carburation	1, sidedraught Solex 30 BFLVS		2, downdraught Solex 32 PBI or BVF 323-1	
Valves	Overhead Rocker, spring & tappet Side camshaft, duplex chain driven		Overhead Rocker, spring & tappet Side camshaft, duplex chain driven	
Crankshaft bearings	4		4	
Cooling	Pump, 9 litres of water		Pump, 9 litres of water	
Lubrication	Pressure, 4.5 litres oil		Pressure, 4.5 litres oil	
Battery	65v 75ah		6v 75ah or 84ah	
Generator	130 Watt		130 Watt	
Transmission	Rear wheel drive		Rear wheel drive	
Clutch	Single dry pressure plate		Single dry pressure plate	
Gear change	Lever, floor mounted	Lever, floor mounted	Column change	
Synchromesh	3rd-4th		2nd-4th Freewheel in 1st & 2nd	
Ratios	1st, 3.70 2nd, 2.22 3rd, 1.51 4th, 1.00		1st, 3.85 2nd, 2.38 3rd, 1.54 4th, 1.00	
Final drive	4.55	3.90	4.55	4.55
Bodywork & chassis	Box frame		Box frame	Box frame
Coachwork	All steel body		Saloon: all steel	Kombi & sanitary wagon: wood, steel construction. Ambulance, box frame/wood
Front suspension	Top wishbones & lower cross spring		Top wishbones & lower cross spring	
Rear suspension	Rigid, half springs		Rigid, three longitudinal location rods, torsion bars	
Steering	Rack & pinion (14.6:1)		Rack and pinion (15.5:1)	
Foot brakes	4 wheel, hydraulic Diam, 280mm, width, 50mm Swept area, 1056cm		4 wheel, hydraulic	
Handbrake	Cable, rear wheels		As 321/327	
Lubrication	Central pressure point		As 321/327	
			As 321/327	
General data	**Saloon**	**Cabriolet & Coupe**	**Saloon**	**Kombi, sanitary & ambulance**
Wheelbase	2750mm	2750mm	3870mm	2884mm
Track (Front/Rear)	1300/1300mm	1300/1400mm	1300/1400mm	1300/1400mm
Length, width, height	4470/1600/1650mm	4500/1600/1420mm	4600/1765/1630mm	Kombi & sanit: 4850/1825/1660mm Ambulance: 4630/1780/1700mm
Tyres	5.25 or 5.50 x 16	5.50 or 5.75x16	5.50 or 5.75x16	6.00x16 extra
Turning circle	11 metres	11 metres	12 metres	12.5 metres
Vehicle weight	1000kg	1100kg	1280kg	1350, Sanit: 1400kg
Max permissible weight	1600kg	1600kg	1700kg	1750kg
Top speed	72mph	78mph	75mph	75mph
Litres/100km	11.5 (24.5mpg)	12 (23.5mpg)	13 (21.7mpg)	14 (20.1mpg)
Fuel tank (rear location)	50 litres	50 litres	65 litres	65 litres

The Soviet-controlled Autovelo organisation was responsible for this 'update' of the BMW 321. Known as the "BMW 340", this Eisenach-product was also made as the EMW (Eisenacher Motoren Werke) 340-2. The production span of this four door model was from 1949-55 and the main changes were in the form of vaguely Americanised styling (grille, rear wings) compared to the original 321. Power unit was the trusty six cylinder of 1971cc.

An EMW 340-4 amounted to the Ambulance version of the 340; this kind of two-door was made between 1951 and 1955.

Another twist to the original BMW theme was this 1951-55 run of two door vans more formally known as the EMW 340-3 range.

Autovelo's authentic rendering of the BMW 321 two door saloon was available even in 1945 and was made in some quantity until 1950. During that period BMW at Munich had the primary problem of getting their factory back into shape and trying to acquire even basic materials to rejoin the car-manufacturing world.

This BMW 340 S prototype appeared in Leipzig in the Spring of 1949. Based loosely on the running gear of the 340 BMW Eisenach product, the 80 horsepower engine was from the earlier BMW 328, but covered with an entirely new – and very satisfactory – lightweight metal body. This car was planned as the successor to the BMW 327, but it never made series production and construction of the BMW 327 in its earlier form continued.

This prototype BMW 342 was also shown at Leipzig, but in the Spring of 1951, when it was intended to replace the 340. It was certainly rather more like a 'proper' BMW with the kidney grille and flowing lines. It had torsion bar front suspension and was 20cm longer than a 340, some 10cm wider and 30cm lower in overall height. It was never produced in volume, though this four door promised much for Eisenach, who were naturally keen to export as much as possible.

Also at Leipzig Show in Spring 1951 was this ugly and badly Americanised "BMW 343" Technically this prototype offered coil spring rear suspension, while the body was basically that of 342 under that garish grille and beaky bonnet. Still using a lot of pre-war BMW know-how, the 343 was the factory's interpretation of what the export markets might demand and came with a 65 horsepower motor. It did not go into production.

The EMW 327-3 Sports
Coupe of 1949 to 1956

The EMW 327-2 Sports
Cabriolet of 1948 to 1956

BMW 328 after 1945: different models and their disguises

Despite the total breakdown and all the ramifications of a complete absence through the war years, motor sports soon awoke to surprisingly vigorous new life in the Western Occupied zone of Germany. By 1946 this had prompted some former BMW employees to found the *Veritas GmbH* in Messkirch/Baden. They worked from the baseline of available or recycled engines and the chassis of the BMW 328 to build competitive racing or sports cars. For a time this was an astonishing success, at least by comparison with what others were doing at the time. Unfortunately the limited availability of suitable materials was a problem, but it was not long before Veritas had the use of a new light alloy motor from Heinkel, which they employed from 1950 onward. A considerable number of cars were made, but the business was badly administered. Their operational base moved to Rastatt and then to Nurburgring, scene of a six-car Veritas racing appearance in 1950. Unfortunately little further luck accrued during these moves and there was always a lack of capital.

After their second bankruptcy in 1953, BMW bought out the Veritas company and with that deal they regained former BMW styling director Ernst Loof, one of the Veritas concern's founders. Loof developed for postwar BMW in Munich a prototype sportscar – shown publicly in 1954. This model did not make production, but a year later Loof was pictured happily working on the preliminary stages of the BMW 507. However, Loof did not have much longer to live and despite the high repute in which the "Veritas" name was held in postwar years, despite their many mistakes – hardly anyone remembers the marque today.

In Germany Alexander Freiherr von Falkenhausen also produced and raced a BMW-based sports car (the AFM), but he returned to work for Munich again in the fifties. The German aristocrat became the most famous influence on the BMW sporting and engines engineering side through the fifties, sixties and early seventies.

England gave the basic BMW 328 design a new lease of life in postwar years, under a variety of names. By 1935 the English sports car firm Frazer Nash had undertaken the entire sales programme, importing some BMW cars complete. Then AFN would install some of their own parts and the car was offered as the Frazer-Nash BMW. Thus business prospered and BMW learned to consider their English partners, for instance the BMW 335 made its debut at the 1938 Olympia Motor Show in London. After the second World War Frazer Nash worked with Bristol, better known for their aeroplanes, on a series of cars derived from the 328. Bristol continued with production of what amounted basically to the BMW straight six in ever more modified form until 1958 – employing the engine within a series of tubular frame/alloy body cars of very sleek and, presumably, aerodynamic line. Once the engine went out of production AFN took until 1959 to stop making their 328-derived sports roadsters, but AFN did experiment with the BMW 2.6-litre and 3.2-litre V8 motors. Finally AFN became the sole importers of BMWs to Britain, a situation that was not to last for AFN went over to a similar arrangement with Porsche before Stuttgart bought out the UK concession.

Meanwhile, it should be noted that right up until 1953 the Bristol was so similar to a BMW concept that it even carried the kidney-shaped radiator grille!

This beautifully sleek Sport-Coupe of 1949 came from the Veritas works and was powered by the 2-litre BMW six. The main problem in producing any cars at all in the Western Germany of that period was simply getting good enough materials, or enough materials, to manufacture the product. Alex von Falkenhausen recalled even in the seventies that his most critical racing need had been for British quality bearings to withstand racing loads, bearings that were not permitted in the Germany of the immediate postwar period.

Oh dear! Spohn coachworks were responsible for this Veritas 2-litre sporting exercise. It was called "Saturn" and was made in 1950.

Spohn also provided the bodywork for this Veritas of Nurburgring 2-litre Cabriolet. This four-seater had an oddly British fifties sporting feel about its style ... one could imagine a touch of Healey inspiration about the front grille, wings and lighting.

71

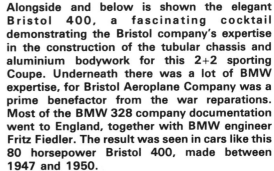

Alongside and below is shown the elegant Bristol 400, a fascinating cocktail demonstrating the Bristol company's expertise in the construction of the tubular chassis and aluminium bodywork for this 2+2 sporting Coupe. Underneath there was a lot of BMW expertise, for Bristol Aeroplane Company was a prime benefactor from the war reparations. Most of the BMW 328 company documentation went to England, together with BMW engineer Fritz Fiedler. The result was seen in cars like this 80 horsepower Bristol 400, made between 1947 and 1950.

Pininfarina was responsible for this 2+2 Cabriolet of 1950-53, based on the same straight six-cylinder 80 horsepower running gear and derived from the Bristol 401.

Coachwork by Touring under licence, this Bristol 401 four-seater also used the 80bhp BMW six-cylinder engine, but was built in Britain from the original Munich plans. The 401 was produced between 1950-53 but the BMW six-cylinder engine was further and further developed both by Bristol and AFN in their separate ways, so that outputs of 130bhp were eventually realised from its 2-litres. Production of the 1971cc unit ceased in 1958 at Bristol, but they continued to use a developed version of the incredible six in 105bhp/2216cc guise, when it still retained that cross pushrod valve gear arrangement of the thirties BMW! The 406 and its long stroke version of the six (68.7mm by 99.6mm, giving 2.2-litres) stayed in production until 1961, when Bristol finally went shopping for Detroit V8 power for their ever more luxurious sporting coupes.

Colour section: The Eisenach Cars from 1900 to 1940

Built around 1900 this Wartburg (constructed under license by Decauville) represented a motorised version of the accommodation that would be offered behind a horse. This chain final drive example is from the Eisenacher Automobile Works Museum.

Roughly ten years on and a more recognisable car has evolved complete with capacious, covered, accommodation for four to five occupants, front engine and spoked metal wheels for the road, plus a recognisable steering wheel in place of the previous tiller. This Dixi R 8 had a four-cylinder power plant rated at 6/14HP. It was built around 1910 and is also to be seen at the Eisenacher Automobile Works Museum.

Opposite, top: True twenties nostalgia! The lady in the striking coat is assisted aboard a Dixi 6/24 OS Town Coupe in this illustration from an advertisement of 1924.

Jaunty little open two-seater is the Dixi 3/15HP, also from 1928 and the Type DA 1 series. Note the wire wheels and Dunlop tyres.

The BMW legend stems from the BMW 3/15HP successors to the Dixi adaptations of Austin Seven. This three to four-seater Cabriolet is from 1930 and the Type DA 2 series.

Opposite, bottom: Perhaps *the* turning point in BMW history was the arrival of the Austin Seven in Germany. This is a 1928 Dixi 3/15HP from the DA 1 series, clothed with the three to four-seater touring body.

Belonging to the BMW Museum in Munich today is this fine example of the 1932-34 production BMW 3/20HP. The two door saloon had coachwork from Sindelfingen and was BMW's own design to succeed the cancelled Austin licencing agreement. The long stroke 782cc development of the engine provided 20bhp.

Ambi-Budd provided the body for this two door 303, a 1933 example of the model that began the BMW six-cylinder legend with its 1.2-litre engine that shared the bore and stroke of the 3/20, but provided an extra two cylinders and 30bhp.

This beautifully preserved BMW 315 Cabriolet is a 1935 four window model, which rather contradicts its 1934 number plate. It had Polish owners, though the 850 plate at the front is from East Germany.

Founder of a great sporting tradition. The BMW 315/1 of the 1934–36 period was an ideal base for sporting activity with its 1.5-litre six-cylinder engine. Some 40bhp was generated by its triple Solex-carburated motor, allowing speeds of 75mph to be reached. This example can normally be found in the BMW Munich museum.

A truly versatile design that lived on under other names during postwar years: the BMW 321. This is the two door saloon from 1939-41 with Ambi-Budd body and the 1971cc six that was the basis of the legendary 328 engine. In this single carburettor form it provided 45bhp, enough for 321 to reach almost 70mph.

Ambi-Budd four door body for the BMW 326, made between 1939-41. A twin Solex carburettor version of the 1971cc six provided 50bhp and 71mph.

The sleek 1938-39 BMW 327/28 sporting coupe with 2+2 seating. As the suffix suggests, power came from the 80bhp six of 328.

The legend that spawned a whole postwar industry of derivatives: the immortal BMW 328.

Property today of BMW Munich is this breathtaking BMW 328 prepared for the 1940 Mille Miglia; a hybrid event held over a closed circuit of just over 100 miles that year. BMW entered five cars, three open roadsters amongst them. This car belonged to the well known Bowler family, British enthusiasts, and was returned to BMW in the seventies. In racing trim weight was reckoned to be below 650kg/1430lb with over 130bhp available from the 2-litre six.

A return to logical numbering: the 3.5-litre BMW 335. This is a four door Cabriolet of 1939/40, its 90bhp six covered by Autenrieth coachwork. As exhibited by the BMW Museum, Munich.

Closed four door Cabriolet of the same period, also by Autenrieth and powered by the 3.5-litre six. This shining example is owned by Peter de Crousaz of Wurselen.

The Bavarian Motor Works from 1945 and the BMW cars from Munich

The complete breakdown in normal life in the years up to 1945 meant not only the production standstill on the car side for BMW, but also the subsequent confiscation and partial dismantling of both Munich business activities and the complete loss of the Thuringen (Eisenach) and Brandenberg (Berlin) factories. The aero engine factory in Munich-Allach was claimed by the US Army and eventually rented as a site for repairing motor vehicles: at first it had looked as though all BMW's business connections would be confiscated.

Only in the Munich press works at Milbertshofen could production of motorcycles (first of all the R 24) commence once again. That took until 1947 to achieve and was preceded by BMW improvising in the manufacture of cooking pots, baking utensils and building fittings. A really good business was made despite the constrictions of those years, but the volume was not sufficient to fully occupy a company of this size. The continuation of any kind of aero engine building could not even be thought about, so the return to four wheel vehicle manufacture by BMW drew nearer — especially as it was in car manufacture that their experience and excellent market reputation lay, despite the long, enforced, absence. BMW motorcycle manufacture began again in 1948 at Munich.

Unfortunately BMW could not take the path of Mercedes-Benz, Opel, VW and Ford in producing a proven and largely unchanged pre-war design again. By the time BMW were in any sort of shape to even think about making cars, too many postwar years had gone by for that simple revival ploy to be valid. Besides BMW did not even have tools to make cars — pretty well everything on the car side had been concentrated at Eisenach.

So, the Munich company acquired a licence to build from a foreign factory before realising their own preferred design. Director Fritz Fiedler returned from England and

joined colleagues Boning and Schimanowski, the latter responsible for the body styling, and they prepared two prototypes. One presented itself in form and technology as a very attractive small car (BMW 331). From the outside it looked similar to a Fiat Topolino, but its twin cylinder engine of 600cc, with fan air cooling, was derived from the large BMW motor cycle of the period. However, BMW Director Hanns Grewenig (from the Deutsche Bank) who was established on the commercial board of the factory felt that such a small car was not dignified for a company such as BMW: "we build for the cream of society", was his comment!

In the long term the problem was that the 331 was a two-seater and not suitable for development into a four-seater, so it never got past the prototype stage. (Some sources refer to this 1949-50 development as the "513", which fits in with the eventual production terminology of the fifties). By this time the members of the BMW board and its Chairman had decided that an integral part of any projected model range would be a luxury car.

Overcoming considerable financial demands from other parts of their business — any of which could have drained their resources — BMW decided to entirely equip their Munich vehicle manufacturing side with new facilities. The biggest chunk of finance went toward their own body and press works, which took until 1955 to construct. To begin with, and for many years subsequently, BMW left part of the bodywork finishing to the firm of Baur in Stuttgart — a link reinstated with the mid-engine M1 of the late seventies.

By 1951 BMW had progressed sufficiently to show a prototype of their new postwar machine (501) at the Frankfurt Show, but they really had no means of mass producing the car when it was displayed. Still the orders came in and BMW, even though they had little option but to initially power the 501 with the now rather outdated 1971cc six, belatedly went into production. It was November 1952 before production BMW 501s were delivered to the public. The model was received with great interest by the public, but only moderate acceptance by the fairly small market. It seemed that the body styling, inspired by Austin in England, required some familiarity before it would be accepted. Yet the most difficult thing to understand, from Werner Oswald's point of view, was why did BMW fall back on such a weak pre-war engine for such a large motor car? Presumably it was because almost any means of getting back into the production of cars quickly had to be found, and used, by the factory.

In 1954, BMW did bring out a thoroughly modern and competitive V8 engine — in fact Germany's first and only postwar eight cylinder engine for a very long time. Now, with more power available for their cars, the men of Munich began to receive many compliments, but far too few sales receipts.

Then came a quickly escalating two-wheeler crisis, for whatever leadership and financial return came from motorcycles was no longer enough to balance out the losses made in building cars. Likewise the Isetta, whose production under licence began in 1955, did not bring the anticipated profits. The BMW 600 evolution of Isetta (made from 1957 to 1959) led to further and considerable losses. The real BMW financial crisis came in the Autumn of 1958. The business was well known to the public as the victim of mismanagement and bad planning. BMW had 'made' 12 million Dm losses in that financial year, paying off 6.5 million Dm through using their last reserves and leaving 5.5 million Dm to be carried forward. Yet, in 1959, there was another 9.2 million Dm deficit resulting in half of the 30 million Dm share capital also being lost. Throughout the year the

BMW statistics	Workforce	Turnover (DMx millions)	Profit/loss (DMx millions)		Share capital (DMx millions)
1946	980	1,8	minus	1,0	
1947	1060	3,2	minus	1,0	
1948	1230	4,2	minus	1,9	
1949	2380	19,9	minus	1,9	
1950	8720	36,5	plus	1,0	30
1951	9300	57,5	plus	0,7	30
1952	9570	82,2	minus	0,1	30
1953	9200	87,9	plus	0,1	30
1954	8000	95,1	plus	1,1	30
1955	6900	138,0	plus	0,1	30
1956	5750	148,6	minus	6,4	30
1957	6040	148,2	minus	6,5	30
1958	6540	195,3	minus	12,0	30
1959	5950	170,3	minus	9,2	30
1960	6960	239,3		–	22,5
1961	6800	248,6		–	60
1962	9200	294,1	plus	2,5	60
1963	10100	433,1	plus	3,8	60
1964	10800	515,1	plus	6,5	60
1965	11070	590,7	plus	9,2	75
1966	13070	755,9	plus	10,7	100
1967	12470	870,8	plus	12,2	100
1968	18040	1032,4*)	plus	17,1	100
1969	21300	1443,4	plus	22,8	100
1970	22900	1724,4	plus	34,2	200
1971	23300	1907,1	plus	32,2	250
1972	24750	2319,3	plus	92,9	250
1973	27730	2608,0	plus	93,2	275
1974	25800	2492,3	plus	42,0	300
1975	29000	3254,5	plus	74,0	300
1976	30200	4287,0	plus	126,0	330
1977	33400	4993,0			330

*) From 1968: nett turnover (no turnover tax)

BMW management made futile efforts to obtain further bank credit and Bavarian state support.

Finally, on December 9, 1959, things came to a head at a memorable and dramatic annual general meeting of the company. Board of directors Chairman Dr Hans Feith (Deutsche Bank) laid out his redevelopment plan. This amounted to a cheap affiliation with Daimler-Benz, in which the Deutsche Bank were large shareholders! Not surprisingly the small shareholders in BMW almost walked out at that suggestion: they fought in such an organised manner that the motion was postponed. Thus this ultimate decision was deferred until another meeting took place.

At this next meeting the board of directors and general management professed that the only alternative to the Mercedes amalgamation was bankruptcy. So it appeared that the sale of BMW to Daimler-Benz was a foregone conclusion. Especially as the Deutsche Bank were authorised to act as deputies for numerous shareholders' votes: well over half the capital in fact. However, it turned out differently ... the MAN works at Allach, suitably encouraged by the resumption of aero factory work, loaned the small shareholders 30 million Dm. The small shareholders declared themselves prepared to find a further 30 million Dm outside capital to see off the Deutsche Bank redevelopment plan.

Obviously, this plan hardly sufficed. Yet, to keep the independence of BMW was the objective of the majority of small stockholders, some of whom were BMW dealers with faith in the product. As their spokesman at the general meeting Frankfurt lawyer and accountant Dr Friedrich Mathern stepped in. Thanks to his sound knowledge of shareholders' rights he succeeded in a brilliant move: at the adjournment of the meeting Dr Richter Brohm was virtually forced to resign, taking with him much of the strong influence of the Deutsche Bank and postponing the fatal decision over amalgamation with Mercedes. The saviour of an independent BMW, Dr. Mathern, belonged to the BMW board from the close of 1960 until the end of 1966. At the age of 61 in 1968, Dr Mathern suffered a fatal heart attack.

BMW was fortunate in the circumstances surrounding its capital revival, for, after that historic general meeting, the Quandt Group emerged as major new shareholders.

Familiar sight from the Munich ring road since 1973 has been BMW's imaginative 22-storey HQ, 'the biggest four-cylinder in the world", according to legend. The outline of this near 100 metre high edifice is that of a cloverleaf, within which it provides space for 2000 staff, some of whom have a magnificent view to the Alps from behind the blue-tinted glass. To the left, the smaller "cup" building, without windows, is the BMW Museum. This is worth seeing because of the attractive way in which it presents historic BMW motorcycles and cars. Inside there's a continuous audio-visual commentary, an escalator and a frequently changed, but always imaginative display of company history.

Dr Herbert Quandt and brother Harald had become a major force by taking over a previous large buyer of then cheap BMW stock: timber magnate from Bremen, Herman Krages and his company Holzkaufmans Krages. This brought the Quandt share of BMW capital to 15 per cent. Leading the rest, Dr Herbert Quandt now took on an entrepreneurial influence over the fate of the works, taking care not to damage the shareholders fortunes whilst also actively interested in the new products BMW needed in order to survive. Primarily Dr Quandt understood that BMW needed the attention of a highly qualified "guiding personality". From 1969 Dr Herbert Quandt held, or controlled, over half the shareholders' capital, including a period as Chairman of the board of BMW directors. Even in the eighties the Quandt influence is in the background at BMW.

At the General Meeting of November 30, 1960, the rebirth of the Munich firm was safely ensured. Dr Johannes Semler who had a legendary reputation for reviving ailing companies was chosen by the BMW board of directors to assist the company in this decisive year. Shortly afterwards, Semler headed for Bremen, where he was charged with averting the threat of bankruptcy that Borgward faced. There, for the first time, success was denied him, but with BMW he coped brilliantly, overcoming a heavy workload.

Obviously it could be seen at the General Meeting in 1960 that the situation was no longer hopeless as it appeared the year before. In the meantime the rear-engined BMW 700 had a surprisingly good introduction,

By 1950 Fritz Fiedler and his team had developed the BMW 331. A small two-seater with an air-cooled boxer engine of two cylinders, it had rear wheel drive. Despite its similarity to the Italian Fiat Topolino, this delightful little character offered great opportunities for BMW. Then came the decision by BMW boss, director Hanns Grewenig in favour of the later Isetta, after which they built the comical BMW 600. The BMW 331 of Fiedler was not thought to be sophisticated enough to carry the white and blue BMW symbol. Thus was production prevented of this promising model.

so that there were at least no further business losses to emerge. The successful revival in BMW fortunes allowed the management, at last, the resources necessary for the production of a "New Class" of BMW the 1500 and its successors ...

Series production of the 1500 began in 1962. It made such an immediate and effective impact that the firm's fortunes began to climb in spectacular fashion. After a gap of 20 years, a modest dividend was paid out in 1963. BMW hardly felt the recession after 1970 and today *Bayerischen Motoren Werke* is counted as one of the healthiest companies in the world.

By 1966 Hans Glas GmbH, of Dingolfing, were at a financial end. This patriarchal family business mainly enjoyed popularity during the manufacturing period of the Goggomobile economy car, but with the demand for more sophisticated vehicles, they found themselves overtaken by events. *Bayerischen Motoren Werke* — without further ado — took over the whole outfit,

BMW left this Pininfarina alternative to one side even before they had styled the six-cylinder 501 saloon. Built by Pininfarina, then the leading coachworks in the world and led by Commendatore Pininfarina himself (he died in 1966), this saloon foretold the shape of saloons to come. Essentially it is in the style of the S-class from Mercedes-Benz — a style BMW followed as competitors 27 years later. Then BMW decided, for the sake of their independence, to press ahead with their own 501. This ignored the bigger possibilities of the Italian line at the time, BMW approval going to the proper English-style of the 501.

following a request from the Bavarian State Government.

BMW paid 10 million Dm to the Glas family and undertook to meet even the highest debts of that firm, which must have amounted to at least 50 million Dm. On one hand this was a risky strongman act but, on balance, it provided the works with a freedom of movement for the imminent necessity of large scale expansion. Primarily the works in Dingolfing made *Bayerische Motoren Werke's* breathtaking expansion in recent years possible. The solitary wooden factory building of Glas was replaced by BMW with two entirely new, highly modern, and fully equipped factories, which became operational in 1973. A further 100 million Dm had been needed to invest in this site. However, today some 10,000 people work at Dingolfing, whereas (at best) Hans Glas employed 4000. BMW were to build cars of the 5, 6 and 7-series at Dingolfing, while Munich's production facility was devoted to 3-series. From 1967 the Berlin-Spandau factory made the very popular motorcycles.

Finally we should record one of the most important events in the postwar BMW story. In 1973 the new administration high rise building was completed. It is known as the "Four-Cylinder" building, but there are company men who feel BMW's later move into six-cylinder engines for the majority of the range should have seen an extra two cylinders added to the magnificent offices too! The 100 metre high structure has space for 2000 employees. Since its erection its unusual architecture has come to symbolise the new power and strength of BMW.

Here it is appropriate to recall the leaders of BMW since 1945: Kurt Donath (1945–1957); Hanns Grewenig (1949-1957); Dr Heinrich Richter-Brohm (1957–1960); Dr Karl Heinz Sonne (1962–1965); Gerhard Wilcke (1965–1969); Eberhard von Kuenheim (from 1970). Similarly for development and design leadership we should remember: Fritz Fiedler (1949–1964); Bernhard Osswald (1965–1975); Dr Ing. Karl-heinz Radermacher (from 1975). Sales chiefs: Paul G. Hahnemann (1961–1971); Robert A Lutz (1972–1974); Hans Erdmann Schonbeck (from 1974). Chairmen of the Board: Dr Hans Karl von Mangoldt-Reiboldt (1946–1959); Dr Hans Feith (1959–1960); Dr Johannes Semler (1960–1961); Dr Hermann Karoli (1962–1972); Dr Phil. h.c. Herbert Quandt (from 1974). Chairman, supervisory Board, Hans Graf von der Goltz (as at December 1981).

BMW 501 six-cylinder (1952-58)

The first BMW passenger car to reach production after the war. The 501's chassis was excellent. A strong collection of tubular and rectangular frames to be exact, but the steering was too nervous over poor roads for some tastes: a bevel gear system was used, with a further linkage on a rack and pinion principle. The body had a distinctive English style, but was above all comfortable, and spacious. From the prewar BMW came the 2-litre engine, rather overtaxed by the demands of the weight and class of car. Notable design features included (not on the grounds of safety, just design limitations!) a short steering column and fuel tank located over the axle.

The prototype 501 was shown at the April, 1951, Frankfurt Show and production started in November 1952. To emphasise the aspirations of exclusivity relating to the 501, it was offered with a standard built-in Becker radio. The 65bhp single Solex engine, was produced until March 1954. This month saw the advent of the BMW 501A and standard use of the 72bhp engine for BMW 501B. From March 1955 the BMW 501/6 was available with an engine block bored to provide 2.1-litres; also a saloon version, with simpler equipment, was provided at lower price than before. Indeed, each successive 501 derivative became cheaper!

Toward the end of 1958, production of the BMW 501 *Sechszylinder* ceased, though 17 further cars were specially made in subsequent years. Altogether 8,936 BMW type 501 cars were made, all with six-cylinder engines. The Baur coachworks provided all the bodies at first, then by 1955 they played a supporting role providing part of production. In total the Stuttgart concern provided 1,870 cars. Furthermore, Baur delivered eight BMW 501A and 37 501/6 models in Cabriolet or Coupe style.

The BMW 501 made its debut in April 1951, but the prototype could not be turned into reality owing to BMW's chronic shortage of suitable tooling. It would be November 1952 before the long-suffering public, some of whom had ordered at the Frankfurt Show more than a year earlier, got their cars. Baur at Stuttgart played a big hand in making even that protracted production run possible. As a design Werner Oswald found the car redolent of the big Austins of the period, while other sources say that Pininfarina, who offered the alternative we detail on an earlier page, reportedly found the overall BMW company 501 look pleasing. Underneath the 501 had a strong separate chassis, torsion bar suspension and a four-speed, column-change manual gearbox set well back in the body – so far, in fact, that it had to be connected to engine and clutch by a short shaft. An overall weight close to 3000lbs meant the 65bhp original engine had to work hard. Later derivatives had the 2.1-litre version of the six and substantially the same car was also propelled by a subsequent V8.

BMW 502 2.6-litre (1954-64)
BMW 501 eight-cylinder (1955-62)
BMW 502 3.2-litre (1955-62)
BMW 502 3.2-litre Super (1957-64)

BMW 502: the first postwar German eight-cylinder passenger car. Chassis and bodywork were as for the BMW 501. However, equipment included more chrome, built-in foglights, indicators instead of trafficators, as well as a wrap-around "Panoramic" rear screen (from September 1955).

BMW made history with the introduction of their V8. Not only was it the first in postwar Germany, but also the major parts were constructed in aluminium. It made its debut at the Geneva Show of 1954 and was built from July 1954 until March 1964. The model name changed in Autumn 1958 to BMW 2.6 Luxury and then in September 1961 to BMW 2600L. The latter had another 10bhp (total 110), was capable of 102mph and had disc brakes: it was recognisable by its round tail lights.

BMW 501 eight-cylinder: This model had a 2.6-litre V8, rated at 95bhp in the 501 body, distinguished by its smaller rear window and lack of additional chrome. Built from March 1955 until Summer 1962, the model was known as the BMW 2.6 from Autumn 1958. From September 1961 it became the BMW 2600 and also took on extra performance, disc brakes (front only) and round tail lights similar to the 502.

BMW 502: 3.2-litre: This amounted to much the same car as the 502, but boosted by the 120bhp enlarged 3.2-litre V8. It was first shown at Frankfurt Motor Show in September 1955. Production stretched from October 1955 until the Summer of 1962. From the Autumn of 1958 it was called BMW 3.2 while in September 1961 it became BMW 3200L. Once more disc brakes and round tail lights were offered at this point, and the 3.2 was uprated to 140bhp, enough to travel at 107mph.

BMW 502 3.2-litre Super: This twin carburettor derivative provided yet higher engine output (140bhp). It was produced from April 1957 to March

1964. As of October 1959 disc brakes became standard, while the model name changed to BMW 3200S from September 1961 and it gained 20bhp, plus the usual model change round tail lamps.

Inside the factory they ignored the marketing names and knew all cars with the 2.6-litre V8 as "Typ 502". All cars with the 3.2-litre V8 were known as "Typ 506". Confusing, but that is how they added up their figures too: production of Typ 502 was 9,109 vehicles, while 3,935 cars of Typ 506 were constructed. All saloons were made by BMW's own pressworks. The coachworks at Baur, Stuttgart, delivered between 1954 and 1955 some 230 Cabriolets and Coupes with the eight-cylinder motor, including 50 four-door Cabriolets. Autenrieth, Darmstadt, managed about 50 further Coupes and Cabriolets. The Autenrieth bodies were unique in their radiator outline and the line of their wings, but this noteworthy departure was not really visually satisfying.

BMW 505 (1955)

Seeking to offer an alternative to the Mercedes 300 "Adenauer Typ" of the period, BMW displayed the BMW 505 at the September 1955 Frankfurt Motor Show. A longer — by some 200 mm — as well as stronger chassis was of 502 origin. Power was provided by a 120 horsepower version of the 3.2-litre V8, but the most important feature was the Pullman luxury coachwork, drawn up by Michelotti of Turin and completed by Ghia-Aigle of Lugano, Switzerland. For luxurious comfort the equipment included electro-hydraulic operation of the side windows and a proper sliding partition: there was an intercom provided for speech between driver and passengers. The rear seats were almost like club chairs, and there was a drinks bar plus a folding writing desk that even had its own lights. As if that were not sufficient, a remote control radio, acres of wood and the use of precious fabrics and carpets completed the picture.

Built on a wheelbase of 3055mm and a front/rear track measurement of 1343 and 1429mm, the total overall dimensions were: length 5100mm; width, 1830mm; height, 1630mm. The tyres were of 6.70-15 measurement and 505 carried the 502 gearbox and BMW 503 final drive ratio. The BMW 505 was seen as the "State Carriage" for West German Chancellor Dr. Adenauer, who was not best pleased with his recently-acquired Mercedes 300. Adenauer himself undertook two long trial drives in the BMW, but he decided on the acquisition of a Mercedes-Benz 300C, built to his ideal specification. For Bayerischen Motoren Werke the risks involved in series production of the 505 were too great. Just two prototypes were made and both saw useful official service around Munich.

BMW 503 (1956-59)

This model came in Coupe and Cabriolet style with a considerably longer bonnet. The result was an almost monstrous and rather flat-decked appearance for this 2+2. Styled by Graf Goertz, the car was displayed at the 1955 Frankfurt Show in September. From May 1956 to March 1959, some 413 examples were constructed.

Production	BMW 501	BMW 501/6	BMW 502 2.6-litre	BMW 506 3.2-litre	BMW 505	BMW 503	BMW 507	BMW 3200 CS	
1952	49								49
1953	1592								1592
1954	3410		186	4					3600
1955	641	1386	2364	157	2	2	2		4554
1956		1080	1999	529		154	13		3775
1957		611	540	358		64	91		1664
1958		150	916	564		143	98		1871
1959		7	1170	528		50	48		1803
1960		5	259	397					661
1961		5	730	780				3	1518
1962			615	269				25	909
1963			315	235				142	692
1964			15	14				253	282
1965								115	115
Totals	5692	3244	9109	3935	2	413	252	538	23185

	BMW 501 1952-1954	BMW 501A 1954-1955	BMW 501 six cyls. 1955-1958	
Motor				
Cylinders	6 inline	6 inline	6 inline	
Bore x stroke	66x96mm	66x96mm	68x96mm	
Capacity	1971cc	1971cc	2077cc	
Power	65bhp @ 4400rpm	72bhp @ 4400rpm	72bhp @ 4500rpm	
Torque	13.2mkg @ 2000rpm	13.3mkg @ 2500rpm	13.8mkg @ 2500rpm	
Compression	6.8:1	6.8:1	7:1	
Carburation	1, twin choke, downdraught Solex 30 PAAJ	1, twin choke, downdraught Solex 30PAAJ	1, twin choke, downdraught Solex 32 PAJTA	
Valves	Overhead Rocker, tappet & spring Side camshaft, duplex chain driven	Overhead Rocker, tappet & spring Side camshaft, duplex chain driven	Overhead Rocker, tappet & spring Side camshaft As 501,501A	
Crankshaft bearings	4	4	4	
Cooling	Pump, 7.25 litres of water	As 501	As 501/501A	
Lubrication	Pressure, 4.5 litres, oil	As 501	As 501/501A	
Battery	12v 50ah	As 501	As 501/501A	
Generator	160W DC	160W DC	160W DC	
Transmission	Rear wheel drive Gearbox under front seats Short secondary propshaft	Rear wheel drive As 501 As 501	Rear wheel drive As 501/501A As 501/501A	
Gearchange	Column linkage	As 501	As 501/501A	
Gearbox	4-speed	4-speed	4-speed	
Synchromesh	1st-4th	1st-4th	1st-4th	
Ratios	1st, 4.24 2nd, 2.35 3rd, 1.49 4th, 1.00	1st, 4.24 2nd, 2.35 3rd, 1.49 4th, 1.00	1st, 4.24 2nd, 2.35 3rd, 1.49 4th, 1.00	
Final drive	4.225	4.225	4.551 or 4.225	
Bodywork & chassis	Box section longitudinal frames; tubular cross beams All steel coachwork, welded from floor up	As 501 As 501	As 501/501A As 501/501A	
Front suspension	Double wishbones, torsion bars	As 501	As 501/501A	
Rear suspension	Rigid axle, torsion bars	As 501	As 501/501A	
Steering	Bevel gears, jointed to rack and pinion			
	Ratio: 16.5:1 Lock to to lock, 3.5 turns.	As 501	As 501/501A	
Footbrakes	Hydraulic Drums, 284mm dia. Swept area, 850cm	Hydraulic Drums, 284mm dia. As 501	Hydraulic Drums, 284mm dia. Swept area, 1050cm	
General data				
Wheelbase	2835mm	2835mm	2835mm	
Track (Front/Rear)	1322/1408mm	1302/1408mm	1302/1408mm	
Length, width & height	4730/1780/1530mm	4730/1780/1530mm	4730/1780/1530mm	
Rims	4.00 E x 16	4.00 E x 16	4.00 E x 16 or 4½K x 15	
Tyres	5.50x16	5.50x16	5.50x16 or 6.40x15	
Turning circle (right)	12 metres	12 metres	12 metres	
Vehicle weight	1340kg	1340kg	1340kg	
Max permissible weight	1725kg	1725kg	1800kg	
Top speed	84mph	87mph	90mph	
0-62mph	27 secs	23 secs	—	
Litres/100km	12.5 (22.5mpg)	13 (21.7mpg)	13 (21.7mpg)	
Fuel tank	58 litres (over back axle)	As 501	As 501/501A	

Externally similar were the four door BMW 501, 501A and 501B saloons, produced between 1952-55.

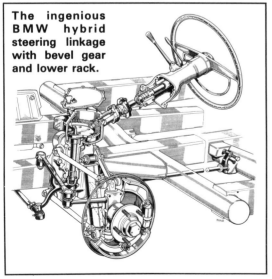

The ingenious BMW hybrid steering linkage with bevel gear and lower rack.

BMW 501 chassis displays gearbox set well back in frame, rear axle linkages, and torsion bar suspension.

	BMW 502 – 2.6-Litre 1954-1961 BMW 501 Eight-Cylinder 1955-1961	BMW 502 – 3.2-Litre 1955-1961	BMW 502 – 3.2-Litre Super 1957-1961	
Motor				
Cylinders	90°V8 Aluminium heads & cylinder block Wet cylinder liners	90°V8 Aluminium heads & cylinder block Wet cylinder liners	90°V8 Aluminium heads & cylinder block Wet cylinder liners	
Bore x stroke	74x75mm	82x75mm	82x75mm	
Capacity	2580cc	3168cc	3168cc	
Power	501: 90bhp @ 4800rpm 502: 100bhp @ 4800rpm	120bhp @ 4800rpm –	140bhp @ 4800rpm –	
Torque	501: 18.0mkg @ 2800rpm 502: 18.4mkg @ 2500rpm	21.4mkg @ 2500rpm –	22mkg @ 3200rpm –	
Compression	7:1	7.2:1	7.3:1	
Carburation	1, downdraught twin choke Solex 30 PAAJ From 1957: Zenith 32 NDIX	As 2.6/501-8 Zenith 32 NDIX	2, downdraught twin choke Zenith 32 NDIX	
Valves	Overhead, central camshaft Rocket, tappet & spring Duplex chain cam drive	As 2.6/501-8 As 2.6/501-8 As 2.6/501-8	Overhead, central camshaft Rocker, tappet & spring Duplex chain cam drive	
Crankshaft bearings	5	5	5	
Cooling	Pump, 10 litres water	As 2.6/501-8	Pump, 10 litres of water	
Lubrication	Pressure, 6.5 litres oil	As 2.6/501-8	Pressure, 6.5 litres oil	
Battery	12v 56ah	As 2.6/501-8	12v 56ah	
Generator	160 Watt	160W,DC	200W,DC	
Transmission	Rear wheel drive Gearbox under front seats Short secondary propshaft for clutch and gearbox	Rear wheel drive As 2.6/501-8 As 2.6/501-8	Rear wheel drive Gearbox under front seats Short secondary propshaft for clutch and gearbox	
Clutch	Single, dry pressure plate	As 2.6/501-8	Single, dry pressure plate	
Gearchange	Steering column	Steering column	Steering column	
Gearbox	4-speed	4-speed	4-speed	
Synchromesh	1st-4th	1st-4th	1st-4th	
Ratios	1st, 3.78	1st, 3.78. From '60: 3.71	As 502-3.2	
	2nd, 2.35	2nd, 2.35. From '60:2.27	As 502-3.2	
	3rd, 1.49	3rd, 1.49	As 502-3.2	
	4th, 1.00	4th, 1.00	As 502-3.2	
Final drive	4.225	3.89 or 3.90	As 502-3.2	
Bodywork & chassis	Box section longitudinal frame, tubular cross beams Floorpan upward, all steel coachwork	As 2.6/501-8	As 502-3.2	
Front suspension	Double wishbones, longitudinal torsion bars	As 2.6/501-8	As 502-3.2	
Rear suspension	Rigid (live) axle, torsion bars & three link locations	As 2.6/501-8	As 502-3.2	
Steering	Bevel gears & linkage to rack & pinion. Ratio: 16.5:1. Lock-to-lock 3.5 turns	As 2.6/501-8	As 502-3.2	
Footbrakes	Hydraulic Drums, 284mm dia. Swept area, 1050cm^2 1959-option:servo 1959-option:front disc brakes (267mm dia.) with servo-assistance	Hydraulic Drums, 284mm Swept area, 1256cm^2 1959 option:servo 1959-option:front discs (267mm dia.) with servo-assistance	Hydraulic Drums, 284mm Swept area, 1256cm^2 Servo-assisted Sept 1959: front discs (267mm dia.) servo-assistance, std.	
General data				
Wheelbase	2835mm	2835mm	2835mm	
Track (Front/Rear)	1330/1416mm	1330/1416mm	1330/1416mm	
Length, width & height	4730/1780/1530mm	4730/1780/1530mm	4730/1780/1530mm	
Rims	4½Kx15	4½Kx15	4½Kx15	
Tyres	6.40 S 15 L	6.40 S 15 L	6.40 S 15L, or (1959) 6.50/6.70 H 15 L	
Turning circle (right)	12 metres	12 metres	12 metres	
Vehicle weight	501:1430kg; 502:1440kg	1470kg	1500kg	
Max permissible weight	1900kg	1900kg	1900kg (1959), 2000kg	
Top speed	100mph	106mph	109mph	
0-62mph	17.5 sec	15 sec	14.5 sec	
Litres/100km	14.5 (19.4mpg)	15 (18.8mpg)	16 (17.6mpg)	
Fuel tank	70 litres (over rear axle)	70 litres (over rear axle)	70 litres (over rear axle)	

BMW 501 proved adaptable to six and eight-cylinder power between 1955-58. The four door saloon was also made from 1958-61 as the BMW 2.6 Luxus. The nearly square bore/stroke ratio of its 2580cc V8 providing up to 110bhp and speeds of more than 100 mph.

Slightly more ornate, the BMW 502 offered the chrome strip below the window line and built-in fog lamps as distinguishing features of Germany's first postwar V8. Both 3.2-litre and 3.2-litre Super versions had four doors, but the Super version offered another 20bhp from its twin carburettor version of the 3168cc short stroke V8. This is a later version of the model, complete with "Panoramic" American-inspired wrap-around rear screen.

Also a late model, this is the four door shape of the BMW 2600L, 3200L and 3200S, as produced between 1961 and 1964, complete with round tail lights.

	BMW 2600 1961-62 BMW 2600 L 1961-64	BMW 3200L 1961-62	BMW 3200 S 1961-63	
Motor				
Cylinders	90°V8 Aluminium cylinder block & heads, wet cylinder liners	90°V8 As 2600	90°V8 As 2600/3200L	
Bore x stroke	74x75mm	82x75mm	82x75mm	
Capacity	2580cc	3168cc	3168cc	
Power (bhp)	2600:100 @ 4800rpm 2600L:110 @ 4900rpm	140 @ 5400rpm	160 @ 5600rpm	
Torque	2600:18.5mkg @ 2500rpm 2600 L: 18.6mkg @ 3000rpm	24.2mkg @ 3000rpm	24.5mkg @ 3600rpm	
Compression	7.5:1	9:1	9:1	
Carburation	1,twin choke downdraught Zenith 32 NDIX	As 2600 Zenith 36 NDIX	2, twin choke, downdraught Zenith 36 NDIX	
Valves	Overhead Central block camshaft Rocker, tappet & spring Duplex chain cam drive	Overhead As 2600 As 2600 As 2600	Overhead Central block camshaft Rocker, tappet & spring Duplex chain cam drive	
Crankshaft bearings	5	5	5	
Cooling	Pump, 10 litres of water	Pump, 10 litres of water	Pump, 10 litres of water	
Lubrication	Pressure, 6.5 litres, oil	As 2600	As 2600/3200L	
Battery	12v 56ah	As 2600	As 2600/3200L	
Generator	160 Watt	160W,DC	200W,DC	
Transmission	Rear wheel drive Gearbox under front seats Short propshaft between clutch and gearbox	Rear wheel drive As 2600 As 2600	Rear wheel drive As 2600/3200 L As 2600/3200 L	
Clutch	Single plate, dry	Single plate, dry	Single plate, dry	
Gearchange	Steering column change	As 2600	As 2600/3200L	
Gearbox	4-speed	4-speed	4-speed	
Synchromesh	1st-4th	1st-4th	1st-4th	
Ratios	1st,3.71 2nd,2.27 3rd,1.49 4th,1.00	1st,3.71 2nd,2.27 3rd,1.49 4th,1.00	1st,3.71 2nd,2.27 3rd,1.49 4th,1.00	
Final drive	4,225	3.90	3.90	
Bodywork & chassis	Box section longitudinal chassis frame; tubular cross beams, with welded, all-steel coachwork	As 2600	As 2600/3200 L	
Front suspension	Double wishbones, longitudinal torsion bars	As 2600	As 2600/3200 L	
Rear suspension	Rigid, live axle with three location rods & longitudinal torsion bars	As 2600	As 2600/3200 L	
Steering	Bevel gears then to rack & pinion, 16.5:1 ratio. 3.5 turns lock-to-lock	As 2600	As 2600/3200 L	
Footbrake	Servo-assisted, hydraulic Front, discs, 267mm dia. Rear, drums, 284mm dia.	As 2600 As 2600 As 2600	As 2600/3200 L As 2600/3200 L As 2600/3200 L	
General Data				
Wheelbase	2835mm	2835mm	2835mm	
Track (Front/Rear)	1330/1416mm	1330/1416mm	1330/1416mm	
Length, width & height	4730/1780/1530mm	4730/1780/1530mm	4730/1780/1530mm	
Rims	4½ Kx15	4½ Kx15	4½ Kx15	
Tyres	6.40 S 15 L	6.40 S 15 L	6.50/6.70 H 15 L	
Turning circle (right)	12 metres	12 metres	12 metres	
Vehicle weight	1440kg	1470kg	1490kg	
Max permissible weight	1900kg	1900kg	2000kg	
Top speed	2600:101mph 2600 L:103mph	109mph	118mph	
0-62mph	2600: 17.5 sec. 2600 L: 17 sec.	14 sec.	14 sec.	
Litres/100km	14.5 (19.5mpg)	15.5 (18.2mpg)	16 (17.7mpg)	
Fuel tank	70 liters, over rear axle	As 2600	As 2600/3200L	

A 1955-built BMW 502 in the guise of control car for the Munich fire service. Similar cars were used as radio patrol cars by the Munich police.

Both pictures on this page are from Werner Oswald's book *Kraftfahrzeuge der Feuerwehr unt des Sanitsdienstes,* dealing with fire and ambulance service vehicles.

Binz and Co of Lorsch, Wurttemberg, were responsible for the construction of this BMW 502 as an ambulance in 1957. This plush and solitary example served the Bavarian Red Cross in Munich and then went to Grafenau.

	BMW 503 1956-59	BMW 507 1956-59	BMW 3200 CS 1962-65
Motor			
Cylinders	V8 90° Alloy block & heads with wet cylinder liners	V8 90° As 503	V8 90° As 503/507
Bore x stroke	82x75mm	82x75mm	82x75mm
Capacity	3168cc	3168cc	3168cc
Power (bhp)	140 @ 4800rpm	150 @ 5000rpm	160 @ 5600rpm
Torque	22mkg @ 3800rpm	24mkg @ 4000rpm	24.5mkg @ 3600rpm
Compression	7.3:1	7.8:1	9:1
Carburation	2, twin choke, downdraught Zenith 32 NDIX	2, As 503 Zenith 32NDIX	2, As 503/507 Zenith 36 NDIX
Valves	Overhead, rocker. Tappet & spring. Central cam & duplex chain cam drive	As 503	As 503/507
Crankshaft bearings	5	5	5
Cooling	Pump, 10 litres water	As 503	As 503/507
Lubrication	Pressure, 6.5 litres oil	As 503	As 503/507
Battery	12v 56ah	As 503	As 503/507
Generator	200W,DC	As 503	As 503/507
Transmission	Rear wheel drive	As 503	As 503/507
Clutch	Single, dry pressure plate	As 503	As 503/507
Gearchange	Steering column change with gearbox under front seats From Sept 1957: gearbox & engine together, floor change	Floor change with gearbox & engine together	Gearbox under front seats, column change or optional floor change
Gearbox	4-speed 4-speed, Sport	4-speed	4-speed
Synchromesh	1st–4th 1st–4th	1st–4th	1st-4th
Ratios	1st,3.78 1st,3.540 2nd,2.35 2nd,2.202 3rd,1.49 3rd,1.395 4th,1.00 4th,1.00	1st,3.387 2nd,2.073 3rd,1.364 4th,1.00	1st,3/71 2nd,2.27 3rd,1/49 4th,1.00
Final drive	3.90 optional 3.42	3.70,also 3.42 or 3.90	3.90 with extra cost 3.70 option
Bodywork & Chassis	Box section longitudinal frame & tubular cross beams with welded skeleton coachwork to take outer skin touring alloy coachwork	As 503, but differing outer skin, short wheelbase	Chassis principles as 503/507 but with welded steel body
Front suspension	Double wishbones & longitudinal torsion bars	As 503 + roll bar	As 507
Rear suspension	Rigid, live, axle, three link location & torsion bars	Live axle with extra links & Panhard Rod, torsion bars	As 507
Steering	Bevel gear ratio 16.5:1 3.5 turns lock-to-lock	As 503 As 503 + steering damper	As 503/507 As 503/507
Footbrakes	Servo-assisted, hydraulic Drums, 284mm diam. Swept area, 1256cm^2	As 503 As 503 As 503	As 503/507 Front, discs, 267mm. Rear, drums, 284mm
General Data			
Wheelbase	2835mm	2480mm	2835mm
Track (front/rear)	1400/1420mm	1445/1425mm	1330/1416mm
Length, width & height	4750/1710/1440mm	4380/1650/1300mm	4380/1720/1460mm
Rims	4.50E x16	4.50E x16	5Jx15
Tyres	6.00 H 16 (6PR)	6.00 H 16 (6PR)	6.00 H 15 L, or 185 HR15
Turning circle (right)	12 metres	10.7 metres	12 metres
Vehicle weight	1500kg	1330kg	1500kg
Max permissible weight	1800kg	1500kg	1900kg
Top speed	118mph	3.90 axle: 118mph 3.70 axle: 124mph 3.42 axle: 137mph	124mph
0-62 mph	13 sec	11.5 sec	14 sec
Litres/100km	16 (17.7mpg)	17 (16.6mpg)	16 (17.7mpg)
Fuel tank	75 litres, in back	65 or 110 litres, in back	75 litres, in back

Baur continued their tradition of association with BMW by producing this Cabriolet version of the 501, seen here with the hood neatly erected.

Hood down, the Baur 501 Cabriolet displays seating that was officially 2+2 in designation, though it looks more generous than that by modern standards. Such Cabriolets were made between 1954-55 and had two door bodies.

Baur also offered this four door Cabriolet in the same 1954-55 period. Accommodation comprised room for five.

In 1960 the open air five-seater tradition continued with four door Cabriolets such as this comparatively 'square-rigged' example from Autenrieth. It was built on the BMW 3.2-litre Super V8 running gear.

A smart 2+2 Hard top Coupe from Autenrieth in 1958. It was based on the 502 V8 and provided 2+2 seating, much in the modern coupe manner.

BMW 507 (1956-59)

Over 20 years later, this fantastically handsome creation of Graf Goertz was to command absolutely top prices from enthusiasts. Its debut was also at the September 1955 Frankfurt Show and production occupied November 1956 to March 1959 and resulted in 252 examples of the 507. About 70 still existed in 1978.

The 507 represented an exciting amalgamation of the large saloons and 503 philosophy. It is difficult today to judge which of the many external influences on Goertz's styling were most important: certainly BMW did not just accept the original drawings.

BMW 3200 CS (1962-65)

Inside the works this was known as the BMW 532. Following the 503, but with a Bertone of Turin body, the car was very solidly built and appeared a little too flashy for its time, though its lines could have been judged brilliant and a possible influence on the later works coupes of 2800 CS type. Today the BMW 3200 CS is highly valued and cherished by experts. It could be said to have established the big BMW coupe tradition.

September 1961, Frankfurt Show, was the debut of this model. From February 1962 until September 1965, exactly 538 cars were delivered.

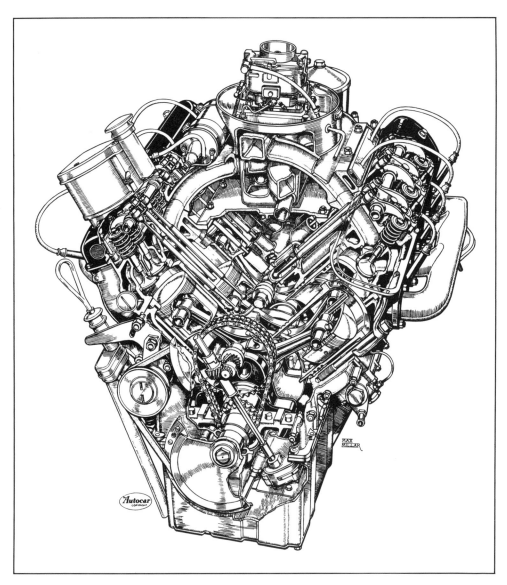

Max Miller *Autocar* cutaway of the V8 engine used for 502 and 501 through the fifties and into the sixties. Note the centre camshaft location for the pushrod valve gear of the aluminium block and cylinder heads of this 2.6 litre unit.

Photographic cutaway job on BMW 502 four door saloon shows plenty of rear seat space, the folding armrests providing a plush touch. Extensive instrumentation was provided and the finish to the side of the rake-adjustable seat backrest at the front is typical of the high chrome quality to be found on many later large BMWs too.

The box frame and tubular section chassis was a feature of BMW 502. As with the 501 there are the top-mounting links for the rear axle to observe and the engine-gearbox shaft connection remains, together with telescopic damping and torsion bar suspension. The umbrella handbrake and steering column gearchange emphasise the period flavour.

BMW 505 Pullman Limousine was constructed on a strengthened and lengthened 502 chassis, carrying this Michelotti style body. Presented in 1955, the prototype lost out in favour of Mercedes transport for West German Chancellor Konrad Adenauer. A second such car was constructed, but production of this V8 variant was felt to be too risky commercially.

An interesting Swiss BMW 502 Coupe of 1962/63 manufacture. For 50,000 Swiss Francs Beutler produced this four-seater, two door from their Thun factory. This Coupe is many years younger than 503, but was in no way more successful.

In 1953 BMW entirely took over the Veritas-Nurburgring concern and with that deal came former works development engineer Ernst Loof, who had been with BMW Eisenach until 1945. Very soon, the return to his old firm brought a new misfortune to Loof. For it was not Loof but Graf Albrecht Goertz who drew up the new big BMW sports car, though Loof was the in-house designer and had been commissioned first. Anyway Loof tried to push his design through by getting a prototype that could be displayed built up. Thus this unusual car was previewed by the public just once at a *concours d' elegance* held in Bad Neuenlich on September 13, 1954. Loof's sports car was built on a BMW 502 chassis and had the 2.6-litre V8 engine. Yet the development of Graf Goertz was essentially a much more elegant and attractive design, though it was certainly more complicated to build and therefore essentially more expensive. So the fate of the Ernst Loof creation was to remain a single prototype.

These cutaway drawings of the BMW 503 show the impressive construction which the works called providing an entirely protected chassis frame: a step toward unitary construction. By now well known, there was further work on the eight-cylinder engine and the power transmission train, including the gearbox under the front seats. Unlike the saloons it was significant that the unconsciously retrograde step of accommodating the fuel tank even further to the rear of the back axle was a feature of both 503 and 507. Later 503s had the engine and gearbox coupled, moving the four speed manual forward and allowing a simpler floor gearchange mechanism, rather than the column arrangement shown here. Note also torsion bar suspension is kept, and the convoluted steering system, the overall approach being similar to today in providing sporting looks over conventional BMW engineering.

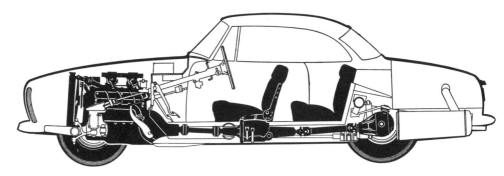

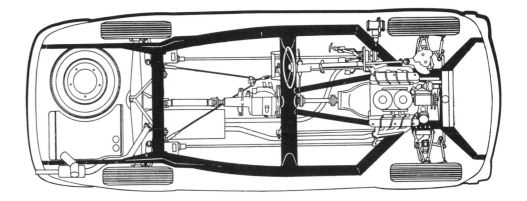

BMW 503 was available in a variety of bodystyles centred upon Coupe or Cabriolet accommodation of the 2+2 school. Here is the straightforward Coupe from the 1956-1959 production run, as are all the 503 illustrations on this page.

Cabriolet shows classic rakish convertible lines with the hood raised, including the traditional long bonnet. The 503 matched its sporty looks with a 140bhp version of the 3.2-litre V8, which powered 503s from rest to 62mph in 13 seconds and allowed up to 118mph.

Hood down on the Cabriolet 2+2 and time to display the properly finished hood tonneau and the distinctive body line from cowled headlamps to boot. Weighing over 3,000 lb the 503 was an expensive, limited production, offering that was reckoned to average 17.2mpg.

Also from the talented Albrecht Goertz was the 507, this a rather idealised artist's view of the two-seater Roadster model made between 1956-1959. This purer sports car still used BMW current engineering underneath, including a short wheelbase, gearbox and engine mated without connecting shaft, an even more convoluted steering system (with a joint before the bevel gear needed to clear the 3.2-litre V8 in this installation) and torsion bar suspension. Disc brakes for the front were added during 1958, toward the close of the production run.

Hardtop in place on the 1956-59 BMW 507 two-seater Roadster, and we gain a good view of the historic front styling. Historic? Yes, the kidney grille is absent, forsaken temporarily in favour of outside styling influences of the period: note too the front wing grilles that would not have looked out of place on the contemporary Chevrolet Corvette. Complete with 150bhp and twin Zenith carburation the 507 was reckoned to be good for 137mph on the 3.42 final drive. It was said to accelerate from 0-62mph in 11.5s (it weighed nearly 375lb less than 503) and travelled at 16.3mpg.

The traditional grille is back for the 1962-65 BMW 3200 CS with its Bertone four-seater body and two doors. Look at the roofline, and particularly the shape of the rear side glass frame and you get a genuine hint of BMWs to come – and later coupe styling. A significant 160bhp/124mph model, but only just over 500 were built ...

BMW Isetta (1955-62)

At the beginning of 1954 the Italian firm of Iso Isetta introduced a tiny two-seater with four wheels. It had a narrow rear track, no differential and a single front door. Although the Isetta achieved little in its homeland, BMW acquired both the licence to build it and the press tools needed for manufacture of the small vehicle.

BMW replaced the original noisy two-stroke with the muffled thuds emitting from a modified version of their single-cylinder R 25 motorcycle four-stroke engine. There were numerous other improvements, so that the BMW Isetta was soon thriving and regarded as a sturdy and respected example amongst the many scooters and micro-cars available at the time.

The Isetta was built from April 1955 around the original glass dome concept, with a folding sunroof (the Isetta 300 was offered from February 1956 with 298cc to replace 245cc) until March 1957. Then the body was modernised with a hardtop roof – though a folding roof could be ordered and was usually fitted. Such Isettas were made from October 1956 to May 1962.

Total production amounted to 161,360 vehicles, from which over half had sub-250cc engines owing to driving licence concessions. Because the British taxation and licensing laws would allow the Isetta to be driven on a motorcycle licence and qualify for lower road tax with three wheels, the Isetta 300 usually went there as a true three-wheeler. The original Isetta was also built under licence in France, while the BMW version of the Isetta was manufactured under licence in Britain and Brazil. Prices were: Isetta 250/(300) – 1955 Dm2580; 1956 Dm 2780 (Dm 2920); 1957 Dm 2780 (Dm 2890); From Oct 1958 Dm 2695 (Dm 2795).

BMW 600 (1957-59)

From the Isetta, BMW developed a small car with a front

The side and rear views of the Isetta on this page are divided into the original model on the left (1955-57) and the BMW modified later Isetta 300 of 1957-62. Neither version was too powerful at 12 and 13bhp respectively, but they could reach over 50mph and consumed only a gallon of fuel every 51.7 miles – according to factory figures. The original 245cc four-stroke engine was oversquare, the later fractionally long stroke unit (72 by 73mm) had 298cc to propel something over 1,200lb.

door and a side door, toward the back on the right of the car. Again a rear-mounted engine was used, but with two boxer-arranged cylinders, derived from the larger BMW bikes. Although the technology was well executed (including a semi-trailing arm rear suspension), the concept lacked conviction.

First shown at the end of August 1957, the model was made between December 1957 and November 1959. Some 35,000 BMW 600s were made at a time when BMW badly needed a bridge between their large V8 range and the Isettas. Price of the four-seater limousine was Dm 3985.

The cutaway clearly displays the rear location of the modified single-cylinder BMW motorcycle engine in the Isetta. Other details include chain final drive in oilbath chaincase. The narrow rear track was usually dispensed with in favour of a single rear wheel for export markets like Britain, where there were tax and driving licence concessions for three-wheelers. The fan cooling for the engine can also be clearly seen.

Below and right we show the bare separate chassis and running gear of the BMW Isetta, including the wheel-arch mounted four-speed gearchange and (right) the way in which the steering column was articulated to move with the front door.

	BMW Isetta 250 1955 – 62	BMW Isetta 300 1956 – 62	BMW 600 1957 – 59	
Motor				
Cylinders	1, four-stroke	1, four-stroke	2, boxer (flat) layout	
Bore x stroke	68 x 68mm	72 x 73mm	74 x 68mm	
Capacity	245cc	298cc	582cc	
Power (bhp)	12 @ 5800rpm	13 @ 5200rpm	19.5 @ 4500rpm	
Torque	1.45mkg @ 4500rpm	1.88mkg @ 4600rpm	3.9mkg @ 2800rpm	
Compression	6.8:1	7:1	6.8:1	
Carburation	1, slide carburettor	As 250	1, sidedraught carb	
	Bing 1/24. From 1957: 1/22	As 250	Zenith 28 KLP 1	
Valves	Rocker, tappet & spring	As 250	As 250/300	
	Overhead	Overhead	V-pattern, overhead	
	Side camshaft, chain	As 250	Central camshaft, gear-	
	driven	As 250	driven	
Crankshaft bearings	2	2	3	
Cooling	Fan-assisted air	As 250	As 250/300	
Lubrication	Pressure, 1.25 litres oil,	Pressure, 1.75 litres oil	Pressure, 2.5 litres oil	
	(from 1956) 1.75 litres oil			
Battery	12v 24ah	As 250	12v 24ah	
Generator	130W, DC	130W, DC	130W, DC	
Transmission	No differential. Drive to		Mid-engine, gearbox in	
	rear wheel by short cross		front of rear axle,	
	shaft from gearbox and		rear drive	
	duplex chain in oil bath	As 250		
Clutch	Single, dry plate	As 250	As 250/300	
Gearchange	Side mounted shift linkage	As 250	Floor change	
Gearbox	4-speed, claw type	As 250	4-speed	
Synchromesh	None	None	1st-4th	
Ratios	1st, 4.35	As 250	1st, 3.54	
	2nd, 2.22	As 250	2nd, 1.94	
	3rd, 1.52	As 250	3rd, 1.27	
	4th, 1.17	As 250	4th, 0.846	
Final drive	2.31	As 250	5.43	
Bodywork & chassis	Steel frame, box and tubular	As 250	As 250/300 but with	
	chassis with all steel		rear, right, side door	
	coachwork, 1 front door		as well as front	
Front suspension	Leading swing arm & coil	As 250	As 250/300	
	springs			
Rear suspension	Narrow live axle with quarter-	As 250	Trailing arm with coil	
	elliptic leaf springs, angled		spring/damper units	
	upright dampers			
Steering	Worm & nut, 15.4:1	As 250	Worm & nut, 15.4:1	
	2.5 turns lock-to-lock	As 250	As 250/300	
Footbrakes	Hydraulic, drums of 180mm	As 250	Hydraulic, drums, 180mm	
	diam. front and single rear		diam. on four wheels	
	wheel drum brake			
	Swept area, 324 cm^2	As 250	Swept area, 432cm^2	
General data				
Wheelbase	1500mm	1500mm	1700mm	
Track (Front/Rear)	1200/520 mm with	1200/520mm with	1220/1160mm	
	twin rear wheels	twin rear wheels		
Length, width & height	1955-57: 2285/	As 250	2900/1400	
	1380/1340mm		1375mm	
	1956-62:2355/1380			
	/1340mm			
Rims	3.00 x 10	3.00 x 10	3.50 x 10	
Tyres	4.80 x 10	4.80 x 10	5.20 x 10	
Turning circle (right)	8.3 metres	8.3 metres	8.3 metres	
Vehicle weight	360kg	360kg	550kg	
Max permissible weight	580, then 600kg	As 250	900kg	
Top speed	53mph	53mph	64mph	
Acceleration	0-50mph: 40 sec	As 250	0-62mph: 58 sec	
Litres/100km	5.5 (51.4mpg)	As 250	6.0 (47mpg)	
Fuel tank	13 litres (in back)	As 250	23 litres (in back)	

BMW 600 (1957-59). This model could be called a grown-up Isetta, having proper four-wheeler track at the rear and a two-cylinder engine of nearly 20bhp. There were seats for four, and two doors – the original front entrance and just one for the rear passengers! The 600 showed BMW knew they needed a middle range car, but lacked the finance to go immediately for that target.

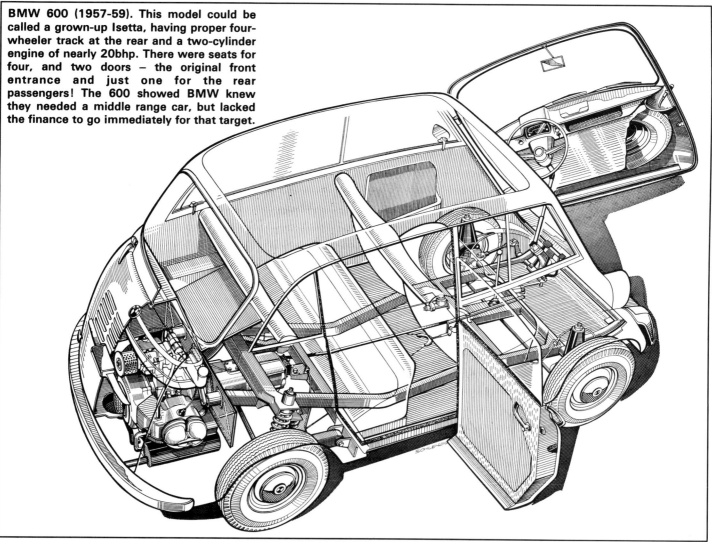

BMW 700 (1959-64)
BMW LS (1962-65)

The BMW 700 was directly derived from the BMW 600 small car, but had conventional and attractive lines by Turin's Michelotti. At last this brought BMW into the

BMW 700 Cabrio Convertible, 2-seater, Dm 6950

BMW LS. Following the BMW 700 saloons this had the same rear engined principle as before, but the wheelbase was augmented by some 160mm and the overall length was around 320mm. Thus this model allowed considerably more legroom for the back seat passengers.

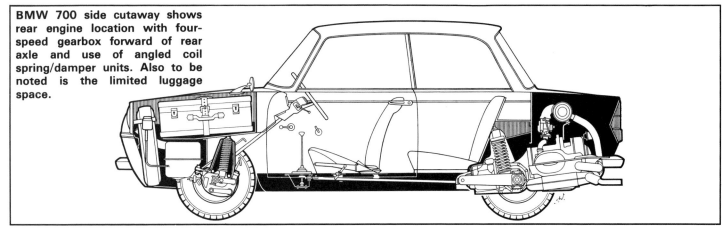

BMW 700 side cutaway shows rear engine location with four-speed gearbox forward of rear axle and use of angled coil spring/damper units. Also to be noted is the limited luggage space.

smaller sporty car market, a move many people had awaited for years. The 700 helped the works achieve their rewarding breakthrough into larger scale production.

The Coupe was built from August 1959 until April 1964; the Saloon from December 1959 (a luxury Saloon version being announced in January 1961) until April 1962. Prices were as follows:

BMW 700 Saloon, 2 door, Dm 4760
BMW 700 Luxury Saloon, 2 door, Dm 4995
BMW 700 Coupe, 2 door, 2+2 seater, Dm 5300 (From 1963: Dm 5500)

BMW 700 Sport. From the outside there was no difference between this model and the BMW 700 Coupe, but the Sport possessed notably higher engine performance (40bhp) and was sportingly equipped. The name was changed to BMW 700 CS from 1963. The model was built from August 1960 until May 1964 and used the same engine power as the BMW 700 Cabrio. The latter was a Baur, Stuttgart, product, and was made from September 1961 until November 1964. Prices were:

BMW 700 Sport Coupe, 2+2-seater, Dm 5850

Just as welcome was a stabilisation in driving characteristics achieved through better springing. Externally the small BMW now appeared to have been stretched, and to be rather more substantial than before. Some 250mm of rear overhang was filled with air because the originally planned four-cylinder version got only as far as construction of a few test examples. The BMW LS luxury was produced between March 1962 and November 1965. The less well equipped BMW LS was produced from February 1963 until September 1963. Prices were:

BMW LS Saloon, 2 door, Dm 4785
BMW LS Luxury Saloon, 2 door, Dm 5320 (From 1964: Dm 4985)

BMW LS Coupe. Successor to the BMW 700 Coupe and the BMW 700 CS, it is relevant to note that — because of the saloon's longer wheelbase — the LS Coupe began to lose its beautiful proportions. Baur, Stuttgart, made the coachwork for the LS Coupe in series production from September 1964 until September 1965. Price was:

BMW LS Coupe, 2+2-seater, Dm 5850

In total BMW completed 181,411 cars of the 700 series, including all types from BMW 700 to LS models.

Produced between August 1959 and September 1965 they can be analysed in rounded off production numbers as follows:

BMW 700, Saloons, 53,000

BMW 700, Coupe, 23,000
BMW 700, Sport and 700 Coupe CS, 11,150
BMW 700, Convertible (Cabriolet), 1,750
BMW LS, Saloons, 90,000
BMW LS, Coupe, 1,750

BMW 700 saloon of 1960-1961 had 30 bhp.

Coupe 700 of 1964-1965 shared earlier Sport 40bhp motor.

Three views of the 700 Cabrio Convertible (1961-1964), which also had 40bhp tune and was said to manage 84mph and 36.5mpg.

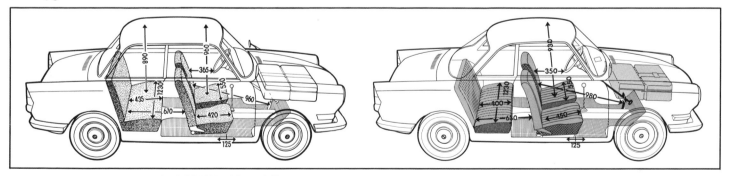

Internal dimensions of original BMW 700 and Coupe.

	BMW 700 1960 – 61 BMW 700 Coupe 1959 – 64	BMW 700 Sport 1960 – 64	BMW LS Luxus 1962 – 65	BMW LS Coupe 1964 – 65
Motor				
Cylinders	Flat twin	Flat twin	Flat twin	Flat twin
	Alloy crankcase	Alloy crankcase	Alloy crankcase	Alloy crankcase
Bore x stroke	78 x 73mm	78 x 73mm	78 x 73mm	78 x 73 mm
Capacity	697cc	697cc	697cc	697cc
Power (bhp)	30 @ 5000rpm	40 @ 5700 rpm	30@ 5000rpm	40 @ 5700rpm
	From Feb 1963:		From Feb 1963:	
	32 @ 5000rpm		32 @ 5000rpm	
Torque	5.1mkg @ 3400rpm	5.2mkg @ 4500rpm	5.1mkg @ 3400rpm	As 700 Sport
Compression	7.5:1	9:1	7.5:1	9:1
Carburation	1, downdraught	2, downdraught	1, downdraught	2, downdraught
	Solex 34 PCI	Solex 34 PCI	Solex 34 PCI	Solex 34 PCI
Valves	Overhead, V-pattern	Overhead, V-pattern	Overhead, V-pattern	Overhead, V-pattern
	Rocker, Tappet & spring	As column 1	As column 1	As column 1
	Central camshaft,	As column 1	As column 1	As column 1
	gear-driven	As column 1	As column 1	As column 1
Crankshaft bearings	3	3	3	3
Cooling	Fan-assisted, air	As column 1	As column 1	As column 1
Lubrication	Pressure, 2 litres of oil	As column 1	As column 1	As column 1
Generator	130W, DC	130W, DC	130W, DC	130W, DC
Transmission	Rear drive, rear engine. Gearbox in front of back axle	As column 1	As column 1	As column 1
Clutch	Single, dry plate	As column 1	As column 1	As column 1
Gearchange	Lever, floor mounted	Lever, floor mounted	Lever, floor mounted	Lever, floor mounted
Gearbox	4-speed	4-speed	4-speed	4-speed
Synchromesh	1st-4th	1st-4th	1st-4th	1st-4th
		Coupe, 1961 Cabriolet		
Ratios	1st, 3.54	1st, 2.667 1st, 3.54	1st, 3.54	1st, 3.54
	2nd, 1.94	2nd, 1.600 2nd, 1.94	2nd, 1.94	2nd, 1.94
	3rd, 1.27	3rd, 1.148 3rd, 1.27	3rd, 1.27	3rd, 1.27
	4th, 0.839	4th, 0.839 4th, 0.839	4th, 0.839	4th, 0.839
Final drive	5.43	5.43	5.43	5.43
Bodywork				
Front suspension	Unitary construction, all steel coachwork			
	Leading arm, coil spring/damper			
Rear suspension	Trailing arm, coil spring/damper			
	Coupe: + anti-roll bar	+ hollow rubber bushes		+ hollow rubber bushes
Steering	Rack & pinion, 17.85:1			
	1.3 turns lock-to-lock			
Footbrakes	Hydraulic, drums, 200mm dia.			
	& 588 cm^2 swept area			
General data				
Wheelbase	2120mm	2120mm	2280mm	2280mm
Track (Front/Rear)	1270/1200mm	1270/1200mm	1270/1200mm	1270/1200mm
Length, width & height	Saloon: 3540/1480/	Coupe: 3540/1480/	3860/1480/1360mm	3860/1480/1300mm
	1345mm	1270mm		
	Coupe: 1270mm hihg	Cabrio: 1290mm high		
Rims	3.50 x 12	3.50 x 12	3.50 x 12	3.50 x 12
Tyres	5.50-12	5.20-12; 5.50-12 from Autumn 1963	5.20-12; from Autumn 1963, 5.50-12	5.50-12
Turning circle (right)	10.1 metres	10.1 metres	10.6 metres	10.6 metres
Vehicle weight	640kg	650: Cabrio, 685kg	680kg	690kg
Max permissible weight	Saloon: 960kg	Coupe: 860kg	1050kg	1050kg
	Coupe: 860kg	Cabri: 910kg		
Top speed	Saloon: 75mph	84mph	75mph	84mph
	Coupe: 78mph			
0-62mph	Saloon: 30 sec	20 sec	33 sec	22 sec
	Coupe: 26.5 sec			
Litres/100km	7 (40.1mpg)	7.5 (37.7mpg)	7.5 (37.7mpg)	7.5 (37.7mpg)
Fuel tank	30 litres (in front)	As column 1	As column 1	As column 1

Original BMW 700 saloon of 1960-61 (furthest away) poses with BMW LS Luxus (1962-65). The BMW LS was a particularly good model in commercial terms and provided BMW with working capital at a time when the grand recovery was underway, but delayed by the interval between show display and production of the new generation 1500. The 700 series went a long way toward restoring public faith in Munich and was their first widely accepted car since the war and the annexation of car production facilities at Eisenach.

Inside the 'floor-gearchange' BMW LS Luxus the amount of rear seat and leg room has increased from the original 670mm to 710mm thanks to a wheelbase of 2280mm instead of 2120mm.

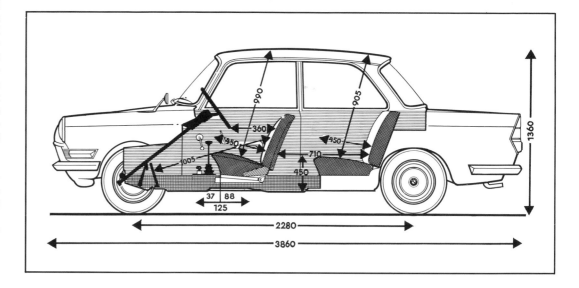

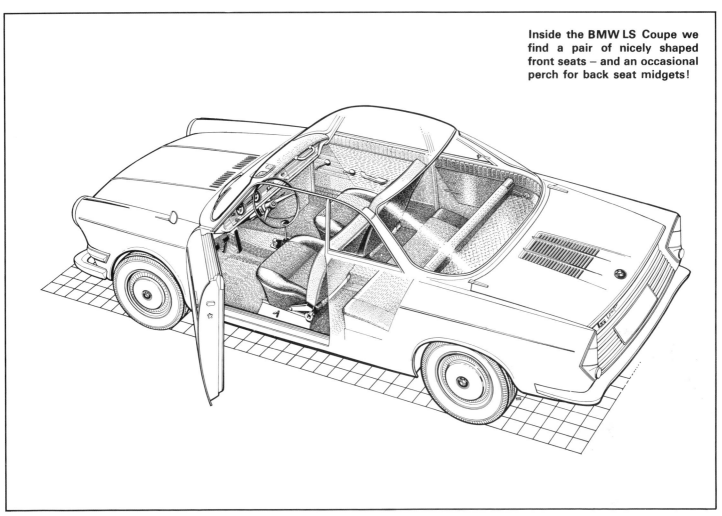

Inside the BMW LS Coupe we find a pair of nicely shaped front seats — and an occasional perch for back seat midgets!

Just as the big coupes contributed towards BMW's eventual full restoration to its role as a sporting marque, so did the smaller series. This LS Coupe of 1964-65 was not quite so pretty or so light as the originals, which excelled in motorsports. Quite frequently the little 700s would humiliate opposition of twice their engine capacity and on one occasion in Britain (in soaking rain) they even pulled off a Jaguar giant-killing act. Normally they had 40bhp at 5700rpm, but BMW's store of motorcycle engine tuning knowledge ensured they competed with over 75bhp and 100mph plus capacity. With such cars were aces like Jacky Ickx and Hubert Hahne trained ...

BMW 1500 (1962-64)
BMW 1600 (1964-66)
BMW 1800 (1963-72)
BMW 2000 (1966-72)

BMW 1500. This was the beginning of a new model range ("Neue Klasse") which brought a new bloom to the corporate cheeks of Bayerischen Motoren Werke. The prototype with 75bhp, 8.2:1 CR and tyres of 5.90 X 13 was displayed at September 1961's Frankfurt Show at a recommended price of Dm 8500. It was clear that this example was not yet ready for series production, but the new technology and style inspired public approval for this new BMW. The general opinion was, "At last we once more have a *real* BMW!"

However, there were all too many problems with the 1500 when it did struggle into production. Company experts agree setbacks like transmission troubles were overcome by 1963, and we must remember that this was the car which founded BMW as it is today, providing a solid and profitable base for the future. Its remarkable SOHC four cylinder engine also provided the basic principles of BMW four and six-cylinder road engines into the eighties. The new four also provided a base for motorsports that has seen unequalled success in European Formula II and which was winning in 1982 turbocharged $1\frac{1}{2}$-litre Grand Prix trim. Truly a significant car and engine!

From February 1962 a preliminary semi-mass-production series of BMW 1500s were made, with full production from October 1962 until December 1964. In production tune the 1499cc slant four had 8.8:1 CR and 80bhp.

BMW 1600. Succeeding the BMW 1500, the 1600 had no external changes, but it was actually maturing the 1500 concept as a much better car in quality details. The engine bore was stretched by 2mm and now provided 83bhp. In fact, there was no comparison, but the 1600 suffered a bit from the bad name of its predecessor and the arrival of BMW 1800. Mass production of the 1600 ran from March 1964 until April 1966.

BMW 1800. This model had the same basic design as the 1500 and 1600, but the 1773cc engine enlargement was denoted by chrome stripes. Debut of this long-running model (which had two versions of 1.8-litres in its life) was September 1963, when it went into production. Also shown at this time but not made until February 1964 was the sportier twin carburettor 1800 TI.

Both models suffered first year teething problems but were destined to earn great respect. From the close of 1964 until Autumn 1965 there was an additional indication of BMW's return to strength with the manufacture of 200 BMW 1800 TI/SA ("TI" for *Touring Internationale*, as used by Alfa, "SA" to denote *Sonderausfuhrung*, meaning an especially sporting special). Often called "Tisa" in racing slang, these 115mph special 1800s were sold only to competition licence holders (Dm 13,500) and offered a basic 130bhp from their twin Weber 1773cc engines, and had five-speed gearboxes.

Manufacture of 1800 TI ceased in Autumn 1968, after which the 1800 started to lose some of its appeal as, in the meantime, the BMW 2000 had been announced. Yet the normal 1800 soldiered on with a faithful clientele for its economy and reliability. August 1968 saw the 1800 hit top form with a new short motor. Whereas the old 1800 used the 1600 bore (84mm), the new 1800 used a 2000 block and pistons for 89mm bore. Conversely the new 1800 utilised a 1600 crankshaft (71mm) instead of its previous 80mm BMW 2000 crank: capacity went from 1773cc to 1766cc. The engine offered the same power (90bhp) and torque (14.6Mkg) as before, but delivered it quietly with a great free-running charm. Also new at this time was a split circuit braking system and a blacked-out grille. As of April 1971 it gained rectangular front lamps from the 2000 as well as rear end and other 2000 styling details. Production ended in July 1972.

BMW 2000. Debuting in late January 1966, the BMW 2000 had 100bhp and the 2000 TI some 120bhp, both utilising the 89 x 80mm bore and stroke that were the heart of the classic 1990cc SOHC unit. BMW 2000 was distinguished by unique rectangular headlights, while the 2000 TI originally had 1800 bodywork. However, this proved a sales obstacle, despite a more attractive price, which was the reasoning behind the July 1966

Production	BMW 1500	BMW 1600	BMW 1800	BMW 2000	
1962	1737				1737
1963	19634		8353		27987
1964	2436	2131	33254 (+2)		37821 (+2)
1965		6395 (+550)	50675 (+847)	57	57127 (+1397)
1966		1202	13397 (+1090)	43431 (+1494)	58030 (+2584)
1967			9312 (+264)	34418 (+1078)	43730 (+1342)
1968			7844 (+2561)	26350 (+1184)	34194 (+3745)
1969			11273 (+1576)	22420 (+1846)	33693 (+3422)
1970			14837 (+878)	17625 (+1670)	32462 (+2548)
1971			7653 (+140)	10603 (+725)	18256 (+865)
1972			– (+205)	337 (+689)	337 (+894)
1973			– (+413)	– (+1036)	– (+1449)
1974			– (+384)	– (+372)	– (+756)
	23807	9728 (+550)	156598 (+8360)	155241 (+10094)	345374 (+19004)
	23807	10278	164958	165335	364378

Totals in brackets show overseas production

introduction of BMW 2000 TI-lux with rectangular lamps. BMW 2000 TI was withdrawn from sale in Summer 1968.

From April 1966 all models came with dual circuit braking. BMW 2000 tilux (originally TI-lux) was made up to March 1970 and was replaced (from the end of 1969 effectively) by the BMW 2000 tii. This additional "i" denoted a fuel-injection (Kugelfischer) engine. However, because of its high price, and uncharacteristically high performance for this solid family car, it was difficult to sell. Yet the normal BMW 2000 was held in high esteem and commanded constant popularity until the end. Generally it should be remembered that, as with all the *Neue Klasse* BMWs, weak headlights and poor springing were inherent snags, but they were far outweighed by the advantages. Public sentiment was in favour of the compact body, which contributed to the car's manoeuvrability and agility. Above all the series bribed favour through wonderful steering and cornering ability, plus good brakes and logical layout. For its time it was particularly attractive and the body was of good quality.

Another point that pleased was the 2000's larger engine, which was especially responsive.

Production of BMW 2000 and the 2000 tii finished in June 1972, the latter selling only 1,952 examples because of the mass appeal of the 2000.

The car that founded BMW's postwar revival and a sporting force: the 1500 Saloon of four doors, made between 1962 and 1964.

	BMW 1500 1962-1964	BMW 1600 1964-1966
Motor		
Cylinders	4 inline Iron block, tilted 30° to right, alloy cylinder head	4 inline Iron block, tilted 30° to right, alloy cylinder head
Bore x stroke	82x71mm	84x71mm
Capacity	1499cc	1573cc
Power (bhp)	80 @ 5700rpm	83 @ 5500rpm
Torque	12.0mkg @ 3000rpm	12.6mkg @ 3000rpm
Compression	8.8:1	8.6:1
Carburation	1, downdraught Solex 34 PCIB 1964:Solex 36-40 PDSI	1, downdraught Solex 36-40 PDSI
Valves	V-pattern, single overhead camshaft with duplex chain drive	V-pattern, single overhead camshaft with duplex chain drive
Crankshaft bearings	5	5
Cooling	Pump, 7 litres of water	Pump, 7 litres of water
Lubrication	Pressure 4.25 litres oil	Pressure 4.25 litres oil
Battery	6v 77ah	6v 77ah
Generator	200 Watts, DC	250 Watts, DC
Transmission	Rear wheel drive short propshaft	Rear wheel drive short propshaft
Clutch	Single plate, dry	Single plate, dry
Gearchange	Floor, central lever	Floor, central lever
Gearbox	4-speed	4-speed
Synchromesh	1st-4th	1st-4th
Ratios	1st, 3.816 2nd, 2.170 3rd, 1.355 4th, 1.00	1st, 3.816 2nd, 2.070 3rd, 1.330 4th, 1.00
Final drive ratio	4.375	4.275
Bodywork	Unitary construction, all steel coachwork	as 1500
Front suspension	MacPherson strut, coil springs	MacPherson strut coil springs
Rear suspension	Trailing arm, coil spring/damper	Trailing arm, coil spring/damper
Steering	Worm, 17.58:1 & 3.75 turns lock-to-lock	Worm, 17.58:1 & 3.75 turns lock-to-lock
Footbrake	Hydraulic Front, discs 268mm Rear, drums 250mm	Hydraulic Front, discs 268mm Rear, drums 250mm
General data		
Wheelbase	2550mm	2550mm
Track (front/rear)	1320/1366mm	1320/1366mm
Length, width, height	4500/1710/1450mm	4500/1710/1450mm
Rims	4½Jx14	4½Jx14
Tyres	6.00-14 Optional: 165 SR 14	6.00 S-14 Optional: 165 SR 14
Turning circle (left/right)	10.6/10.8 metres	10.6/10.8 metres
Vehicle weight	1060kg	1070kg
Max permissible weight	1450kg	1450kg
Top speed	92mph	96mph
0-62mph	16 sec.	14 sec.
Litres/100km	11.0, 25.7mpg (to 1964) 11.5 Super (24.6mpg)	12.0 (23.5mpg)
Fuel tank	53 litres, at rear	53 litres, at rear

BMW 1800 1963-1968	BMW 1800 TI 1964-1966	BMW 1800 TI/SA 1964-1965	BMW 1800 1968-1972	
4 inline Iron block, tilted 30° to right, alloy cylinder head 84x80mm 1773cc 90bhp @ 5250rpm 14.6mkg @ 3000rpm 8.6:1 1, downdraught Solex 36-40 PDSI As 1500/1600	4 inline Iron block tilted at 30° to right side 84x80mm 1773cc 110 @ 5800rpm 15.1mkg @ 4000rpm 9.5:1 2, double sidedraught Solex 40 PHH V-pattern with single overhead camshaft, duplex chain driven	4 inline Iron block tilted at 30° to right side 84x80mm 1773cc 130 @ 6100rpm 16.0mkg @ 5250rpm 10.5:1 2, double sidedraught Weber 45 DCOE V-pattern with single overhead camshaft, duplex chain driven	4 inline Iron block tilted at 30° to right side 89x71mm 1766cc 90 @ 5250rpm 14.6mkg @ 3000rpm 8.6:1 1, downdraught Solex 36-40 PDSI V-pattern with single overhead camshaft, duplex chain driven	
5 Pump, 7 litres of water Pressure 4.25 litres oil 6v 77ah 250 Watts, DC Rear wheel drive Short propshaft Single plate, dry Floor, central lever 4-speed 1st-4th 1st. 3.816 2nd, 2.070 3rd, 1.330 4th, 1.00 1966-option: ZF automatic with hydraulic operation and planetary gears, central floor lever 1st, 2.56; 2nd, 1.52; 3rd, 1.00. 1.94 multiplication factor 4.22 Automatic, 4.11 As 1500/1800	5 Pump, 7 litres of water Pressure 5.25 litres oil 6v 66ah Alternator, 360 Watts, AC Rear wheel drive Short propshaft Single plate, dry Floor, central lever 4-speed 1st-4th 1st, 3.816 2nd, 2.070 3rd, 1.330 4th, 1.00 4.11 or 3.89 Unitary construction	5 Pump, 7 litres of water Pressure 5.25 litres oil 6v 66ah Alternator, 360 Watts, AC Rear wheel drive Divided propshaft Single plate, dry Floor, central lever 5-speed 1st-5th 1st, 3.330 2nd, 2.150 3rd, 1.565 4th, 1.225 5th, 1.00 Optional: limited slip differential 4.11/4.22/4.75 or 5.86 Unitary construction	5 Pump, 7 litres of water Pressure 5.25 litres oil 12v 44ah Alternator, 490 W, AC Rear wheel drive Divided propshaft Single plate, dry Floor, central lever 4-speed 1st-4th 1st, 3.835 2nd, 2.053 3rd, 1.345 4th, 1.00 Optional: ZF auto with hydraulic operation & planetary gears, 3-speed 1st, 2.56; 2nd, 1.52; 3rd, 1.00. multiplication factor, 1.94 4.11 Unitary construction	
MacPherson strut, coil springs + anti-roll bar option Trailing arm Coil spring/damper Worm, 17.58:1 & 3.75 turns lock-to-lock Hydraulic, servo-assist Front, discs 268mm Rear, drums 250mm	all steel coachwork MacPherson strut, coil springs + anti-roll bar Trailing arm Coil spring/damper Optional: anti-roll bar Worm & roller, 17.58:1 & 3.75 turns lock-to-lock Hydraulic, servo-assist Front, discs 268mm Rear, drums 250mm	all steel coachwork MacPherson strut, coil springs + anti-roll bar Trailing arm Coil spring/damper Optional: anti-roll bar Worm & roller, 14.5:1 & 3 turns lock-to-lock Hydraulic, servo-assist Front, discs 272mm Rear, drums 250mm	all steel coachwork MacPherson strut, coil springs Option: anti-roll bar Trailing arm Coil spring/damper Optional: anti-roll bar Worm & roller 17.58:1 & 3.75 turns lock-to-lock Hydraulic, twin circuit, servo Front, discs 272mm Rear, drums 250mm	
2550mm 1320/1366mm 4500/1710/1450mm 4½Jx14 6.00 S-14 Optional: 165 SR 14	2550mm 1330/1376mm 4500/1710/1450mm 5JK 14 6.00 S 14	2550mm 1330/1376mm 4500/1710/1450mm 5JK 14 165 HR 14 or 6.00 14 race	2550mm 1330/1376mm 4500/1710/1450mm 5J x 14 6.56/165 S 14. Extra cost option, July 1970 series production with 165 SR 14	
10.6/10.8 metres 1090kg 1470kg 101mph/99mph (auto) 13 sec. 15 sec. (auto)	10.6/10.8 metres 1120kg 1440kg 109mph 11 sec.	10.6/10.8 metres 1050kg 1440kg 116mph 9 sec.	10.6/10.8 metres 1130kg 1500kg. From 1971: 1550kg 103mph/101mph (auto) 13 sec./15 sec. (auto)	
12.0/13.0 (auto, 21.7mpg)	14.0 (20.2mpg)	16.0 (17.7mpg)	12.0 (23mpg)/13.0 (21.7mpg for automatic)	
53 litres, at rear	53 litres, at rear	53 litres, at rear 105 litre option	53 litres, at rear	

117

		BMW 2000 C 1965-69	BMW 2000 CS 1965-69
Motor			
	Cylinders	4 inline Iron block tilted 30° to right side; alloy cylinder head	4 inline Iron block tilted 30° to right side;, alloy cylinder head
	Bore x stroke	89 x 80mm	89 x 80mm
	Capacity	1990cc	1990cc
	Power (bhp)	100 @ 5500rpm	120 @ 5500rpm
	Torque	16.0mkg @ 3000rpm	17.0mkg @ 3600rpm
	Compression	8.5:1	9.3:1
	Carburation	1, downdraught Solex 40 PDSI	2, sidedraught Solex 40 PHH
	Valves	V-pattern, overhead. Single overhead camshaft with duplex chain drive	V-pattern, overhead. Single overhead camshaft with duplex chain drive
	Crankshaft bearings	5	5
	Cooling	Pump, 7 litres water	Pump, 7 litres water
	Lubrication	Pressure, 4.25 litres of oil	Pressure, 4.25 litres of oil
	Battery	12v 44ah	12v 44ah
	Generator	Alternator, 490 Watts	Alternator, 490 Watts
Transmission		Rear wheel drive Divided propshaft	Rear wheel drive Divided propshaft
	Clutch	Single, dry plate	Single, dry plate
	Gearchange	Floor, central lever	Floor, central lever
	Gearbox	4-speed	4-speed
	Synchromesh	1st-4th	1st-4th
	Ratios	1st, 3.835 2nd, 2.053 3rd, 1.345 4th, 1.00 Optional:ZF automatic with hydraulic operation and 3-speed planetary gears, selected by central lever. 1st, 2.56; 2nd, 1.52; 3rd, 1.0. Multiplication factor, 1.94	1st, 3.835 2nd, 2.053 3rd, 1.345 4th, 1.00
	Final drive	4.11	3.90
Bodywork		Unitary, all-steel, construction	Unitary, all-steel, construction
	Front suspension	MacPherson struts, coil springs Optional:anti-roll bar	MacPherson struts, coil springs +Anti-roll bar
	Rear suspension	Trailing arms, coil springs Optional:anti-roll bar	Trailing arms, coil springs +Anti-roll bar
	Steering	Worm and roller, 17.58:1 3.75 turns lock-to-lock	Worm and roller, 17.58:1 3.75 turns lock-to-lock
	Footbrakes	Hydraulic, servo-assisted From July 1968:hydraulic twin circuit Front discs 272mm Rear drums 250mm	Hydraulic, servo-assisted As 2000 C Front discs 272mm Rear drums 250mm
General data			
	Wheelbase	2550mm	2550mm
	Track (front/rear)	1330/1376	1330/1376mm
	Length, width & height	4530/1675/1360mm	4530/1675/1360mm
	Rims	5½J x 14	5½ x 14
	Tyres	6.95/175 S 14 (4 PR) Optional:175 SR 14	6.95/175 H 14 (6 PR) 175 HR 14
	Turning circle	10.6 metres (left), 10.8 metres (right)	As 2000 C As 2000 C
	Vehicle weight	1200kg. Auto; 1220kg	1200kg
	Max permissible weight	1580kg	1580kg
	Top speed	107mph Auto:104mph	115mph
	0-62mph	13 sec auto:14 sec	12 sec
	Litres/100km	13.0 (21.7mpg) Auto: 13.5 (20.9 mpg)	13.5 (20.9mpg)
	Fuel tank	53 litres (11.7 galls) Placed at rear	53 litres (11.7 galls) Placed at rear

BMW 2000 1966-72	BMW 2000 TI 1966-68 BMW 2000 tilux 1966-70	BMW 2000 Tii 1969-72	
4 inline	4 inline	4 inline	
Iron block tilted 30°	Iron block tilted 30°	Iron block tilted 30°	
to right side; alloy	to right side; alloy	to right side; alloy	
cylinder head	cylinder head	cylinder head	
89 x 80mm	89 x 80mm	89 x 80mm	
1990cc	1990cc	1990cc	
100 @ 5500rpm	120 @ 5500rpm	130 @ 5800rpm	
16.0mkg @ 3000rpm	17.0mkg @ 3600rpm	18.1mkg @ 4500rpm	
8.5:1	9.3:1	9.5:1	
1, downdraught	2, sidedraught	Kugelfischer injection	
Solex 40 PDSI	Solex 40 PHH	Kugelfischer PL04 pump	
V-pattern, overhead. Single	V-pattern, overhead. Single	V-pattern, overhead. Single	
overhead camshaft with	overhead camshaft with	overhead camshaft with	
duplex chain drive	duplex chain drive	duplex chain drive	
5	5	5	
Pump, 7 litres water	Pump, 7 litres water	Pump, 7 litres water	
Pressure, 4.25 litres	Pressure, 4.25 litres	Pressure, 4.25 litres	
of oil	of oil	of oil	
12v 44ah	12v 44ah	12v 44ah	
Alternator, 490 Watts	Alternator, 490 Watts	Alternator, 490 Watts	
Rear wheel drive	Rear wheel drive	Rear wheel drive	
Divided propshaft	Divided propshaft	Divided propshaft	
Single, dry plate	Single, dry plate	Single, dry plate	
Floor, central lever	Floor, central lever	Floor, central lever	
4-speed	4-speed	4-speed	
1st-4th	1st-4th	1st-4th	
1st, 3.835	1st, 3.835	1st, 3.835	
2nd, 2.053	2nd, 2.053	2nd, 2.053	
3rd, 1.345	3rd, 1.345	3rd, 1.345	
4th, 1.00	4th, 1.00	4th, 1.00	
Optional: ZF automatic with			
hydraulic operation & 3-speed			
planetary gears, central lever			
selection. 1st, 2.56; 2nd, 1.52;		3.90	
3rd, 1.00. Multiplication factor, 1.94	3.90		
4.11			
Unitary, all-steel construction	Unitary, all-steel construction	Unitary, all-steel construction	
MacPherson struts & coil springs	MacPherson struts & coil springs	MacPherson struts and coil springs	
Aug'68 option:anti roll-bar	Anti-roll bar	Anti-roll bar	
Trailing arms, coil springs	Trailing arms, coil springs	Trailing arms, coil springs	
Optional:anti-roll bar	+Anti-roll bar	+Anti-roll bar	
Worm & roller, 17.58:1	Worm & roller, 17.58:1	Worm & roller, 17.58:1	
3.75 turns lock-to-lock	3.75 turns lock-to-lock	3.75 turns lock-to-lock	
Hydraulic, servo-assisted	Hydraulic, servo-assisted	Hydraulic, twin circuit	
July 1968:twin circuit	July 1968:twin circuit	servo-assisted	
Front discs 272mm	Front discs 272mm	Front discs 272mm	
Rear drums 250mm	Rear drums 250mm	Rear drums 250mm	
2550mm	2550mm	2550mm	
1330/1376mm	1330/1376mm	1330/1376mm	
4500/1710/1450mm	4500/1710/1450mm	4500/1710/1450mm	
5J x 14	5½J x 14	5½J x 14	
6.45/165 S 14 (4 PR)	6.95/175 H 14 (6 PR)	175 HR 14	
Option: until July 1970,			
165 SR 14 (then std)			
10.6 metres (left)	10.6 metres (left)	10.6 metres (left)	
10.8 metres (right)	10.8 metres (right)	10.8 metres (right)	
1170kg. Auto:1190kg	TI: 1150kg. Tilux: 1170kg	1170kg	
1550kg	1540kg	1560kg	
104mph. Auto:102mph	112mph	115mph	
13 sec. Auto:14 sec	12 sec	11 sec	
13.0 (21.7mpg)	13.5 (20.7mpg)	13.5 (20.7mpg)	
Auto:13.5 (20.7mpg)			
53 litres (11.7 galls)	53 litres (11.7 galls)	53 litres (11.7 galls)	
Placed at rear	Placed at rear	Placed at rear	

BMW 2000 C, 2000 CS (1965-69)

Over 7 months before the BMW 2000 saloons, the 2-litre engine appeared (June 1965) in a new Coupe, which foretold the future by BMW development and Karmann of Osnabruck construction. As a concept it was less convincing than the saloons, but the distinctive headlamps were a 'red herring' – for when they were replaced by round lamps for the later six-cylinder Coupes, much of the original line remained to provide BMW's most famous postwar Coupes. By 1969 some 2,837 BMW 2000 C (mostly automatic gearbox) and 8883 BMW 2000 CS had been made.

Inside the 1500 we can see the principles BMW have followed for over two decades: slant-mounted SOHC engine; strut front and semi-trailing arm rear suspension, with a logical cabin layout and excellent boot space. Essential parts of the quality sporting character.

BMW 1500 four door saloon on 1962-1964. The slant (by 30°) engine had a slight increase in compression between prototype and full production, so the public got an extra 5bhp. The 1.5-litre was capable of 92mph, 0-62mph in 16 seconds and some 24.8mpg overall, according to factory figures. It was no lightweight at 2232lb.

Maybe the author did say the original was unreliable but waving for help seems an over-dramatic reaction! This is the improved quality BMW 1600, four door, made between 1964-66.

Above: Outwardly the 1800 four door saloon had only some extra chrome body strips to denote its 1.8-litres in place of 1.5 or 1.6. Its 90bhp was enough to allow just over 100mph and acceleration from rest to 62mph occupied some 13 seconds. An automatic version was offered optionally from 1966, based on a ZF three-speed unit.

The 1968-1971 BMW 1800 series retained the four door saloon principles with some styling changes, but more important was a new short stroke engine. This increased capacity from 1773cc to 1766cc and represented an alliance of 1600 short stroke crankshaft and large bore 2000 cylinder block. The result was a quieter and more responsive engine, but no material difference in performance was reported compared to the original 1800.

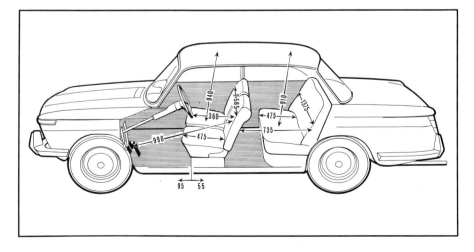

Internal dimensions of the BMW 1500, 1600 and 1800 series were the same, offering — amongst many other benefits — another 25mm extra between front seat backs and rear seat backs, compared to the 700 saloon series in its longer wheelbase form.

A sure indication of BMW's fast recovering confidence was the announcement of a sporty 1800 TI alongside the ordinary model. Complete with twin Solex 40mm carburettors and a 9.5:1 CR (instead of 8.6:1), the TI model promised an extra 20bhp and 109mph compared to the 1800's 101mph. Fuel consumption was put at just 20mpg for this 2464lb pacesetter of 1964-68.

From the rear the extended taillights and trademark rear side window line, could have belonged to BMW 2000 (1966-72); BMW 2000 tilux (1966-70); BMW 2000 tii (1969-72) or the 1971-72 BMW 1800 series. All had four doors and spread BMW's reputation a little further, but the car illustrated is actually the straightforward 2000.

The 2000 ti shown here reflects how the company went for lower case model definition on the badgework during the later sixties (eg: tilux and tii). The 2000 ti twin carburettor model offered 112mph, acceleration from rest to 62mph in 12 seconds and an official 21mpg overall. The model won the Munich factory the prestigious Belgian Spa-Francorchamps 24 hours race in 1966. Drivers Jacky Ickx/Hubert Hahne averaged nearly 105mph for the road circuit and could call on over 160bhp, compared with a standard 120bhp. The racing car had the original 1800 styling, whereas this example has the later 2000 rectangular lamps.

As at many points in BMW's history an indifferent model preceded a classic design. The 2000 C and 2000 CS four-seater, two door coupes of 1965-69 did not inspire Werner Oswald's support, but the main bodywork line, especially that pillarless cabin, was substantially the form of the later six-cylinder Coupes. In 2-litre form they were underpowered at 100 or 120bhp in something over 2400lb, frequently with automatic transmission.

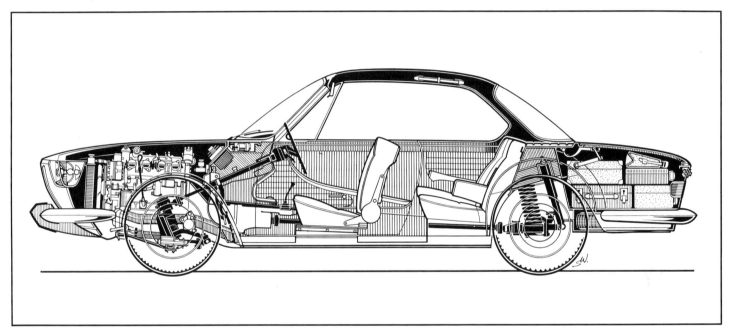

Cutaway shows the way the four-cylinder was crammed into the Coupe lines with minimal bonnet clearance of some components. The Coupe was created 'in-house' by BMW and drew something from the earlier 3200 CS by Bertone, while remaining firmly based upon the dimensions (wheelbase and track most importantly) of the *Neue Klasse* 1800.

A 2000 CS of the 1965-69 run displays the large areas of glass and inset, wrap-around tail lights that were to stay on sale in Germany as part of the six-cylinder Coupe style until the 1976 arrival of the 6-series!

BMW 1600-2, 1602 (1966-75)
BMW 1802 (1972-75)
BMW 2002 (1968-75)
BMW 1502 (1975-77)

The "02" model range utilised the same engine as, and similar running gear to, the BMW 1600/1800/2000 four door saloons, but styling-wise were more along the lines of a coupe with their two door bodies. From a styling viewpoint they were perhaps not outstanding, but their straightforward and neat lines found favour with customers, who also enthused over the performance abilities and generally sporting character. Overall the car offered a lower weight and more affordable cost as its chief home market attractions, breaking below the Dm 10,000 barrier convincingly. The March 1966 Geneva Motor Show, was the chosen debut for the 1600-2, the "-2" designation a comparison with the previous four door models. Production began just a few weeks later. In September 1967 the BMW 1600 TI became reality with a twin carburettor (105bhp) motor, servo-assisted braking, front and rear anti-roll bars — offered optionally on lesser models — opening rear quarterlights and a tachometer.

1600 TI had a short life for, in the meantime, the BMW 2002 and 2002 ti were born: the 1600 TI ceased production in November 1968. Incidentally, in September 1967 the 1600-2 received 12 volt electrics and an alternator, while in September 1968 dual circuit brakes and servo-assistance became standard. April 1971 marked the now official model name "1602", an example which the complete 02 line followed, the later 1602 distinguished externally by rubber inserts along the side chrome and the bumpers.

The BMW 2002 with the 2-litre (100bhp) motor came in January 1968 and became another BMW sporting legend. By September 1968 it gained the dual circuit braking system: a year later an automatic was offered (September '69). It shared the April 1971 rubber inserts with the 1602. Naturally the example of the 1600 ti was followed and the BMW 2002 ti with twin carburettor motor (120bhp) soon became popular. Emphasising the sheer versatility and competence of the basic design, the injection 2002 tii, announced in February 1971, brought 130bhp and shared the improved running gear of the ti, including bigger front discs and 5J instead of $4\frac{1}{2}$J steel wheels.

As of March 1971 the short stroke BMW 1800 motor was available as the 1802. This proved the ideal compromise between 2002 power and 1600 economy, a car to serve a wider cross section of customers.

Production	BMW 1502	BMW 1602-2 / BMW 1602	BMW Touring 1600	BMW 1600 GT	BMW 1802	BMW Touring 1800/1802	BMW 2002	BMW Touring 2000/2002	
1966		13244 (+219)							13244 (+219)
1967		38560 (+3916)		58			12		38630 (+3916)
1968		34255 (+2587)		1201			28674 (+1383)		64130 (+3970)
1969		26336 (+2583)					39847 (+2204)		66183 (+4787)
1970		33952					55734		89686
1971		26176	1998		14675	269	59857	7795	110769
1972		26549	2341		25420	1633	62613	6567	125123
1973		21804	40		21022	1856	54992	6077	105791
1974	18	38000			19353	317	56916	1314	115918
1975	41337	9139			2881		26121		79478
1976	22034						10081		32115
1977	9243								9243
	72632	258015 (+9305) 277320	4379	1259	83351	4075	394847 (+3587) 398434	21753	850311 (+12892) 863203
Totals in brackets are overseas production									

An unusual twist to this adaptable design came with the February 1971 production of the 1600, 2000 and 2000 ti Touring, which had the normal two side doors augmented by what is familiar today as a hatchback third door. Additionally September 1971 brought an 1800 Touring, which effectively ended the 1600 derivative's production.

In 1973 the model marking changed to BMW Touring 1802, 2002 and 2002 tii. The Touring offered some practical and obvious advantages, but was more sensitive to crosswinds and generally less pleasant to drive than the saloons, owing to a slight tail-heaviness. They did not sell for very long, nor as well as was expected, disappearing out of the line in July 1974.

Very soon we had yet another 02 derivative, the September 1967 BMW 1600 Cabriolet. This Baur creation had a fully folding hood and was echoed in 1982 3-series production. From the end of 1967 until early 1971 some 1,681 such cars were made.

It was from April 1971 that the BMW 2002 Cabriolet appeared and also introduced the now fashionable central roll-over bar: the 1600 had been a full convertible with no centre pillar. The bar offered greater body strength and allowed the more powerful engine to be used with greater safety. Against this could be balanced the pleasure of driving an entirely open car. About 2,300 2002 Cabriolets were made by Baur.

The complete 02 line was reworked in September 1973. Externally the blacked out grille, headrests, safety belts and use of square rear lights service to identify these later cars. Yet the Touring models retained round tail lamps. Frankfurt Motor Show, September 1973, saw the ultimate sporting 2002 displayed. Like the twin carburettor and injection models, this 2002 traced its ancestry to saloon car racing. Instead of the 250 plus horsepower of the 1969 turbo racer, BMW had produced 170bhp and a piece of motoring history for this 2002 was the roadgoing turbo model, Europe's first (the Porsche 911 turbo variant came in 1975). Unfortunately the mechanically-injected, KKK turbocharged 2002 could not have chosen a worse moment to thrust its gaily painted mirror-written front spoiler to the public's attention. For this was fuel crisis time and in the ensuing economic recession and general anti-car feeling, BMW's aggressive new model was not appreciated in Germany.

The normal road manners of this vehicle left something to be desired too, with its distinct turbo lag and the same disc-drum braking layout that served on cars of 50bhp less. Only 1,672 of these 130mph 2002 turbos were manufactured before production ceased at the end of 1974. According to *Autocar,* this remarkable 2002 could reach 100mph from rest in 20.7s, its engine boosted at 7psi by the KKK unit. A five-speed gearbox was optional, $5\frac{1}{2}$ inch wide wheels standard as was LHD. In an appreciation that appeared in *Car* during the Summer of '82, the magazine thought that this was the finest BMW this side of 507!

The original 1600-2 that went into production in 1966 and started BMW upon another successful series, but this time with two doors.

The 1600 ti and its clean lines to best advantage. Once more twin Solex 400mm carburettors provided a power boost, this time in association with a 9:5:1 CR. The ti was quite a spritely model – able to reach the best part of 110mph and accelerate from rest to 62mph in 11 seconds – but it was really overshadowed by the advent of the 2002 series.

BMW 1502. Responding to the fuel-conscious climate, BMW announced the emaciated 1602 as a 1502. At the opposite extreme to the turbo this economy model actually had the 1602 engine of 1573cc but with lower CR (8:1) and 75bhp. It was only 1000 Dm or so cheaper than the 1602, but it was astonishingly well received and continued even after the July 1975 announcement of 3-series, to finally die in early August 1977.

In total, a majestic 863,000 units of the 02 range were made ...

The shape was the same for 2002 and 2002 ti made between 1968-71, a square tail lamp 2002 surviving until 1975 while the 1.6-litre models spanned over a decade. The 2-litre models attracted new lustre to the BMW name, both on the road and track, where they scored numerous European Championship successes, particularly when the factory raced the model in 1968-69 — the latter season with a turbocharged version.

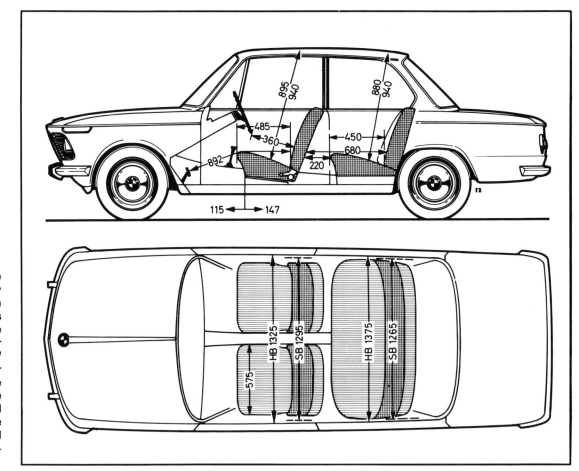

Inside the 02 range the dimensions, particularly of the rear seat (which offered less accommodation than the *Neue Klasse* with its four doors) revealed BMW had shifted their approach to a more sporting and affordable vehicle. Those long-lived *Neue Klasse* cars were not really replaced until the seventies arrival of 5-series.

	BMW 1502 1975-77	BMW 1600-2/1602 1966-75 BMW 1600 Cabriolet 1967-71	BMW 1600 Touring 1971-72	BMW 1600TI 1967-68
Motor				
Cylinders	4 inline, iron cylinder block slants 30° to right side, alloy head	4 inline, iron cylinder block slants 30° to right side, alloy head	4 inline, iron cylinder block slants 30° to right side, alloy head	4 inline, iron block slanting 30° to right side, alloy cylinder head
Bore x stroke	84 x 71mm	84 x 71mm	84 x 71mm	84x71mm
Capacity	1573cc	1573cc	1573cc	1573cc
Power (bhp)	75 @ 5800rpm	85 @ 5700rpm	85 @ 5700rpm	105 @ 6000rpm
Torque	12mkg @ 3700rpm	12.6mkg @ 3000rpm	12.6mkg @ 3000 rpm	13.4mkg @ 4500rpm
Compression	8.0:1	8.6:1	8.6:1	9.5:1
Carburation	1, downdraught Solex 38 PDSI	1, downdraught Solex 38 PDSI	1, downdraught Solex 38 PDSI	2, twin choke, sidedraught Solex 40 PHH
Valves	V-pattern OHV SOHC, duplex chain driven	V-pattern OHV SOHC, duplex chain driven	V-pattern OHV DOHC, duplex chain driven	V-pattern, OHV & duplex chain-driven SOHC
Crankshaft bearings	5	5	5	5
Cooling	Pump, 7 litres water	Pump, 7 litres water	Pump, 7 litres water	Pump, water, 7 litres
Lubrication	Pressurised, 4.25 litres oil	Pressurised, 4.25 litres oil	Pressurised, 4.25 litres oil	Pressurised, 4.25 litres of oil
Battery	12v 36ah In engine bay	6v 77ah In engine bay	12v 36ah In engine bay	12v 44ah
Generator	Alternator, 490 Watt	Dynamo 250Watt Sept '67 on: 490W, AC	Alternator, 490 W, AC	Alternator, 490 Watt
Transmission				
Clutch		Rear wheel drive, divided propshaft Single dry pressure plate		Rear wheel drive Divided propshaf Single dry plate
Gearchange		Floor, central lever		Floor, central lever
Gearbox		4-speed		4-speed. Optional 5sp 1st-4th/1st-5th
Synchromesh	1st-4th	**To 1971** 1st-4th **From 1971**	1st-4th	**4-speed 5-speed**
Ratios	1st, 3.764	1st, 3.835 1st, 3.764	1st, 3.764	1st,3.835 1st,3.368
	2nd, 2.020	2nd, 2.053 2nd, 2.020	2nd, 2.020	2nd,2.053 2nd,2.160
	3rd, 1.320	3rd, 1.345 3rd, 1.320	3rd, 1.320	3rd,1.345 3rd,1.579
	4th, 1.00	4th, 1.00 4th, 1.00	4th, 1.00	4th,1.00 4th,1.241
				5th,1.00
Final drive ratio	4.11	4.11	4.11	3.90
Bodywork		Unitary construction, all steel		Unitary construction all steel
Front suspension		MacPherson struts, coil springs Optional 1600 TI: alternative roll bar		MacPherson struts, coil springs Tubular anti-roll bar
Rear suspension		Trailing arms, coil springs Optional 1600 TI: alternative roll bar		Trailing arms, coil springs Anti-roll bar option
Steering		Worm & roller, 17.58:1,3.75 turns lock-to-lock		Worm & roller, 17.58:1 3.75 turns lock-to-lock
Footbrake	Twin circuit, hydraulic Servo-assisted Front discs 240mm Rear drums 230mm	Hydraulic, Twin circuit. From Sept '68 Servo-assisted Front discs 240mm Rear drums 200mm	Twin circuit, hydraulic Servo-assisted Front discs 240mm Rear drums 230mm	Twin circuit, hydraulic Servo-assisted Front discs 240mm Rear drums 200mm
General data				
Wheelbase	2500mm	2500mm	2500mm	2500mm
Track (front/rear)	1330/1330mm	1330/1330mm. From Sept '73:1342/1342mm	1330/1330mm	1330/1330mm
Length, width & height	4230/1590/1410mm	4230/1590/1410mm Cabriolet:1360mm height	4110/1590/1380mm	4230/1590/1410mm
Rims	4½J x 13	4½J x 13. From Sept '73:5J x 13	4½J x 13	4½Jx13
Tyres	165 SR 13	6.00 S 13. Optional & then Std from Aug 1970:165 SR 13	165 SR 13	165 SR 13
Turning circle	10.4 metres	10.4 metres	10.4 metres	10.4 metres
Vehicle weight	980kg	940kg. From Sept '73 980kg. Cabriolet 980kg	1030kg	960kg
Max permissible weight	1380kg	1320kg. From Sept '70 1370kg. Cabrio:1320kg	1450kg	1335kg
Top speed	97mph	101mph	101mph	109mph
0-62mph	14.5 sec	13.5 sec	13.5 sec	11 sec
Litres/100km	12.0 (23.5mpg)	11.5 (24.6mpg)	11.5 (24.6mpg)	12.5 (22.6mpg)
Fuel tank	Rear, 50 litres (11 galls)	Rear, 46 litres (10.1 galls) to Sept '73 then 50 litre	52 litres (11.45 galls) Rear-mounted	46 litres (10.1 galls) Placed in rear

	BMW 1802 1971-75	BMW 1800 Touring 1971-74	BMW 2002 1968-75 BMW 2002 Cabriolet 1971-75	BMW 2000 Touring 1971-74
Motor				
Cylinders	4 inline block slanting 30° to right side, alloy cylinder head	4 inline block slanting 30° to right side, alloy cylinder head	4 inline, iron block tilted @ 30° to right side, alloy cylinder head	4 inline, iron block tilted @ 30° to right side, alloy cylinder head
Bore x stroke	89x71mm	89x71mm	89x80mm	89x80mm
Capacity	1766cc	1766cc	1990cc	1990cc
Power (bhp)	90 @ 5250rpm	90 @ 5250rpm	100 @ 5500rpm	100 @ 5500rpm
Torque	14.6mkg @ 3000rpm	14.6mkg @ 3000rpm	16mkg @ 3500rpm	16mkg @ 3500rpm
Compression	8.6:1	8.6:1	8.5:1	8.5:1
Carburation	1, downdraught Solex 38 PDSI	1, downdraught Solex 38 PDSI	1, downdraught Solex 40 PDSI	1,downdraught Solex 40 PDSI
Valves	V-pattern OHV & duplex chain-driven SOHC	V-pattern, OHV & duplex chain-driven SOHC	V-pattern OHV & duplex chain-driven SOHC	V-pattern OHV & duplex chain-driven SOHC
Crankshaft bearings	5	5	5	5
Cooling	Pump, water, 7 litres	Pump, water, 7 litres	Pump, 7 litres water	Pump, 7 litres water
Lubrication	Pressurised, 4.25 litres of oil	Pressurised, 4.25 litres of oil	Pressurised, 4.25 litres of oil	Pressurised, 4.25 litres of oil
Battery	12v 44ah	12v 44ah	12v 44ah	12V 44ah
Generator	Alternator, 490 Watt. April 1971 on: 630 Watt.	As 1802	Alternator, 490 Watt. April '71:630 Watt.	Alternator, 490 Watt. April '71:630 Watt.
Transmission	Rear wheel drive Divided propshaft	Rear wheel drive Divided propshaft	Rear wheel drive Divided propshaft	Rear wheel drive Divided propshaft
Clutch	Single dry plate	Single dry plate	Single, dry plate	Single, dry plate
Gearchange	Floor, central lever	Floor, central lever	Floor, central lever	Floor, central lever
Gearbox	4-speed. Optional 5sp	4-speed. Optional 5sp	4-speed or optional 5-speed	4-speed or optional 5-speed
Synchromesh	1st-4th/1st-5th	1st-4th/1st-5th	1st-4th or 1st-5th	1st-4th or 1st-5th
Ratios	**4-speed** 1st,3.764 2nd,2.020 3rd,1.320 4th,1.00	**5-speed** 1st,3.368 2nd,2.160 3rd,1.579 4th,1.241 5th,1.00	**Ratios (4 and 5 speed)** As for 1802/1800 Touring Optional ZF automatic with hydraulic operation and 3-speed planetary gears selected by central lever. 1st, 2.56; 2nd, 1.52; 3rd, 1.00. Multiplication factor, 1.94	**Ratios (4 and 5 speed)** As for 1802/1800 Touring
Final drive ratio	4.11	4.11	3.64	3.64
Bodywork	As 1600 TI	As 1600 TI/1800 Touring	Unitary construction, all steel	Unitary construction, all steel
Front suspension	MacPherson struts, coil springs As 1600 TI	MacPherson struts, coil springs Tubular anti-roll bar	MacPherson strut, coil springs Tubular anti-roll bar (Optional for Cabriolet)	MacPherson strut, coil springs Tubular anti-roll bar
Rear suspension	Trailing arms, coil springs Tubular anti-roll bar	Trailing arms, coil springs Tubular anti-roll bar As 1600 TI/1802	Trailing arms, coil springs Tubular anti-roll bar (Optional on Cabriolet)	Trailing arms, coil springs Tubular anti-roll bar
Steering	Worm & roller, 17.58:1 3.75 turns lock-to-lock Twin circuit, hydraulic Servo-assisted	As 1600 TI/1802 Servo-assisted	Worm & roller, 17.58:1 3.75 turns lock-to-lock Twin circuit, hydraulic	Worm & roller, 17.58:1 3.75 turns lock-to-lock Twin circuit, hydraulic
Footbrake	Front discs 240mm Rear drums 200mm	Front discs 240mm Rear drums 200mm	Front discs 240mm Rear drums 230mm	Front discs 240mm Rear drums 230mm
General data				
Wheelbase	2500mm	2500mm	2500mm	2500mm
Track (front/rear)	1330/1330mm From Sept '73: 1342/1342mm	1330/1330mm From Sept '73: As 1802	1330/1330mm. From Sept '73: 1342/1342mm	1330/1330mm. From Sept '73: 1342/1342mm
Length, width & height	4230/1590/1410mm	4110/1590/1380mm	4230/1590/1410mm Cabrio: 1360mm high	4110/1590/1380mm
Rims	4½Jx13 From Sept '73: 5Jx13	4½Jx13 From Sept '73: 5Jx13	4½Jx13. From Sept '73: 5Jx13	4½Jx13. From Sept '73: 5Jx13
Tyres	165 SR 13	165 SR 13	165SR 13	165 SR 13
Turning circle	10.4 metres	10.4 metres	10.4 metres	10.4 metres
Vehicle weight	980kg	1030kg	990kg. Cabrio: 1040kg Automatic: 20kg extra	1030kg Automatic: 20kg extra
Max permissible weight	1370kg	1450kg	107mph. Auto: 105mph	As 2002
Top speed	104mph	104mph	11sec. Auto: 12s	As 2002
0-62mph	12 sec	12 sec	12.5 (22.6mpg) or 13.0 (21.7mpg) for auto	As 2002
Litres/100km	12.0 (23.5mpg)	12.0 (23.5mpg)		
Fuel tank	46 litres (10.1 galls) From Sept '73: 50 litres (11 galls)	52 litres 11.5 galls) Placed in rear	46 litres (10.1 galls) Sept '73: 50 litres (11 galls) All placed in rear	52 litres (11.5 galls) Placed in rear

BMW 2002 TI (ti) 1968-71	BMW 2002 Tii 1971-75	BMW 2002 Tii Touring 1971-74	BMW 2002 Turbo 1973-74
4 inline, iron block tilted @ 30° to right side, alloy cylinder head	4 inline, iron block tilted @ 30° to right side, alloy cylinder head	4 inline, iron block tilted @ 30° to right side, alloy cylinder head	4 inline, iron block tilted @ 30° to right side, alloy cylinder head
89x80mm 1990cc 120 @ 5500rpm 17mkg @ 3600rpm 9.3:1	89x80mm 1990cc 130 @ 5800rpm 18.1mkg at 4500rpm 9.5:1	89x80mm 1990cc 130 @ 5800rpm 18.1mkg at 4500rpm 9.5:1	89x80mm 1990cc 170 @ 5800rpm 24.5mkg @ 4500rpm 6.9:1
2,sidedraught, twin Choke, Solex 40 PHH V-pattern OHV and duplex chain-driven SOHC	Kugelfischer injection Pump, PLO4 V-pattern OHV & duplex chain-driven SOHC	Kugelfischer injection Pump, PLO4 V-pattern OHV & duplex chain-driven SOHC	Kugelfischer injection + KKK Turbocharger BLD. Kugelfischer pump, PLO4 V-pattern OHV & duplex chain-driven SOHC
5 Pump, 7 litres water Pressurised, 4.25 litres of oil 12v 44ah Alternator, 490 Watt. April '71:630 Watt.	5 Pump, 7 litres water Pressurised, 4.25 litres of oil 12v 44ah Alternator, 630 Watt	5 Pump, 7 litres water Pressurised, 4.25 litres of oil 12v 44ah Alternator, 630 Watt	5 Pump, 7 litres water Pressurised, 4.25 litres of oil 12v 44ah Alternator, 630 Watt
Rear wheel drive Divided propshaft Single, dry plate Floor, central lever 4-speed or optional 5-speed	Rear wheel drive Divided propshaft Single, dry plate Floor, central lever 4-speed or optional 5-speed	Rear wheel drive Divided propshaft Single, dry plate Floor, central lever As for 2002 tii	Rear wheel drive Divided propshaft Single, dry plate Floor, central lever 4-speed or optional 5-speed
1st-4th or 1st-5th **4-speed** / **5-speed** 1st, 3.835 / 1st, 3.368 2nd, 2.053 / 2nd, 2.160 3rd, 1.345 / 3rd, 1.579 4th, 1.00 / 4th, 1.241 5th, 1.00 3.64	**4-speed** 1st, 3.764 2nd, 2.020 3rd, 1.320 4th, 1.00	**5-speed** 1st, 3.368 2nd, 2.160 3rd, 1.579 4th, 1.241 5th, 1.00 3.64	As for 2002 tii/tii Touring 3.36
Unitary construction, all steel	Unitary construction, all-steel	Unitary construction, all-steel	Unitary construction, all steel except for front & rear spoilers
MacPherson strut, coil springs Tubular anti-roll bar	MacPherson struts, coil springs & tubular anti-roll bar	As 2002 tii	Uprated MacPherson struts, coil springs (lower ride height) & tubular anti-roll bar
Trailing arms, coils Tubular anti-roll bar	Trailing arms, coil springs & tubular anti-roll bar	As 2002 tii	Trailing arms, coil springs & tubular anti-roll bar with uprated dampers (Optional: gas) & lowered ride height As 2002 tii & Touring
Worm & roller, 17.58:1 3.75 turns lock-to-lock Twin circuit, double second circuit failsafe, hydraulic	Worm & roller, 17.58:1 3.75 turns lock-to-lock Twin circuit, double second circuit failsafe hydraulic	As 2002 tii	As 2002 tii & Touring
Front discs, 256mm Rear drums 230mm	Front discs 256mm Rear drums 230mm	Front discs 256mm Rear drums 230mm	Front discs 256mm Rear drums 250mm
2500mm 1342/1342mm	2500mm 1342/1342mm	2500mm 1342/1342mm	2500mm 1375/1362mm
4230/1590/1410mm	4230/1590/1410mm	4110/1590/1380mm	4220/1620/1410mm
5Jx13	5Jx13	5Jx13	Steel, 5½Jx13 or extra cost aluminium 6Jx13
165 HR 13 10.4 metres 990kg	165 HR 13 10.4 metres 1010kg 1410kg	165 HR 13 10.4 metres 1050kg 1450kg	185/70 HR 13 10.5 metres 1080kg 1440kg
115mph 10 sec 13.0 (21.7mpg)	118mph 10 sec 13.0 (21.7mpg)	118mph 10 sec 13.0 (21.7mpg)	131mph 8 sec 14.5 (19.5mpg)
46 litres (10.1 galls) Placed in rear	46 litres (10.1 galls). From Sept '73: 50 litres (11 galls) All placed in back	52 litres (11.5 galls) Placed in back	70 litres (15.4 galls) Rear tank

The rubber rubbing strips of later models are visible on the bumpers and sides of this 1971-73 BMW 1602 saloon.

A 1971-73 BMW 2002 shows more elaborate wheel trims but little else to denote extra status.

BMW 1802 from the same period as above. This 1.8-litre represented a nice balance between 2002 speed (1802 managed 104mph) and 1602 economy, the 1802 recording 23.8mpg overall.

The 2002 tii was a successful marriage between the Kugelfischer mechanical injection motor and 02 chassis providing acceleration from rest to 60mph in nine seconds or less, according to contemporary road tests, as well as providing 118mph and 25mpg plus economy under British conditions.

The 1973-75 series of 1602, 1802, 2002 and 2002 tii shared these blacked out grilles and also had square rear lamps instead of round.

The 1502 was an astonishing success but a bit misleading as it shared the 1602 engine of 1573cc. It was made from 1975 to 1977.

130

Gorgeous with the hood down, the Baur Cabriolet 2+2 coachwork for BMW 1600 provided a true convertible (above and top right). Such cars were made between 1967 and 1971. As a basic design the 2002 must have been one of the most versatile ever, allowing the factory to offer convertibles, sporting estates and two door road cars from 75 to 170bhp.

Middle right. A flat roof panel and a folding hood were features of the stylish Baur BMW 2002 Cabriolet 2+2 of 1971-73.

From the rear and side you can make up your own mind about the success of the Baur Cabriolet styling for the 2002, and compare the squared-off later model tail lamps with those used earlier. This model may not have had the sleekness of line provided by the earlier 1.6-litre Baur convertibles, but extra engine power was a compensation.

Top left. BMW 1600 Touring of 1971-72 was externally similar to 1800 Touring. Both foretold the era of the hatchback, but were not claimed to be pioneers, just another demonstration of basic design adaptation.

Top right; The bigger-engined Touring 2000 and 2000 tii from the same period also had fancier wheel trims as external identification.

Right. From the 1973-1974 series of Touring 1802, 2002 and 2002 tii we note the arrival of slotted steel wheels, which were of 5J section instead of the previous 4½J.

Right. Presumably named after the Garmisch area of outstanding beauty (less than an hour by motorway from Munich), this interesting prototype was concocted by Bertone upon a 2002 ti base.

BMW 2002 turbo (1973-74), now a very collectable car. Perhaps the worst-judged introduction in the company's history? That mirror writing on the spoiler saying "turbo" and "2002" was judged by many critics to be too aggressive and it was swiftly removed.

BMW 1600 GT (1967-68)

Those elegant, competitively designed and proportionately cheap Glas 1300 GT and 1700 GT coupes were the most successful models to emerge from the original Hans Glas GmbH at Dingolfing. The bodies were designed and made by Frua at Turin in Northern Italy. Glas made 5,378 such cars between March 1964 and September 1967. It could be said these cars were the only tangible asset Glas were offering, aside from their premises and the bigger GT also described on this page. Yet it was another year before the BMW 1600 GT could be built. Far from just placing a BMW kidney grille and badges on this stylish fastback, BMW also inserted the engine, gearbox and rear suspension/axle layout of BMW 1600 TI. From the original came the body, front suspension and the remaining fittings.

From September 1967 to August 1968 BMW produced only 1,259 examples of this model. Price of the BMW 1600 GT was Dm 15,850 which, from October 1968, was discounted to Dm 10,900.

(BMW) Glas 3000 V8 (1967-68)

Nicknamed the "Glaserati" this ambitious project was taken over during its Glas production run by BMW. Glas had built 277 examples of the 2600 V8, a sporty four-seater coupe with advanced eight cylinder engine (it included transistorised ignition and belt driven overhead camshafts); De Dion rear axle and Frua body with touch of Maserati about it – thus the nickname. Snags included a short wheelbase that spoiled it visually and upset the handling.

Yet the car was competitively priced and BMW decided to continue with the project, enlarging the V8 to 3-litres, as planned by Glas. Externally the Glas became a BMW with badges on the bonnet, boot lid and hub caps emblazoned with the whirling propeller insignia, yet it continued to be marketed as the Glas 3000 V8. Production ran from September 1967 to May 1968 and 389 of the 120 plus mph Glas 3000 V8s were delivered. Price was Dm 23,850.

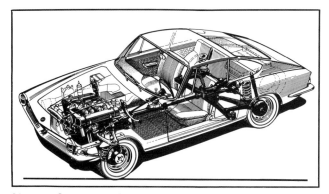

Above. Cutaway of the BMW-Glas hybrid that became the BMW 1600 GT. The styling, fittings and front suspension were Glas, but the 105bhp engine, rear suspension and final drive arrangements were all from BMW 1600 TI. Gearboxes were provided by BMW with a four or five-speed manual option.

Our two pictures (right) show the Frua lines and proliferation of BMW insignia for the BMW 1600 GT of 1967-68. In its original 1300 and 1700 form the Glas had 75bhp from 1289cc or 112bhp from 1682cc, both four-cylinder Glas units utilising toothed belt drive to their single overhead camshafts, nowadays widespread practice around the automotive world. With chain drive SOHC BMW-power the 1600 GT was said to reach 115mph and attain 62mph from rest in 11 seconds.

From the front, the Glas 3000 had a slightly muddled style, its identity not helped by both BMW and Glas badging. The high roofline allowed a genuine four-seater cabin. Overall fuel consumption was recorded as 17.7mpg from the triple Solex-carburated V8.

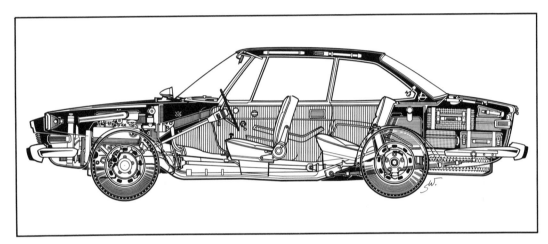

From its accommodating boot to its 90° V8, mounted low in the front bodywork, the 160bhp Glas 3000 was a clever compromise between carrying capacity and sheer speed. For BMW it was very much a stop gap step as they had their own six-cylinder coupes impending.

Very cleanly styled hindquarters emphasised dual identity with BMW badge above that of Glas. In fact the bodies were designed and built by Frua, as with the four-cylinder coupes. Advanced features included four wheel disc braking, the rear discs mounted inboard, and transistorised ignition for the V8, which had a separate belt to drive the SOHC on each cylinder bank.

134

	BMW 1600 GT 1967-68	BMW Glas 3000 V8 1967-68	
Motor			
Cylinders	BMW 4 inline, iron block tilted @ 30° to right side, alloy cylinder head	Glas-BMW V8 of 90° vee	
Bore x stroke	84x71mm	78x78mm	
Capacity	1573cc	2982cc	
Power	105 @ 6000rpm	160 @ 5100rpm	
Torque	13.5mkg @ 4500rpm	24mkg @ 3900rpm	
Compression	9.5:1	9.2:1	
Carburation	2, sidedraught, twin choke	3, downdraught, twin choke (2 in later cars)	
	Solex 40 PHH	Solex 35 DDIS	
Valves	V-pattern OHV with chain (duplex)-driven SOHC	V-pattern OHV with belt-driven SOHC per bank	
Crankshaft bearings	5	5	
Cooling	Pump, 7 litres water	Pump, 15.5 litres water	
Lubrication	Pressurised, 4 litres oil	Pressurised, 6.5 litres of oil	
Battery	12v 44ah	12v 55ah	
Generator	Alternator, 35 Amp	Alternator, 500 W	
Ignition	Battery ignition	Transistorised	
Starter	1 HP	1 HP	
Transmission	Rear wheel drive Split propshaft	Rear wheel drive Split propshaft	
Clutch	Single, dry plate	Single, dry plate	
Gearchange	Floor, central lever	Floor, central lever	
Gearbox	4 or 5-speed	4-speed	
Synchromesh	1st-4th or 1st-5th	1st-4th	
Ratios	**4-speed** **5-speed** 1st, 3.835 1st, 3.368 2nd, 2.053 2nd, 2.160 3rd, 1.345 3rd, 1.579 4th, 1.00 4th, 1.241 5th, 1.00	1st, 3.918 2nd, 2.133 3rd, 1.361 4th, 1.00	
Final drive ratio	3.64	3.364	
Bodywork	Unitary construction, all-steel	Unitary construction, all-steel	
Front suspension	Double wishbones Coil springs, anti-roll bar (transverse mount)	Double wishbones Coil springs, anti-roll bar (transverse mount)	
Rear suspension	Trailing arms, coil springs	De Dion axle, three half leaf springs, Panhard rod	
Steering	ZF Gemmer 16.45:1 3.5 turns lock-to-lock	Worm & roller, 15.7:1, servo-assisted, 3 turns lock-to-lock	
Footbrake	Hydraulic, servo-assisted Front discs 268mm Rear drums 230mm	Hydraulic, servo-assisted Front discs 272mm Rear discs 268mm (inboard)	
Handbrake	Mechanical, to rear wheels	Mechanical, to rear wheels via disc and special drum combination	
General data			
Wheelbase	2320mm	2500mm	
Track front/rear	1260/1260mm	1432/1412mm	
Length, width, height	4050/1550/1280mm	4600/1750/1380mm	
Rims	4½Jx14	5½JKx14	
Tyres	155 HR 14	185 H 14 or 185 HR 14	
Turning circle (left/right)	10.6/10.7 metres	12.6/11.1 metres	
Vehicle weight	970kg	1350kg	
Max permissible weight	1330kg	1800kg	
Top speed	115mph	121mph	
Acceleration, 0-62mph	11 sec.	10 sec.	
Consumption, litres/100km	12.5 (22.6mpg)	16.0 (17.7mpg)	
Fuel tank (rear mounted)	55 litres (12.1 galls)	80 litres (17.6 galls)	

BMW 1800 SA, 2000 SA (1968-72) BMW 1804, 2004 (1973-75)

Frua of Turin also designed a four door saloon for Hans Glas GmbH, who made 13,789 examples at Dingolfing in 1967. After that single series, *Bayerischen Motoren Werke* took over all the manufacturing tools and passed them on to the South African BMW Concessionaire in Pretoria. South Africa's laws are similar to Australia's in that it is impossible to sell in real volume unless you manufacture a high percentage of the car within the country concerned.

The South Africans built the BMW 1800 GL from July 1968, which became the BMW 1800 SA and from 1970 they made the 2000 SA. These cars had the body and running gear of the Glas 1700, but their 1.8 and 2.0-litre (four-cylinder) engines and gearboxes were shipped from Munich. The SA models differed externally from the Glas 1700 only in BMW badges for the front, back and wheel trims. During 1973 to 1975 both models were identified as the 1804 and 2004 and continued in production with a correct BMW 'face' (kidney grille and quad lamps) with reworked rear styling too. In 1974 BMW took over the South African plant completely and began the installation of a line to make the new 5-series (518 to 530 models). Production of the Glas-based cars ended in 1975, when it was estimated that some 12,000 had been built — some of them going to Rhodesia, incidentally.

In proportion to the size of their South African market, the number of BMW cars sold was unimportant. They were very expensive, but enjoyed a good marque reputation.

Top. Frua style certainly comes through on the grille and lamp arrangements for this South African BMW 1800 SA. Also of four doors and similar looks were the 2000 SA models of 1968-72.

Middle. The BMW 1804 and 2004 with four doors took their BMW parentage seriously and adopted this corporate face. They were made from 1973-75.

Bottom. Rear end of the original Frua style, but BMW-badged, 2000 SA.

BMW 2500, 2800 (1968-77)
BMW 3.0 S (1971-77)
BMW 2.8 L, 3.0 L, 3.3 L (1974-77)

An entirely new range of big saloons went into production from September 1968. They were the 2500 and 2800, whose style, size, weight and performance corresponded almost exactly with the similar Mercedes range. In balance the big BMWs offered an engine that was more responsive and which revved like a turbine, plus sportier handling on harder springs. Against this they offered less comfort and less attention to many details than the Stuttgart marque.

Until the end of 1971 the BMW 2800 was essentially more extensively equipped than the 2500, possessing standard suspension ride height levelling and limited slip differential. First impressions are what count and the 2800 was always bound to be the performance model of the two originals, but it did lose the LSD and rear levelling device, so that the standard specification of 2500 and 2800 was ultimately very similar.

April 1971 marked the arrival of BMW 3.0 S with another 30bhp over the 2500 and 10bhp more than the 2800. By September 1971 the quick 3.0 Si fuel-injected 3-litre gave another 20bhp over its carburettor cousin and brought these fleet four door saloons to 200bhp and 130mph capability.

From September 1973 model range styling changes included black grilles, new wheel trims, plus front seat height and steering column adjustment, as well as headrests and automatic reel safety belts. The 2800 struggled to the end of the year, by which time most buyers were opting for 3-litres.

A range of long wheelbase L-suffixed saloons began in August 1973 with the 3.3 L, which had a 10cm longer wheelbase and a corresponding favourable effect on rear seat room. Overall length was up too, and extra luxury equipment provided. Production began in March 1974, while from February 1975 the same body could be had as a 2.8 L or 3.0 L.

Production of the L models ran until February 1977, but only shortly before that date (September 1976) a new fuel-injection engine of 3205cc replaced the 3295 unit of 3.3 L and became 3.3 Li. There was a 7bhp gain and a slight torque loss, but the move was prompted by the need for a price increase rather than an engineering desire to run a shorter stroke with the 89mm bore.

By now both basic and long wheelbase big BMWs were beginning to look a little amateur when compared to the latest Mercedes S-class opposition. Not in price, nor comfort, nor prestige could they compete – though a BMW 3.3 L cost as much as a Mercedes 450 SE V8! Nevertheless BMW recorded a considerable sales success for the entire range. Alex von Falkenhausen's basic approach of adding another two cylinders to the already reputable four had taken BMW back into the prestige market with a vengeance, less than a decade after the merger with Mercedes had been proposed.

The original BMW 2500/2800 four door body. Made between 1968 and 1973 these larger six-cylinder saloons further boosted BMW's fortunes. Less than 10 years after total financial collapse seemed imminent the Bavarians were back; brimming with financial vigour, based on a logical product line.

BMW 2800 CS (1968-71)
BMW 3.0 CS (1971-75)
BMW 2.5 CS (1974-75)

The elegant BMW Coupe shape was defined at the September 1968 debut of 2800 CS which went into series production from December 1968. Like the earlier 2000 CS it was made at the Karmann body factory, but reworked to have a longer bonnet and an essential frontal facelift with quadruple lamps replacing the previous flush units. The result was a very handsome, sporting coupe which laid the foundations of a long-lived range, some 9,400 of the original 2800 CS being delivered before April 1971.

As with the saloons the successors had 3-litre engines becoming 3.0 CS (April 1971) and 3.0 CSi, which went on German sale in September 1971. From the exterior they differed little from 2800 series, but the factory reckoned these 200bhp CSi coupes were good for 136.6mph. Just as important was that they could stop too, thanks to the adoption of four wheel ventilated disc brakes.

From the 3.0 CS there originated the initial lightweight coupes (CSL) with a May 1971-announced 3.0 CSL of 180 carburated horsepower. In August 1972 they installed a 200bhp injection engine (3003cc) and a year later (August '73) there was a third version with 3153cc, which had 'Batmobile' aerodynamic wings. All CSLs were the basic model from which cars for racing could legally be taken (a process known as homologation), but most CSLs were purchased for road use. The 3.0 CS was fully road equipped while later models had the oversize engines to allow up to 3.5-litres in competition trim. For the British market some 500 CSLs were ordered and these featured electric winding windows and other normal luxury equipment that UK customers had become used to. The definitive CSL is the 206bhp model of 3.2-litres with the full wing kit (front spoiler, front wing strakes, rear window hoop and raised three-section rear wing/raised spoiler lip) and an interior featuring bucket seats with sports wheel and alloy door panels – which get dented very easily in ordinary use! A few, *very* few, were imported into the UK in this form and readers are advised to check engine and chassis number with BMW before proceeding with any CSL purchase! Some are quite genuine, even though they offer no performance or aerodynamic advantage, others are deliberate fakes of the Batmobile type that dominated European saloon car racing from 1973-1979. Incidentally winged CSLs were not allowed in Germany, so the wing kit was packed in the boot for use at the customer's discretion!

It was in 1972 that Jochen Neerpasch moved from Ford to reform BMW motorsporting ambitions with the formation of *BMW Motorsport GmbH.* The CSL idea had existed prior to his arrival but his enthusiasm and the aerodynamic imagination of Martin Braungart provided the big engine, winged versions that finally defeated all opposition and won every European Touring Car Championship title between 1973 and 1979. At their peak the BMW Motorsport factory cars developed over 470bhp from 24 valve fuel-injected engines with a 1976 CSL turbo generating upward of 750bhp and able to reach 190mph at Le Mans!

As the public reacted so fiercely to the fuel crisis in Germany (see also BMW 2002 turbo story) a completely opposite Coupe development arrived. This was the cheaper – by over 10,000 Dm compared to CSL– BMW 2.5 CS, complete with 150bhp six. Production of all Coupes came to an end at the close of 1975. A magnificent 44, 254 had been built, an enormous success for a sporting design.

Production	BMW 2500	BMW 2800	BMW 3,0	BMW 3,3 L	
1968	2560	140			2700
1969	20004	16611			36615
1970	17210	19260			36470
1971	10241	7645	16921		34807
1972	14166	2571	26872		43609
1973	13184	2371	26200		41755
1974	5099	948	11642	1131	18820
1975	5536	2455	8837	895	17723
1976	5249	2360	9339	927	17875
1977	957	236	915	77	2185
Totals	94206	54597	100726	3030	252559
					Saloons: 208305
					CS-Coupes: 44254

Right. The 1973-77 BMW 2500 and 1973-74 BMW 2800 models shared blacked-grilles and similar equipment levels. The major difference was beneath the bonnet and consequent performance. The 2.5 and 2.8-litre engines shared the same 86mm bore, but the 2.8 had an 80mm stroke instead of the 2.5's 71.6mm. The larger engine was – and is in 528i fuel-injected guise – one of the nicest BMW have ever made, combining power with not unreasonable economy.

Middle. Deceptively rapid were these capacious four door 3-litre BMWs that succeeded the original 2.8. The carburettor model (shown in 1971-77 guise) was based on the same bore and stroke as the 1990cc four, providing 180bhp in twin carburettor trim and 200bhp with Bosch D-Jetronic injection.

Below. The L-suffixed big BMWs (L for *Lang*; long in German) had stretched wheelbase in rather the same way as the Mercedes and Jaguar rivals. They were very much more comfortable in the rear and, in the case of the £10,000 plus UK models, beautifully equipped with items like electric sunroof and the alloy wheels shown here, all part of the standard specification. Britain took the 3.3 L, and Lia (auto) but also available were 2.8 and 3.0 L (1975-77) plus the 3.3 Li in manual form (1976-77). The cars were sold in Britain from April 1974.

139

	BMW 2500 1968-77	BMW 2800 1968-74	BMW 2.8L 1975-77
Motor			
Cylinders	6 inline, iron block tilted 30° to right, alloy head	6 inline, iron block tilted 30° to right, alloy head	6 inline, iron block tilted 30° right, alloy head
Bore x stroke	86 x 71.6mm	86 x 80mm	86 x 80mm
Capacity	2494cc	2788cc	2788cc
Power (bhp)	150 @ 6000rpm	170 @ 6000rpm	
Torque	21.5mkg @ 3700rpm	23.8mkg @ 3700rpm	
Compression	9:1	9:1	
Carburation	2, downdraught, progressive choke Zenith 35/40. From Sept '73:32/40 INAT with automatic choke	2, downdraught, progressive choke Zenith 35/40 INAT with automatic choke	
Valves	V-pattern OHV with duplex chain-driven SOHC	V-pattern OHV with duplex chain-driven SOHC	
Crankshaft bearings	7	7	
Cooling	Pump, 12 litres water	Pump, 12 litres of water	
Lubrication	Pressurised, 6 litres oil	Pressurised, 6 litres of oil	
Battery	12v 55ah	12v 55ah	
Generator	Alternator, 500 Watt From March 1970: 630 or 700 Watt	Alternator, 500 Watt From Mar '70:630 or 770 Watt	Alternator, 630 or 770 Watt
Transmission	Rear wheel drive Split propshaft	Rear wheel drive Split propshaft	Rear wheel drive Split propshaft
Clutch	Single, dry plate	Single, dry plate	Single, dry plate
Gearchange	Floor, central lever	Floor, central lever	Floor, central lever
Gearbox	4-speed	4-speed	4-speed
Synchromesh	1st-4th	1st-4th	1st-4th
Ratios	To April 1971: 1st, 3.85; 2nd, 2.08; 3rd, 1.375; 4th, 1.00 From April 1971: 1st, 3.855; 2nd, 2.202; 3rd, 1.401; 4th, 1.00 Optional: ZF automatic with hydraulic operation & 3-speed planetary gears. Central lever selection, driver ratio display Ratios for auto: 1st, 2.56; 2nd, 1.52; 3rd, 1.00 Torque Multiplication factor, 1.94		
Final drive ratios	3.64	3.45	3.64
Bodywork	Unitary construction, all-steel coachwork		
Front suspension	MacPherson struts, coil springs, additional rubber spring mounts. Original option (then production, 1971) tubular anti-roll bar		
Rear suspension	Trailing arms, damper legs & coil springs with rubber mounts. The 2800 had Boge self-levelling rear suspension & rear anti-roll bar as standard until 1971, when it became optional.		
Steering	ZF Gemmer worm & roller, 22.5:1 with 4.5 turns lock-to-lock Optional: servo-assisted power steer, 18.5:1 and 4 turns lock-to-lock		
Footbrake	Servo-assisted, hydraulic, twin circuit with secondary failsafe circuit. Discs (front & rear) 272mm diam.		
General data			
Wheelbase	2692mm	2692mm	2792mm
Track front/rear	1446/1464mm	1466/1464mm	1480/1486mm
Length, width & height	4700/1750/1450mm	4700/1750/1450mm	4800/1750/1450mm
Rims	6J 14 H 2	6J 14 H 2	6J 14 H 2
Tyres	175 HR 14	195/70 HR 14	195/70 HR 14
Turning circle (left/right)	11.0/11.2 metres	11.0/11.2 metres	11.2/11.4 metres
Max permissible weight	1830kg	1830kg	1900kg
Vehicle weight	1360kg (auto: + 20kg)	1360kg (auto: + 20kg)	1440kg (auto: + 20kg)
Max speed	118mph	124mph	121mph
0-62mph	11 sec	10 sec	10 sec
Litres/100km	16 (17.7mpg)	16.5 (17.1mpg)	As for 2800
Fuel tank	75 litres (16.5 galls) Placed in rear	75 litres (16.5 galls) Placed in rear	As for 2800 As for 2800

BMW 3.0 S 1971-77	BMW 3.0 L 1975-77	BMW 3.0 Si 1971-77	BMW 3.3 L 1974-76	BMW 3.3 Li 1976-77	
6 inline, iron block tilted 30° to right, alloy head 89 x 80mm 2985cc 180 @ 6000rpm 26mkg @ 3700rpm 9:1 2, progressive, downdraught Zenith 35/40 INAT with automatic choke operation	6 inline, iron block tilted 30° to right, alloy head 89 x 80mm 2985cc 200@ 5500rpm Sept '76: 195bhp 27.7mkg @ 3700rpm Sept '76:27.2mkg 9.5:1 to Sept '76 then 9:1 Electronic fuel-injection. Bosch D-Jetronic to Sept 76, then Bosch L-Jetronic		6 inline, construction as before 89 x 88.4mm 3295cc 190 @ 5500rpm 29.5mkg @ 3700rpm 9:1 2, progressive, downdraught Zenith 35/40 INAT	6 inline, construction as before 89 x 86mm 3210cc 195 @ 5500rpm 28.5mkg @ 4300rpm 9:1 Electronic fuel-injection. Bosch L-Jetronic	

V-pattern OHV with single overhead camshaft, chain-driven

7
Pump, 12 litres of water
Pressurised, 6 litres of oil
12v 55ah (engine bay)
Alternator, 630 Watt or 770 Watt

Rear wheel drive, split propshaft

Single, dry plate
Floor, central lever
4-speed
1st-4th
1st, 3.855; 2nd, 2.202; 3rd, 1.401; 4th, 1.000
Optional: Borg Warner automatic transmission
with hydraulic operation & 3-speed planetary gears
Central selector, ratio selected displayed in front
of driver within instrument binnacle.
Ratios: 1st, 2.39; 2nd, 1.45; 3rd, 1.00. Multiplication of torque factor, 2.00
3.45

Unitary construction, all-steel coachwork
MacPherson struts, coil springs, rubber supplementary springs
Tubular anti-roll bar
Trailing arms, damper leg struts, coil springs
supplementary rubber springs

ZF-Gemmer Worm & roller, 18.5:1 with servo-power assistance
4 turns lock-to-lock

Twin circuit, hydraulic with secondary failsafe
circuit, servo power assistance
Front and rear disc brakes, 272m diameter

BMW 3.0 S	BMW 3.0 L	BMW 3.0 Si	BMW 3.3 L	BMW 3.3 Li	
2692mm 1446/1464mm 4700/1750/1450mm 6J x 14 H 2 195/70 HR 14 11.0/11.2 metres 1420kg (auto: + 20kg) 1800kg 127mph 9 sec 17.5 (16.1mpg)	2792mm 1480/1486mm 4800/1750/1450mm 6J x 14 H 2 195/70 HR 14 11.2/11.4 metres 1470kg (auto: + 20kg) 1900kg 124mph 9.5 sec 17.5 (16.1mpg)	2692mm 1446/1464mm 4700/1750/1450mm 6J x 14 H 2 195/70 VR 14 11.0/11.2 metres 1440kg (auto: + 20kg) 1880kg 130mph 8.5 sec 17.5 (16.1mpg)		2792mm 1480/1486mm 4800/1750/1450mm 6J x 14 H 2 (alloys) 195/70 VR 14 11.2/11.4 metres 1520kg (auto: + 20kg) 1980kg 127mph 9.0 sec 17.5 (16.1mpg)	

75 litres (16.5 imperial gallons) Super grade (97 RM) petrol, placed in rear, all models.

	BMW 2.5 CS 1974-75	BMW 2800 CS 1968-71	BMW 3.0 CS 1971-75 BMW 3.0 CSL 1971-72
Motor			
Cylinders	6 inline with iron cylinder block tilted 30° to right. Alloy head.		
Bore x stroke	86 x 71.6mm	86 x 80mm	89 x 80mm
Capacity	2494cc	2788cc	2985cc
Power (bhp)	150 @ 6000rpm	170 @ 6000rpm	180 @ 6000rpm
Torque	21.5mkg @ 3700rpm	23.8mkg @ 3700rpm	26.0mkg @ 3700rpm
Compression	9:1	9:1	9:1
Carburation (or fuel injection)	2, progressive downdraught Zenith 32/40 INAT, auto-choke	2, progressive downdraught Zenith 35/40 INAT, auto-choke	2, progressive choke downdraught Zenith 35/40 INAT, auto-choke
Valves	V-pattern OHV with duplex chain-driven SOHC		
Crankshaft bearings	7		
Cooling	Pump, 12 litres of water		
Lubrication	Pressurised, 6 litres of oil		
Battery	12v 55ah		
Generator	Alternator, 630 Watt	Alternator 500 Watt March '70:630 Watt	Alternator, 630 or 770 Watt
Transmission	Rear wheel drive, split propshaft		
Clutch	Single dry plate		
Gearchange	Floor, central lever		
Gearbox	4-speed		
Synchromesh	1st-4th		
Ratios	1st, 3.855 2nd, 2.202 3rd, 1.401 4th, 1.00	1st, 3.85 2nd, 2.08 3rd. 1.375 4th, 1.00	1st, 3.855 2nd, 2.202 3rd, 1.401 4th, 1.00
		Optional: ZF automatic with hydraulic operation & 3-speed planetary gears, central selector. 1st, 2.56; 2nd, 1.52; 3rd, 1.0. Torque multiplication factor, 1.94	Optional: Borg Warner auto Hydraulic torque convertor, 3-speed planetary gearbox & cenral selector. 1st, 2.39; 2nd, 1.45; 3rd, 1.00 Torque multiplication factor, 2.0
Final drive	3.64	3.45	3.45
Bodywork	Unitary construction, all steel coachwork (CSL lightweight, door, boot, bonnet panels in alloy, thin glass etc)		
Front suspension	MacPherson struts, coil springs, tubular anti-roll bar		
Rear suspension	Trailing arms, damper struts, coil springs & anti-roll bar (no rear bar on 2.5 CS)		
Steering	ZF Gemmer worm & roller, 22.5:1 with 4.5 turns lock-to-lock	ZF-Gemmer worm & roller + power assistance, 18.5:1 4 turns lock-to-lock	As 2800 CS
Footbrake	Twin circuit hydraulic with servo power assistance and secondary failsafe circuit		
	Front & rear discs 272mm Internally ventilated	Front discs 272mm Rear drums 250mm	Front & rear discs 272mm Internally ventilated
General data			
Wheelbase	2625mm	2625mm	2625mm
Track (front/rear)	1446/1398mm	1446/1402mm	1446/1402mm
Length, width & height	4660/1670/1370mm	4660/1670/1370mm	4660/1670/1370mm
Rims	6J x 14 H2 (steel)	6J x 14 H2 (steel)	CS: 6J x 14 H2 (alloy) CSL: 7J x 14H2 (alloy)
Tyres	175 HR 14	195/70 HR 14	195/70 VR 14
Turning circle (left/right)	10.6/10.8 metres	10.6/10.8 metres	10.6/10.8 metres
Vehicle weight	1400kg. Auto: 1420kg	1355kg. Auto: 1375kg	CS: 1400kg. Auto: 1420kg CSL: 1200kg
Max permissible total weight	1770kg	1770kg	CS: 1750kg. CSL: 1650kg
Top speed	125mph	128mph	CS: 132mph. CSL: 134mph
0-62mph	10.5 sec	10 sec	CS: 9 sec. CSL: 8 sec
Litres/100km	16.0 (17.7mpg)	16.5 (17.1mpg)	17.5 (17.1mpg)
Fuel tank	All models: 70 litres (15.4 galls) Super grade, located at rear.		

BMW 3.0 CSi 1971-75	BMW 3.0 CSL 1972-73	BMW 3.0 CSL 1973-75	
6 inline, iron block tilted at 30° to right, alloy head			
89mm x 80mm	89.25 x 80mm	89.25 x 84mm	
2985cc	3003cc	3153cc	
200 @ 5500rpm	200 @ 5500rpm	206 @ 5600rpm	
27.7mkg @ 4300rpm	27.7mkg @ 4300rpm	29.2mkg @ 4200rpm	
9.5:1	9.5:1	9.5:1	
Electronic fuel-injection	Electronic fuel-injection	Electronic fuel-injection	
Bosch D-Jetronic	Bosch D-Jetronic	Bosch D-Jetronic	

V-pattern OHV, duplex chain-driven SOHC
7
Pump, 12 litres of water
Pressurised, 6 litres of oil
12v 55ah
Alternator, 770 Watt

Rear wheel drive, split propshaft
Single dry plate
Floor, central lever
4-speed
1st-4th
1st, 3.855; 2nd, 2.202; 3rd, 1.401; 4th, 1.00

Optional: Borg-Warner automatic with hydraulic torque convertor, 3-speed planetary gearbox, central selector. 1st, 2.39; 2nd, 1.45; 3rd, 1.00. Torque multiplication factor: 2.0			
3.25	3.25	3.25	
Unitary construction, all-steel	Unitary construction, all-steel (except for lightweight panels as per original CSL, but not for UK RHD)	Basic construction as other coupes but lightweight CSL parts joined by standard aerodynamic front & rear wing kit, bonnet strakes and rear window hoop. All aero parts in plastics	

MacPherson struts, coil springs & tubular anti-roll bar Trailing arms, coil springs & tubular anti-roll bar		MacPherson struts (gas inserts), coil springs & tubular anti-roll bar Trailing arms, coil springs, gas dampers & tubular anti-roll bar	

ZF Gemmer worm & roller, 18.05:1 + power-assistance. 4 turns lock-to-lock	ZF-Gemmer worm & roller, 22.5:1 & 4.5 turns lock-to-lock. Optional: 18.05:1 power assisted steering with 4 turns lock-to-lock (as CSi) 3-spoke sports steering wheel on CSL		

Mastervac power-assisted, twin circuit, hydraulic system with secondary failsafe circuit
Discs front and rear of 272mm diameter & with internal ventilation (as per 3-litre)

2625mm	2625mm	2625mm	
1446/1402mm	1426/1422mm	1470/1426mm	
4660/1670/1370mm	4630/1730/1370mm (Width + CSL spats)	4630/1730/1370mm (Width + CSL spats & height + hoop, where fitted)	
6J x 14 H 2 (alloys)	7J x 14 H 2 (alloys)	7J x 14 H 2 (alloys)	
195/70 VR 14	195/70 VR 14	195/70 VR 14	
10.6/10.8 metres	10.6/10.8 metres	10.6/10.8 metres	
1400kg. Auto: 1420kg	1270kg	1270kg	
136mph	136mph	138 (140 +mph claimed) with wings erected)	
8 sec	7.5 sec	7.5 sec	
17.5 (16.1mpg)	17.5 (16.1mpg)	17.5 (16.1mpg)	

All models: 70 litres (15.4 imperial gallons) of Super grade located at rear.

Introduced with new big BMW Saloons were the six-cylinder Coupes. Shown here is the later 3.0 CSi, which made good use of the 2985cc straight-six engine, leaping from rest to 60mph in eight seconds or less and able to exceed 130mph.

Another view of the 1971-75 BMW 3.0 CSi, showing how the original Karmann line for the 2000 series was only really elaborated with extra chrome at the rear: the front was restyled, primarily to accommodate six-cylinders and new, wider track, front suspension.

Below (left) is one of the fabled CSL series of 1971-74, this is the more familiar non-winged, standard 3.0 CSL guise which became well known in Britain too. Below (right) is the reaction after the fuel crisis—a 2.5-litre version of the SOHC six, which lived between 1974 and 1975 and was still reckoned to be able to top 120mph.

144

Colour section: Munich BMW Automobiles from 1952-78

The flowing lines of the BMW 502 were rarely to be seen in this colour, or against a Mediterranean backdrop, but the 2.6 and 3.2-litre V8s of aluminium construction did a great deal to re-establish BMW prestige. The problems started when BMW had nothing to bridge the gap between these luxury limousines and their later economy car ventures. The 502 was made between 1952 and 1961.

She is happy, and so would any owner be today with the Goertz-styled BMW 503 in this pristine condition. The 2+2 convertible, officially known as a Cabriolet, was powered by the 3.2-litre development of the V8 motor.

A radical styling departure for BMW was the Goertz styled, management-modified, two-seater roadster. The BMW 507 sports tourer reflected the American and Italian styling trends of its 1956-59 manufacturing period. Also powered by the 3.2-litre V8 it was, like the 503, a strictly limited volume model at a time when BMW desperately needed to get back to their pre-war middle class stamping grounds, but lacked the financial means to do so.

Based on the torsion bar suspended saloons of the late fifties, the BMW 507 cutaway shows the front mounted double carburettor version of the 3.2 V8, the sturdy chassis frame enclosed within the near-3000lb body. All drum braking and complicated steering linkage for the bevel and rack system were features of this sports car, which could be persuaded to between 124 and 136mph according to the choice of axle ratio.

BMW looked to the economy Isetta to restore their finances at one stage. Although the strange little four wheelers with a very narrow track at the rear (eliminated for UK exports and turned into a three-wheeler) were popular, there was not really enough money in such activities to support a company such as BMW. The Isetta was sold in 250 and 300 models, both versions powered by a rear-mounted BMW single-cylinder modified ex-motorcycle engine and made between 1957 and 1962.

Halfway to a real car! BMW 600 had a full width rear track and a single rear passenger door in addition to the usual front opening entrance. This four-seater had a BMW engine based on the legendary flat twin motorcycle variety, giving nearly 20bhp to push it along.

A turning point, but not enough on its own. BMW 700 series of rear-engined machines included these Coupes in their 1959-64 production span. The Coupe was a fine little road car and a worthy track competitor capable of tremendous giant-killing feats in the early sixties.

BMW 1800 in original 1963-68 form, this four cylinder, 1.8-litre model was another long-lived BMW variation on the theme of sporting practicality. Sports versions reasserted BMW's claims to overall victory in international events once more, a process begun by the 700's sporting small class successes.

BMW 2000 CS of 1965-69 was certainly stylish and established the basic framework around which later Karmann BMW coupes, but of six cylinders, would follow.

A classic in one of the popular colours of the 1968-71 production span: BMW 2002.

The open and shut case for the BMW 2002 Cabriolet, this 2+2 with centre rollover hoop was made between 1971 and 1973.

The BMW 2000 Touring found favour with the fire services as a patrol vehicle: note optional alloy wheels.

An original example of the BMW 2800 first series, complete with chrome grille and 170bhp, double Zenith carburated engine. These four door six-cylinder machines established Munich's ability to compete in the Mercedes area of the market.

The white finish of this BMW 2800 model highlights the exceptionally clean lines of the original body: later chrome strips would adorn its flanks. The boot was enormous, but favoured length over depth.

The mid-engined BMW Turbo was an interesting design study that could travel at speeds in excess of 150mph according to the factory publicity. It brought together the 2-litre turbo engine—in slightly more powerful tune than would be seen in production for the 2002, but still short of its competition potential – and styling that was highlighted by gullwing doors and safety-conscious designs for front and rear bodywork. By the close of the decade BMW would be involved in a 160mph mid-engine supercar that was sold to the public...

In Germany the 3-series became reality in 1975, the original four-cylinder models of 316, 320 carburated and fuel injected 320i arriving for sale in Britain from October of that year in RHD form. The 1.6-litre 316 came with single instead of the quad headlamps shown on this 2-litre model. Later, the same basic shape gained the small six-cylinder engines bringing back to BMW belt-driven overhead camshafts after years of loyalty to chain drive. It was over a decade since Glas had shown how such things might be done, but conservative quality is a key element in success on the German market.

From 1972 onward BMW had a new mid-range, four door, family saloon to offer the public. Like all the best BMWs the 5-series proved versatile and long-lived. Originally capable of taking anything from a four-cylinder, 1.8-litre four to the 2.8-litre six used in the 165bhp BMW 528 derivative illustrated, this model was later developed to provide a docile, roadgoing, 140mph with the 735i power plant installed (M535i of 1980). It was 1981 before the 5-series was replaced by a new 5-series that looked much the same, save from the angle at which we view this original 1975-76 series 528. These twin carburettor models were tricky to keep in tune and were superseded by a single carburettor version before the adoption of fuel-injection (528i) in 1977.

Back in the big league again with the prestigious 7-series, the four door design that has been with us since 1977 in shape, though it has undergone many mechanical changes. The original series came with carburated 2.8-litre (728) and 3-litre (730) or with a fuel-injected 3.3-litre – using the 3210cc motor (733i). Fuel-injection was adopted throughout the UK range in 1980, giving the 728i, 732i and 735i model names. The latter was another 130mph plus BMW four door, but the useful Bosch Motronic engine management system was initially reserved for 732i. Not available in Britain at all was the turbocharged BMW 745i, another 1980 development that offered 252bhp from 3210cc, usually mated to automatic transmission.

BMW Turbo (1972 prototype)

As a styling and rolling chassis exercise and an experimental "lab-on-wheels" BMW presented, in August 1972, a gullwing mid-engined Coupe to an astonished public. The Turbo anticipated future safety developments with the use of crumple zones that would slowly recover their original shape after an impact. The flourescent colouring in a number of shades served to give extra warning of the vehicle's presence and there was a rubber protective strip right around the waistband. The Turbo also had an extremely low centre of gravity and a radar installation to warn when the car in front was too close for comfort!

Transversely across the rear of the car was mounted the BMW 2002 engine, its turbocharger mounted alongside the cylinder head. The dramatic lines were by then-BMW styling chief, Frenchman Paul Bracq, and were such a success that a second example was built for further studies. This example was built at Michelotti and remained there—the original is in the BMW museum, Munich.

Specification included a 2400mm wheelbase; track 1550mm front and 1530mm rear; length, 4144mm; width, 1880mm; height, 1100mm; Dunlop tyres, 4.75/11.2-14 in diameter; weight 980kg. Top speed, 155mph and acceleration from 0-62mph in 7 seconds (factory figures).

	BMW 316 1975-1980 316-badged 1.8 1980 on 315-badged 1.6 1981 on	BMW 318 1975-1980 BMW 318i 1980 on 320i-badged 1.8i USA 1981 on	BMW 320 1975-1977	BMW 320i 1975-1977	BMW 320 1977 on	BMW 323i 1977 on
Motor						
Cylinders	4 inline, iron block tilted 30° to right. Alloy head.	4 inline, iron block tilted 30° to right. Alloy head.	4 inline, iron block tilted 30° to right. Alloy head.	4 inline, iron block tilted 30° to right. Alloy head	6 inline, iron block tilted 30° to right side. Alloy head	6 inline, iron block tilted 30° to right side. Alloy head
Bore x stroke	316:84x71mm 316/1/8:89x71mm 315/1.6:84x71mm	89x71mm	89x71mm	89x80mm	80x66mm	80x76.8mm
Capacity	316 & 315/1.6:1574cc 316/1.8:1766cc	1766cc	1990cc	1990cc	1990cc	2315cc
Power (USA by SAE)	316:90bhp @ 6000rpm 316/1.8:90bhp @ 5500rpm 315/1.6:75bhp @ 5800rpm	318:98bhp @ 5800rpm 318i:105bhp @ 5800rpm USA 320i:102bhp @ 5800rpm	125bhp @ 5500rpm	125 @ 5700rpm	122 @ 6000rpm	143 @ 6000rpm
Torque (USA: SAE)	316:12.5mkg @ 4500rpm 316/1.8:14.3mkg @ 4300rpm 315/1.6:11.2mkg @ 3200rpm	318:14.5mkg @ 4000rpm 318i:14.8mkg @ 4500rpm USA 320i:13.8mkg @ 4500rpm	17.5mkg @ 4350rpm	17.5mkg @ 4350rpm .3mkg @ 4000rpm 19.4mkg @ 4500rpm	16	
Compression	316:8.3:1. 316/1.8 & 315/1.6:9.5:1	318:8.3:1. 318i:10:1. USA 320i:8.8:1	8:1	9.3:1	9.2:1	9.5:1
Carburation	316:1, Solex 32/32 DIDTA downdraught 316/1.8:1, Solex 2B4 downdraught 315/1.6:1, Pierburg 1b2 downdraught	318:1, Solex 32/32 DIDTA downdraught 318i:Bosch K-Jetronic mechanical fuel-injection USA 320i:As above, Lambda sensor, 3-way catalyst.	1, Solex 32/32 DIDTA downdraught, progressive twin choke carburettor with auto-choke, as fitted 316/318, rejetted	Continuous petrol injection, Bosch K-Jetronic	1, downdraught, progressive choke carburettor. Solex 4 A1. Automatic choke	Continuous petrol injection, Bosch K-Jetronic
Valves		V-pattern OHV with duplex chain-driven SOHC		V-pattern OHV & duplex chain-driven SOHC	V-pattern OHV & belt-driven SOHC	V-pattern OHV & belt-driven SOHC
Crankshaft bearings		5		5	7	7
Cooling		Pump, 7 litres of water		Pump, 7 litres of water	Pump, 12 litres of water	Pump, 12 litres of water
Lubrication		Pressurised, 4.25 litres of oil		Pressurised, 4.25 litres of oil	Pressurised, 4.75 litres of oil	Pressurised, 4.75 litres of oil
Battery	316:12v 36ah. 315 & 316/1.8:12v 36 or 45ah	318:12v 36ah 318i:12v 36 or 44ah. 320i: (US):12v 55ah	12v 36ah	12v 44ah	12v 44ah	12v 55ah
Alternator	316:630W,AC. 315 & 316/1.8 have either 45 or 55A	318:630W,AC. 318i & USA 320i: 55A/910W	630W,AC	Alternator, 770 watt	Alternator, 910 Watt	Alternator, 910 Watt
Transmission		Rear wheel drive, split propshaft			Rear wheel drive, split propshaft	
Clutch		Single plate, dry			Single, dry plate	
Gearchange		Floor, central lever			Floor, central lever	
Gearbox	Original 316, 318 & 320, 4-speed. 315,316/1.8, 318i, USA 320i 5-speed optional or standard, according to period & market			320i & original 320/323i: 4-speed – 1st, 3.764; 2nd, 2.022; 3rd, 1.320, 4th, 1.00 Optional, 320 only, ZF HP 22 automatic gearbox with hydraulic torque convertor & 3-speed planetary gearbox. Central lever selector (P-R-N-D-2-1) Ratios:		
Synchromesh		1st-4th or 1st-5th		1st, 2.478; 2nd, 1.478; 3rd, 1.00. Torque multiplication factor given as 2.0 originally & 2.36 (1981)		
Ratios	Original 316, 318, 320: 1st, 1.3764; 2nd, 2.022; 3rd, 1.320; 4th, 1.00 315, 316/1.8, 318i: As 4-speed ratios except 2.043, 2nd gear. USA 320i: standard 5-speed (optional elsewhere) 1st, 3.681; 2nd, 2.002; 3rd, 1.329; 4th, 1.00; 5th, 0.805 Optional: ZF HP 22 hydraulic torque converter, 3-speed planetary gearbox (not 315) with ratios (USA in brackets): 1st, 2.478 (2.73); 2nd, 1.478 (1.56); 3rd, 1.00 (1.00)			Optional originally & later standard on many markets (UK 1981) was wide ratio 5-speed: 1st, 3.681; 2nd, 2.002; 3rd, 1.329; 4th, 1.0; 5th, 0.805 Sports option (320 & 323i) 5-speed: 1st, 3.764; 2nd, 2.325; 3rd, 1.612; 4th, 1.229; 5th, 1.00		
Final drive	316:4.10. 315:4.11. 316/1.8:3.91	318:3.90. 318i:3.91. USA 320i:3.91 or 3.64 (latter auto)	3.64	3.64	3.64 (Opt.LSD)	3.45 (Opt.LSD)
Bodywork		Unitary construction, all-steel with single or twin headlamps & optional USA Sport body parts			Unitary construction, all-steel. Factory Sport spoiler options (front & rear).	
Front suspension		MacPherson struts, coil springs, anti-roll bar and rubber mountings (USA gas damper Sport pack)			MacPherson struts, coil springs, anti-roll bar. Sports spring & gas damper options.	
Rear suspension	Trailing arms, damper legs (USA gas Sport pack), coil springs & anti-roll bar, rubber mounts. Original 316/318 optional rear roll bar until March 1976, when made standard.			Trailing arms, coil springs & telescopic dampers & anti-roll bar. Rubber bushings & mountings, front & rear. Sports damper & spring options		
Steering		ZF rack & pinion, 19:1 on all but USA 320i (21:1) 4 turns lock-to-lock		ZF rack & pinion, 19.01 4 turns lock-to-lock	ZF rack & pinion, 19.01 4 turns lock-to-lock Optional: power assist.	ZF rack & pinion, 19.01 4 turns lock-to-lock Optional: power assist.
Footbrake		Servo-assisted, hydraulic, twin circuit Front discs 255mm. Rear drums 250mm		Twin circuit, hydraulic Servo-assisted Front discs 255mm Rear drums 250mm	Twin circuit, hydraulic Servo-assisted Front discs 255mm Rear drums 250mm	Twin circuit, hydraulic Servo-assisted Vented front discs 255mm Rear discs 258mm
General data						
Wheelbase	2563mm	2563mm	2563mm	2563mm	2563mm	2563mm
Track (front/rear)	316:1364/1377mm 315/1.6:1365/1375mm. 316/1.8:1365/1375mm.	318:1364/1377mm 318i:1365/1375mm. USA 320i:1387/1397mm	1364/1377mm	1386/1399mm	1386/1399mm	1386/1390mm
Length, width & height	4355/1610/1380mm	As column 1, except USA 320i:4508/1610/1379mm	As column 1	4355/1610/1380mm	4355/1610/1380mm	4355/1310/1380mm
Rims	316: 5Jx13J 315/1.6:optional 5½Jx13 316/1.8:optional 5½Jx13	318: 5Jx13. 318i:5½J option. USA 320i:5½J steel std, 5½J H 2 alloy option	5Jx13	5½Jx13	5½Jx13 (alloy option)	5½Jx13 (alloy option)
Tyres	316:165 SR 13. 315/1.6:optional 185/70HR. 316/1.8:optional 185/70HR	318:165 SR 13. 318i:option, 185/70. USA 320i:std 185/70	165 SR 13	185/70 HR 13	185/70 HR 13	185/70 HR 13
Turning circle (left/right)	10.4/10.8 metres	10.4/10.8 metres	10.4/10.8 metres	10.4/10.8 metres	10.4/10.8 metres	10.4/10.8 metres
Vehicle weight	316: 1040kg. 315/1.6: 1010kg. 316/1.8: 1020kg	318: 1040kg. 318: 1030kg. USA 320i: 1130kg	1060kg	1080kg	1180kg (+20kg, auto)	1150kg
Max weight	316: 1420kg. 315/1.6: 1440kg. 316/1.8: 1440kg	318: 1420kg. 318i: 1440kg. USA 320i: 1561kg	1440kg In all cases add 20kg for automatic transmission	1460kg	1550kg	1570kg
Top speed	316: 100mph. 315/1.6: 96mph	318: 104mph. 318i: 106mph. No USA figures, auto 1.8i: 103mph	107mph	114mph	114mph	119mph
0-62mph	316:14 sec. 315:14.8 sec. 316/1.8: 12.5 sec	318:12 sec. 318i:11.5 sec.	11.5 sec.	10 sec.	10.5 sec.	9.5 sec.
Litres/100 km	316:11.5 (24.6mpg). 315/1.6:10.5 (26.9mpg) 316/1.8:11.0 (25.7mpg)	318:12 (23.5mpg). 318i:10.4 (27.2mpg) USA 320i:N/A. Auto 1.8i:9.3 (30.4mpg)	12.5 (22.2mpg). Auto: 13 (21.7mpg)	13.0 (21.7mpg)	13.0 (21.7mpg). Auto: 13.5 (20.9mpg)	13.5 (20.9mpg)
Fuel tank	52 litres (11.5 galls) to Sept '77: then 58 litres (12.8 galls) Under back seats	As column 1 15.3 US gallons Unleaded fuel	52 litres (11.5 galls)	52 litres (11.5 galls) Under rear seats	58 litres (12.8 galls) Under rear seats	58 litres (12.8 galls) Under rear seats

BMW 3-series (from 1975)

The 3-series replaced the 02 models which ceased production in July 1975 (except 1502). Production of the elegant 3-series began on May 2, 1975; the new body offering, essentially, a slightly roomier rear seat space within a slightly bigger two door saloon. Just as with the 02 series there were normal carburated models and a higher performance injection derivative (320i) but this model was not quite so quick as the 2002 tii.

In effect BMW were offering a design that had grown-up. The model's lines, similar to 5-series, looked attractive and prestigious, winning over many (compared with its predecessor), though for a car of this class customers admittedly paid enormously high prices. Yet, because of the brand name and its inherent sportiness a large circle of prosperous customers was found.

Externally the various 3-series saloons were almost identical. Yet the 316 (carburated, four-cylinder: 1563cc) and 318 (1754cc and 8bhp more) were defined by two headlamps while the 320 (carburated, four-cylinder: 1990cc) and 320i (injected, four-cylinder: another 16bhp) had quadruple lamps, as did the later six-cylinder 320 and 323i.

From September 1977 the four-cylinder engines in 320 and 320i were superseded by a new generation of sixes. These new powerplants, from a design engineering team that included Formula 2 engine wizard Paul Rosche, a lifetime BMW employee, had modern construction, modest weight, high performance, and a joy in running to high rpm that was accompanied by a surprising degree of civilisation (particularly in later models). With this new six-cylinder unit BMW proved a renewed ability to supply the world with the finest of car engines, though there were British reports of unreliability in early 320/6 and 323i; usually associated with the cylinder head, or valve gear.

From the end of 1977 Baur built a series of BMW 3-series Cabriolets at Stuttgart. Between the front windshield and the roll bar these had a removable section in man-made materials that matched the folding hood over the rear seats. Admittedly the rather high and solidly built side sections gave occupants a sensation of being closed in, but to get a completely open air feeling a convertible with less body strength would have been required. Incidentally, the hardtop BMW Baur Cabriolet cost 6000 Dm (more than £1600 at the then-current rate of exchange) more than the corresponding saloon: In Britain the price situation was considerably worse, as had become tradition.

Production year	BMW 316	BMW 318	BMW 320/4	BMW 320/6	BMW 323
1975	10,629	10,446	22,274	–	–
1976	42,166	14,618	74,037	–	–
1977	52,833	20,369	75,113	18,389	37
1978	53,802	20,897	28,414	61,798	18,467
1979	46,418	16,961	28,002	66,305	31,123
1980	55,900	53,755	–	60,247	36,424
1981	45,435	71,739	–	45,338	33,205

*BMW 315 added to range in 1981:33,115 manufactured

Above: The headlamp differences for the 316/318 (the latter not exported to Britain) can be clearly seen with the more luxurious and powerful 320/320i closest to camera. Later the 320 and 323i six-cylinder replacements also carried quadruple headlamps, the 143bhp, 120mph plus 323i being a much-needed replacement for 2002 tii. BMW suffered some British and German criticism over the less sporting characteristics of 3-series compared particularly to 2002, 2002 tii and 2002 turbo, but the concept of a "grown-up" small car was to sell more units than even the legendary 02 series mustered.

Middle: From the side a 323i displays a clean but angular body line. By the eighties BMW had their own wind tunnel and such bluff shapes were being modified in the light of aerodynamic experience. Here the small front spoiler and wide use of rubber side protection can be seen.

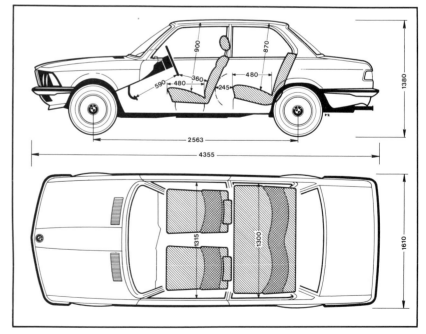

A little more internal room and the general feel of a big car with two doors were hallmarks of the 3-series BMWs. Possibly the first European machines to understand that the prosperous public *would* buy smaller cars, but that they would not forego luxury equipment or performance. Electric sunshine roofs, electric window operation, leather trim, power steering, all were offered either as standard or optional trim (depending on market) by BMW for 3-series.

156

The M60-coded small sixes of 2 and 2.3-litres were introduced in the September 1977 revisions of 3-series. Principal departure from normal BMW practice was the use of belt-driven overhead camshafts, a feature shared by the 1981 2.7-litre Eta engine for 5-series in America. The M60 has also provided a base for BMW's diesel engine work in Austria.

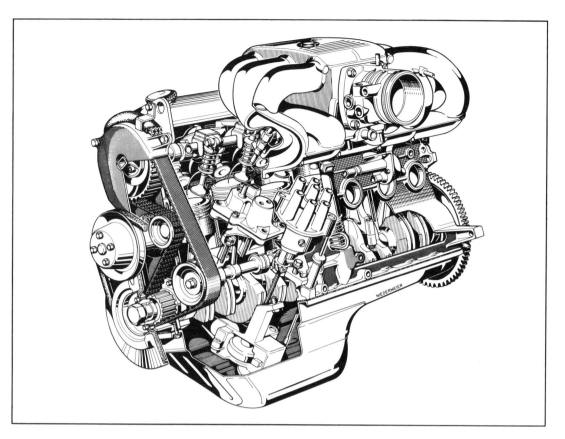

Baur at Stuttgart continued their BMW association with this very neat Cabriolet version of 3-series. This example is an RHD 323i model from the first batch brought into Britain by BMW, shortly after the factory takeover of the UK concession in January 1980.

BMW 5-series (from 1972)

Called the "five twenty" in German slang the production of 5-series began in September 1972 with the BMW 520, which was designed to replace the 2000 *Neue Klasse* of the sixties that had performed so well, for so long. Engine, gearbox and running gear were the same in principle as before, but the body was entirely new. It offered more carrying capacity and a more substantial air, marking BMW's progress toward more prestige for its cars.

The object was to provide a new crisp and modern style with more comfort, while retaining the Pleasure in Driving *(Freude am Fahren)* that is part of the BMW philosophy and advertising. Largely, they succeeded, but (of course!) prices crept ever upward ...

The price and size of the cars was really decided in advance, but when the 5-series became available it was apparent that a considerable number of customers wanted higher performance. The extra power was in no proportion to the extra price, but that didn't stop versions like the September 1973 BMW 525 providing an extra 25bhp over 520i. That led directly to another six: instead of 2.5-litres of the 525 (note the return to pre-war logic with 5-series) there came the 2.8-litre 528 six-cylinder, which began with 165bhp. As fillers between BMW 520 and the larger 2500/2800 series then in production, they were a success.

Perhaps as a following act to BMW 1800 the 518 was logical, but it was also an extremely successful sales weapon for use in its introduction time during the fuel crisis years (1974 onward). One could hardly expect a great economy saving from a 1.8-litre four compared to the 520's 2-litre four but from September 1975 compression was lowered to allow the 518 to run on two star fuel, which had the psychological effect of convincing people they were buying an economy model, even if it did have a BMW badge! From August 1977 the unknowing hypocrisy of the 518 buyer was increased by the acceptance of an automatic gearbox option, despite the obvious adverse effect on economy. Yet there were many who demanded this combination ...

August 1976 marked the arrival of some minor styling changes, though (happily) the overall visual impression of the car was not markedly altered. The bonnet was equipped with a central 'peak'; there were larger rear lights, wheel rim trims (as well as hubcaps) and the fuel filler was moved from alongside the rear number plate to a side position, on the right rear wing. Many basic changes were wrought in September 1977 without altering the exterior (a theme BMW continued into the eighties: the 5-series look appears sacrosanct). Then the 520 gained the six-cylinder carburated unit also used in 320. Of course it attracted a higher price, but the significance lay in an extra degree of refinement imparted by this modern six. At this point the 520i was shuffled off the programme and the 528 became an injected 528i with 176bhp. In Werner Oswald's opinion 528i was immensely expensive and the additional performance (compared to a 525) could not be practically used. Only the choice between 520 and 525 was valid because of the big differences in specification.

The 2.8 model continued to sell through to the eighties and was as successful in production saloon car racing events across Europe as one would expect such a potent combination to be, even though its engine was far from

Production year	BMW 518	BMW 520/4	BMW 520/6	BMW 525/i	BMW 528/i/e	BMW 530i	BMW M535i
1972	–	12,895	–	–	–	–	–
1973	–	44,862	–	3,667	–	–	–
1974	9,848	19,660	–	18,416	19	2000	–
South Africa	–	2,124	–	1,344	60		
1975	23,784	22,178	–	15,859	19,885	5,202	
South Africa	1980	252	–	708	900		
1976	18,484	24,452	–	17,946	13,638	7,353	–
South Africa	2,856	1,692	–	1848	1,008		
1977	19,098	17,229	5973	18,792	12,125	7,648	–
South Africa	2,508	1,248	–	1,104	588		
1978	17,025	1,168	36,116	15,125	13,628	5,667	–
1979	16,540	605	40,860	18,477	22,387	–	–
1980	15,491	5,160	37,746	11,602	17,825	–	919
1981	12,839	24,377	13,967	12,446	22,610	–	887

the biggest offered in 5-series. Built in considerable numbers, but not for the German market, was the 5-series with a 3-litre engine. This six-cylinder was built in the BMW assembly plant of South Africa with a carburated engine. In America the same 2985cc unit was used with fuel injection (530i) and this provided the basis of a very effective competition car as well as a genuine export-only special. The 3-litre engine gave some 175bhp, though the emission equipment used in the USA led to poor throttle response and lack of performance compared to the European 528i of similar power.

New 5-series (from 1981) BMW 518, BMW 520i, BMW 525i, BMW 528i

In June of 1981 BMW lavishly launched their successor to the nine-year-old original 5-series, which had sold approaching three-quarters of a million units. The surprise was that, after five years development and millions of Dm R&D expenditure they had come up with a car that — to the untutored eye — looked exactly like its predecessor!

In fact the changes to the body, though subtle and highlighted by the raised bootline with wrap-round tail lights, were claimed to vastly improve aerodynamics. The 5-series was actually BMW's best performer in the wind tunnel prior to its replacement, but until the company set up their own aerodynamic facility it was an area in which they returned mediocre figures. From an average 0.44 the 5-series in its revised form dropped to 0.385. Add in a weight loss of nearly 200lb, some of that coming from abandoning the traditional rear-opening multiple-linkage bonnet, and it becomes easier to understand why the current 5-series is such a formidable performer in the mph/mpg stakes. Even the top of the range 528i, which also benefited from a 13° rake to the rear trailing arms and an additional

transverse linkage to tame the legendary oversteer, showed itself capable of an overall 23mpg plus. This while on test at *Autocar* during a period that saw its 133mph capability exploited and the acceleration measured at a convincing 8 seconds or so from 0-60mph.

With the exception of the four-cylinder 90bhp 518 model the 5-series went over to fuel-injection at this point. The Bosch mechanical K-Jetronic layout was used for the delightfully smooth 520i 125bhp while the L-Jetronic with fuel cut-out on the overrun was a standard feature on the L-Jetronic-equipped 525i (150bhp, as before, officially for German insurance reasons!) while the 528i shared L-Jetronic and offered 184bhp, as for 728i and 628i.

Changes within included an obvious increase in company awareness of electronics with a Service Interval Indicator showing the need for maintenance rather than using prescribed intervals, and there was also a check light system like that of 6 and 7-series, though there was no need to press a button to find a fault as there had been before. The interiors were thoroughly overhauled to emphasise the traditional strengths of excellent ergonomics (though rather cluttered when the complicated and expensive computer installation was specified) and clear instrumentation. The four spoke steering wheel was an entirely new pattern with horn buttons in each spoke and power steering was standard for all but 518, which was not available on the British market until 1982, whereas RHD injected Fives began to be registered in Britain from October 1981 onward.

On the road the "new 5-series" proved a great improvement over the previous models and earned unanimous praise for quieter and more economical running with extra reserves of roadholding. In this connection optional Michelin TRX tyres improved matters considerably.

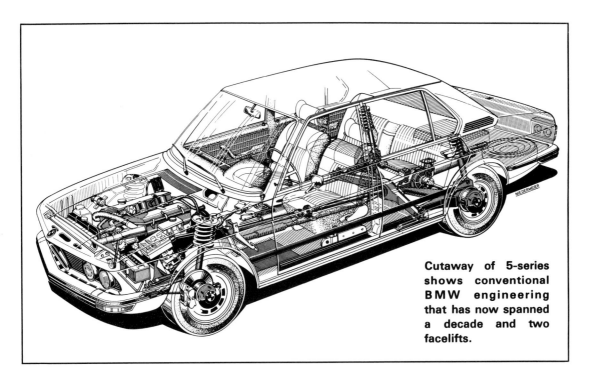

Cutaway of 5-series shows conventional BMW engineering that has now spanned a decade and two facelifts.

Internal dimensions of capacious 5-series four door.

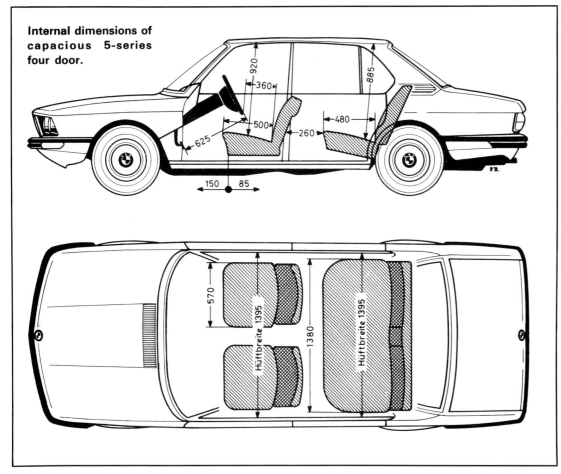

Motor
Cylinders

Bore x stroke
Capacity
Power (bhp)

Torque
Compression
Carburation or fuel-injection

Valves

Crankshaft bearings
Cooling

Lubrication

Battery
Generator

Transmission
Clutch
Gearchange

Gearbox
Synchromesh
Ratios

Final drive ratio

Bodywork
Front suspension

Rear suspension

Steering

Footbrake

General data
Wheelbase
Track (front/rear)
Length, width & height
Rims (five nut)
Tyres
Turning circle (left/right)
Vehicle weight

Max permissible weight
Top speed
0-62mph
Litres/100km

Fuel tank (rear)

BMW 518 1974-75	BMW 518 1975-81	BMW 520 1972-77	BMW 520i 1972-75	BMW 520i 1975-77	BMW 520 1977-81
4 inline, iron block tilted 30° Alloy cylinder head 89x71mm 1766cc 90 @ 5500rpm	4 inline, iron block tilted 30° Alloy cylinder head 89x71mm 1766cc 90 @ 5500rpm	4 inline, iron block tilted 30° Alloy cylinder head 89x80mm 1990cc 115 @ 5800rpm	4 inline, injected, iron block tilted 30° to right. Alloy head 89x80mm 1990cc 130 @ 5800rpm	4 inline, injected, iron block tilted 30° to right. Alloy head 89x80mm 1990cc 125 @ 5700rpm	6 inline, carburated, iron block tilted 30° to right. Alloy head 80x66mm 1990cc 122 @ 6000rpm
14.5mkg @ 4300rpm 8.6:1 1, downdraught Solex 38 PDSI	14.3mkg @ 4300rpm 8.3:1 (9:1, Oct '80) 1, downdraught Solex 32/32 DIDTA. Solex 284 from Oct 80	16.5mkg @ 3700rpm 9:1 1, sidedraught Stromberg 175 CDET	18.1mkg @ 4500rpm 9.5:1 Mechanical petrol-injection FAG Kugelfischer PLO4	17.5mkg @ 4350prm 9.3:1 Continuous petrol-injection Bosch K-Jetronic	16.3mkg @ 4000rpm 9.2:1 1,downdraught, progressive carburettor, Solex 4 A1.Auto-choke
Manual choke	Automatic choke	Automatic choke			

<table>
V-pattern OHV with duplex chain-driven SOHC (BMW 518 cols & BMW 520 1972-77)
</table>

V-pattern OHV with duplex chain-driven SOHC (BMW 520i cols)

V-pattern OHV with belt- driven SOHC (BMW 520 1977-81)

BMW 518 1974-75	BMW 518 1975-81	BMW 520 1972-77	BMW 520i 1972-75	BMW 520i 1975-77	BMW 520 1977-81
5			5	5	7
Pump, 7 litres of water			Pump, 7 litres of water		Pump, 12 litres water
Pressurised, 4.25 litres of oil			Pressurised, 4.25 litres of oil		Pressurised, 4.75 litres of oil
12v 36 or 55ah Alternator, 630 Watts	12v 44 or 55ah		12v 44 or 55ah Alternator, 770 Watt		

Rear wheel drive, split propshaft
Single dry plate
Floor, central lever (BMW 518 / 520 1972-77)

Rear wheel drive, split propshaft
Single, dry plate
Floor, central lever (BMW 520i / 520 1977-81)

BMW 518 1974-75	BMW 518 1975-81	BMW 520 1972-77	BMW 520i 1972-75	BMW 520i 1975-77	BMW 520 1977-81
4-speed 1st–4th			4-speed 1st–4th		Getrag 242
1st, 3.764; 2nd, 2.02; 3rd, 1.32; 4th, 1.00			1st, 3.764;2nd,2.02;3rd,1.32;4th,1.00		

Optional (after Aug 1977 on 518) :ZF HP 22 automatic transmission with hydraulic torque convertor & 3-speed planetary gearbox, central selector. 1st, 2.56; 2nd, 1.52; 3rd, 1.00. Torque multiplication factor, 1.94

Optional on 1977-520:ZF HP 22 automatic gearbox with hydraulic torque convertor and 3-speed planetary gearbox. 1st,2.56;2nd,1.52;3rd,1.00 Central lever selector. Torque multiplication factor 1.94

BMW 518 1974-75	BMW 518 1975-81	BMW 520 1972-77	BMW 520i 1972-75	BMW 520i 1975-77	BMW 520 1977-81
4.44	4.44 (4.27, Oct '80)	4.11	3.90	3.90	3.90

Unitary construction, all-steel coachwork
MacPherson struts, coil springs, rubber mounts, anti-roll bar
Trailing arms, telescopic dampers, coil springs, rubber mounts.
Optional:tubular anti-roll bar

Unitary construction, all-steel coachwork
MacPherson struts, coil springs, rubber mounts, tubular anti-roll bar
Trailing arms, telescopic dampers, rubber mounts, coil springs, tubular anti-roll bar (optional on 1977-81 520)

ZF-Gemmer worm & roller, 22.3:1. $4\frac{1}{3}$ turns lock-to-lock

Optional:power-assist, 16.9:1. $3\frac{2}{3}$ turns lock-to-lock
Servo-assisted, twin circuit with secondary failsafe, hydraulic
Front discs 272mm. Rear drums 250mm

ZF-Gemmer worm & roller, 22.3:1.$4\frac{1}{3}$ turns lock-to-lock

Optional:16.9:1, power-assist. $3\frac{2}{3}$ turns lock-to-lock
Twin circuit, secondary failsafe, power-assisted, hydraulic
Front discs 272mm. Rear drums 250mm

BMW 518 1974-75	BMW 518 1975-81	BMW 520 1972-77	BMW 520i 1972-75	BMW 520i 1975-77	BMW 520 1977-81
2636mm	2636mm	2636mm	2636mm	2636mm	2636mm
1406/1442mm	1406/1442mm	1406/1442mm	1406/1442mm	1406/1442mm	1406/1446mm
4620/1690/1425mm	4620/1690/1425mm	4620/1690/1425mm	4620/1690/1425mm	4620/1690/1425mm	4620/1690/1435mm
$5\frac{1}{2}$Jx14H2	$5\frac{1}{2}$Jx14H2	$5\frac{1}{2}$Jx14H2	$5\frac{1}{2}$Jx14H2	$5\frac{1}{2}$Jx14H2	$5\frac{1}{2}$x14H2
175 HR 14	175 HR 14	175 SR 14	175 HR 14	175 HR 14	175 SR 14
10.7/11.1 metres	10.7/11.1 metres	10.7/11.1 metres	10.7/11.1 metres	10.7/11.1 metres	10.7/11.1 metres
1260kg	1275kg. Auto: + 20kg	To Sept'75:1260kg From Sept'75:1275kg	1280kg	1295kg	1350kg. Auto:+ 20kg
1700kg	1700kg	1700kg	1700kg	1700kg	1770kg
101mph	99mph. Auto: 96mph	109mph. Auto: 106mph	114mph	112mph	112mph
15 sec.	15 sec. Auto: 16 sec.	13 sec. Auto: 14 sec.	12 sec.	12 sec.	12 sec.
12.5 (22.6mpg)	13.0 (21.7mpg) Auto: 13.5 (20.9mpg)	13.5 (20.9mpg) Auto: 14.0 (20.2mpg)	13.5 (20.9mpg)	13.5 (20.9mpg)	13.5 (20.9mpg) Auto: 14.0 (20.2mpg)
56 litres (12.3 galls)	70 litres (15.5 galls)	To Sept'75:56 litres (12.3 galls) Sept'75 on:70 litres (15.5 galls)	70 litres (15.5 galls)	70 litres (15.5 galls)	70 litres (15.5 galls)

Indisputably a BMW with its quad lights and distinctive grille, the 5-series brought BMW a very strong position in the middle ground of the market. Engines from 1972-81 varied from 90bhp fours to 218bhp from the ex-735i six of 3½-litres (M535i).

The unique BMW rear window line is emphasised in this rear shot of an original 520. The 518 was made from 1974-76 and the 520/520i between 1972 and 1976. As tested in Britain the 520i provided an exceptional performance and economy balance: *Autocar* got 114mph, 0-60mph in 10½ seconds and 22.4mpg in their test of 1973.

By contemporary standards the original 115bhp 2-litre four cylinder engine of the 520 was extremely economical, giving around 26.5mpg in normal use.

162

Top: The slight bonnet hump of the 525 and 528 sixes can be compared with the flat bonnets of the four-cylinder originals opposite. The 525 was made from 1973-76 and the 528, with two types of carburated motor, from 1975-76.

Middle: The first facelift was minor and dominated by the peaked bonnet of August 1976. This is actually a 1977 BMW 528i, a potent near 130mph performer that reached 60mph from standstill in less than 9 seconds. Visually the 5-series range all looked much like this from August 1977 until the Summer 1981 replacement 5-series. On these August '77 models just wider wheels and larger diameter exhausts identified the more potent models. The injected 528i also had a twin exhaust as external identification.

A facelifted 1976 BMW 525 displays the angular and larger tail lights that identify the later versions of the original series. In 1981 the boot line was raised considerably in search of a better aerodynamic drag factor, but it is worth noting that independent tests in Germany established that the 5-series, even in its original form, had a better drag factor than its younger stablemates (3 and 7-series) prior to the '81 changes. However none of the BMWs were remarkable in this respect prior to '81 ...

Top: The squared-off tail and wraparound lamps belong to the "New" 5-series, launched in June 1981 with three injection models and the carburated 518 after nearly three-quarters of a million of the original fives had been manufactured.

Middle: From the front the 1981 5-series looked only slightly different to its predecessors, the larger outer headlamps and the slight droop of the 'cleaner' bonnet metalwork being the largest clues to much improved aerodynamics.

The ultimate version of the original 5-series was the 1979-80 M535i. Complete with the top-of-the-UK-range 735i engine of 218bhp it was capable of 140mph and 20mpg plus economy.

	BMW 525 1973-1981	BMW 528 1975-1977	BMW 528i 1977-1981	
Motor	6 inline, iron block, tilted 30° to right Alloy head.	6 inline, iron block, tilted 30° to right Alloy head.	6 inline, iron block, tilted 30° to right Alloy head.	
Bore x stroke	86x71.6mm	86x80mm	86x80mm	
Capacity	2494cc	2788cc	2788cc	
Power (bhp)	145 @ 6000rpm From Aug '76: 150 @ 5800rpm	165 @ 5800rpm From Aug '76: 170 @ 5800rpm	176 @ 5600rpm From July '79: 184 @ 5800rpm	
Torque	21.2mkg @ 4000rpm	25.8mkg @ 4000rpm	24.0mkg @ 4300rpm From July '79:24.5mkg @ 4200rpm	
Compression	9:1	9:1	9:1 (July '79:9.3:1)	
Carburation or fuel-injection	2, downdraught progressive.Zenith 32/40 INAT. From Aug '76:1, downdraught progressive Solex 4A1. Auto-choke	2, downdraught progressive.Zenith 35/40 INAT. From Aug '76:1, downdraught progressive Solex 4A1. Auto choke	Electronic petrol- injection.Bosch L-Jetronic	
Valves	V-pattern OHV with duplex chain-driven SOHC			
Crankshaft bearings	7			
Cooling	Pump, 12 litres of water			
Lubrication	Pressurised, 6 litres of oil			
Battery	12v 55ah Alternator, 770 Watt			
Transmission	Rear wheel drive, split propshaft			
Clutch	Single, dry plate			
Gearchange	Floor, central lever			
Gearbox	Originally 4-speed for range, then 5-speed options			
Synchromesh	1st – 4th. 1st – 5th			
Ratios	4-speed: 1st, 3.855; 2nd, 2.202; 3rd, 1.401; 4th, 1.00 5-speed 'overdrive': 1st, 3.822; 2nd, 2.203; 3rd, 1.398; 4th, 1.00; 5th, 0.812 5-speed 'close ratio': 1st, 3.717; 2nd, 2.403; 3rd, 1.766; 4th, 1.263; 5th, 1.00 Automatic ZF HP 22, hydraulic torque converter and 3-speed planetary gearbox: 1st, 2.56; 2nd, 1.52; 3rd, 1.0, factor 1.94. Later automatics (ZF 3 HP 22): 1st, 2.478; 2nd, 1.478; 3rd, 1.0 & 2.06 torque multiplication factor			
Final drive	3.64	3.64	3.64 or 3.45	
Bodywork	Unitary contruction, all-steel			
Front suspension	MacPherson struts, rubber mounts, coil springs, tubular anti-roll bar. Gas damper inserts, option, 528i			
Rear suspension	Trailing arms, telescopic dampers, rubber mounts, tubular anti-roll bar. Gas damper option, 528i			
Steering	ZF-Gemmer worm & roller 4.1/3 turns lock-to-lock Optional: 16.9:1 + power assistance, 3.2/3 turns	ZF recirculating ball, power assisted, 16.9:1 with 3.2/3 turns lock-to-lock		
Footbrake	Twin circuit hydraulic with secondary failsafe, servo-assisted			
	Front discs 280mm Rear discs 272mm	Front discs 280mm Rear discs 272mm	Vented front discs 280mm Rear discs 272mm	
General data				
Wheelbase	2636mm	2636mm	2636mm	
Track (front/rear)	1406/1446mm	1420/1460mm	1420/1460mm	
Length, width & height	4620/1690/1425mm	4620/1690/1425mm	4620/1690/1425mm	
Rims (five nut)	5½Jx14H2	6Jx14H2. Alloy option	6Jx14H2. Alloy option	
Tyres	175 HR 14 Optional:195/70 HR 14	195/70 HR 14	195/70 VR 14	
Turning circle (left/right)	10.7/I1.1 metres	10.7/11.1 metres	10.7/11.1 metres	
Vehicle weight (+20kg,auto)	1380kg	1415kg	1450kg	
Top speed	119mph	123mph	129mph	
0-62mph	10.5 sec.	9.8 sec.	9.5 sec.	
Litres/100km	15.5 (18.2mpg)	16.0 (17.7mpg)	16.0 (17.7mpg)	
Fuel tank (rear)	70 litres (15.5 galls)	70 litres (15.5 galls)	70 litres (15.5 galls)	

	BMW 518 1981 on	BMW 520i 1981 on	BMW 525i 1981 on	BMW 528i 1981 on	BMW 528e (USA) 1981 on
Motor Cylinders	4 inline, iron block tilted 30° right. Alloy head	6 inline, iron block tilted 30° right. Alloy head	6 inline, iron block tilted 30° right. Alloy head	6 inline, iron block tilted 30° to right. Alloy head	6 inline, iron block tilted 30° to right. Alloy head
Bore x stroke	89 x 71mm	80 x 66mm	86 x 71.6 mm	86 x 80mm	84 x 81mm
Capacity	1766cc	1990cc	2494cc	2788cc	2693cc
Power (bhp)	90 @ 5500rpm	125 @ 5800rpm	150 @ 5500rpm	184 @ 5800rpm	121 (SAE) @ 4250rpm
Torque	14.2mkg @ 4000rpm	16.9mkg @ 4500rpm	22.0mkg @ 4000rpm	24.5mkg @ 4200rpm	23.5mkg (SAE) @ 3250rpm
Compression	9.5:1	9.8:1	9.6:1	9.3:1	9:1
Carburation or fuel injection	1, downdraught, 2-choke Solex 2 B4	Mechanical petrol-injection. Bosch K-Jetronic	Electronic petrol-injection; over-run cut-off. L-Jetronic	Electronic petrol injection Bosch L-Jetronic. Over-run fuel cut-off.	Electronic petrol injection Bosch L-Jetronic 960rpm over-run cut-off. 3-way emissions catalyst. Lambda sensor.
Valves	V-pattern OHV & duplex chain-driven SOHC	V-pattern OHV & belt-driven SOHC	V-pattern OHV & duplex chain-driven SOHC	V-pattern OHV & chain-driven SOHC	V-pattern OHV & belt driven SOHC
Crankshaft bearings	5	7	7	7	7
Cooling	Pump, 7 litres water	Pump, 12 litres of water	Pump, 12 litres of water	Pump, 12 litres water	Water-cooled, pump
Lubrication	Pressurised, 4.25 litres of oil	Pressurised, 4.75litres of oil	Pressurised, 6.0 litres of oil	Pressurised, 6 litres oil	Pressurised oil
Battery	12v 44ah	12v 44ah	12v 55ah	12v 55ah	12v 55ah
Generator	Alternator, 630 Watt	Alternator, 910 Watt	Alternator, 910 Watt	Alternator, 910 Watt Breakerless, transistor ('hybrid')	Alternator, 910 Watt Breakerless with second stage Motronic computer control system
Transmission	Rear wheel drive, split propshaft.		Automatic or manual gearboxes	Rear wheel drive, split propshaft. Choice of two 5-speed gearboxes and automatic according to market	
Clutch	Hydraulic operation, membrane spring, single dry plate		As 518/520i + self centre bearing & over-centre spring	Hydraulically operated membrane spring with self-centre bearing & over-centre spring. Single dry plate.	Hydraulically operated single dry plate with torsional dampers & self-adjustment.
Gearchange	Floor, central lever. Auto with driver display				Floor, central lever.

Ratios:

	BMW 518 4-speed	BMW 520i 4-speed	BMW 520i UK 5-speed	BMW 525i 4-speed	BMW 525i UK 5-speed	BMW 528i 5-speed	BMW 528i 5-speed Sport	BMW 528e 5-speed
						1st-5th		1st-5th
1st	3.764	3.764	3.682	3.855	3.822	3.822	3.717	3.822
2nd	2.043	2.043	2.202	2.203	2.202	2.202	2.403	2.202
3rd	1.320	1.320	1.329	1.402	1.398	1.398	1.766	1.398
4th	1.00	1.00	1.00	1.00	1.00	1.00	1.263	1.00
5th			0.805		0.813	0.813	1.00	0.813

Optional: 3-speed ZF 3 HP 22 with hydraulic torque convertor & planetary gears. 1st, 2.478; 2nd, 1.478; 3rd, 1.00. Torque multiplication factor 2.28 for 518/520i, 2:1 for 525i

5-speed wide ratio overdrive is standard 528i gearbox. Optional automatic is 3-speed ZF with hydraulic torque convertor & planetary gears. 1st, 2.478; 2nd, 1.478 3rd, 1.00. Torque multiplication factor, 2.0:1

	BMW 518	BMW 520i	BMW 525i	BMW 528i	BMW 528e
Final drive	4.27	3.91	3.45	3.45 (optional LSD)	2.93 (Optional (LSD)
Bodywork Front suspension	Unitary construction, all-steel MacPherson struts, double pivot linkage (7-series principles) with coil springs, anti-roll bar, braking anti-dive compensation and positive scrub radius, 11.5mm			Unitary construction, all-steel coachwork MacPherson struts, double pivot linkage (7-series principles) with eccentrically mounted coil springs, anti-roll bar, braking anti-dive compensation and positive scrub radius 11.5mm (528i, 17mm + roll bar)	
Rear suspension	Semi-trailing arms (20° angle), telescopic dampers with coil springs and anti-lift braking compensation. Rubber-isolated			Semi-trailing arms (13° swept angle), telescopic dampers with coil springs, camber compensating linkage, anti-lift (braking & acceleration) compensation	
Steering	Unassisted ZF- Gemmer worm & roller 21.4:1	ZF recirculating ball power steering 16.2:1 ratio		Power-assisted ZF recirculation ball with 16.2:1 overall ratio.	
Footbrake	Diagonally split twin circuit, hydraulic systems with vacuum power assistance on 518/520i and integrated power steering additional hydraulic regulator and accumulator on 525i			Diagonally split, twin circuit, hydraulic with power assistance integrated into power steering regulator and accumulator.	
	Solid Front discs 284mm & single piston calipers. Self-adjusting rear drums 250mm	Solid Front discs 284mm & single piston calipers. Self-adjusting rear drums 250mm	Ventilated front discs, 284mm & single piston calipers. Solid rear discs, inc drum handbrake. Disc 250mm	Vented front discs 284mm single piston calipers Rear: solid discs 250mm & integrated hand brake drum.	Vented front discs 300mm, single piston calipers, auto-adjustment Rear: solid discs 300mm, with 180mm handbrake drum; auto-adjustment
General data Wheelbase		2625mm		2625mm	2625mm
Track (front/rear)		14301470mm		1430/1460mm	1430/1470mm
Length, width, height		4620/1700/1415mm		4620/1700/1415mm	4785/1700/1415mm
Rims		5½J x 14 H 2 (alloys optional)		6J x 14 H2 (alloy)	6½J x 14 H2 (alloy)
Tyres	175 SR 14	175 HR 14	175 HR 14	195/70 VR 14	195/70 14
Turning circle	10.4 metres	10.4 metres	10.4 metres	10.4 metres	10.4 metres
Vehicle weight	1160kg	1220kg	1290kg	1320kg	1530kg (USA '80-'81)
Max permissible weight	1670kg	1730kg	1800kg	1830kg	1800kg
Top speed	102mph	115mph	122mph	130mph	Circa 110mph
0-62mph	14.0 sec	11.8 sec	9.9 sec	8.9 sec	6.6 sec (0-50mph)
Litres/100km (City: DIN70030)	11.1 (25.5mpg)	12.5 (22.96mpg)	14.1 (20.0mpg)	14.9 (18.96mpg)	
Fuel tank	70 litres/18.5 USA gallons/15.4 Imperial gallons			70 litres (15.4 galls)	16.6 US gallons

BMW 6-series (from 1976)

By March 1976 and the Geneva Motor Show, BMW were ready to debut their successor to the range of CS, CSi and CSL six-cylinder coupes. Both 3-litre carburettor version (630 CS) and 3210cc fuel-injected model (633 CSi) looked elegant but were rather heavier than their predecessors which seemed to rule out any competition use. Nevertheless the public and press gave it the thumbs up, though initial sales certainly were not up to the levels of its predecessor.

Production of the 6-series harked back to some of the earlier postwar BMWs in that there were a lot of teething troubles in the first year. Karmann workmanship was called into question, with the result of BMW moving production out of Osnabruck to Dingolfing (August 1977). Now only bare coupe bodies come from Osnabruck.

Additions to the 6-series theme acknowledged a sporting heritage with the middle of July 1978 production of 635 CSi. This logical use of the big bore block (as used in M1, but with two valve per cylinder head layout in this case) was combined with a five-speed gearbox, front and rear spoilers, lowered and stiffened suspension and wider wheels. German prices began at something over £12,000 at the 1978 exchange rate.

Another addition to the line from September 1979 was the 184bhp 628 CSi. A neat cocktail between the engine used in 5 and 7-series and the normal 6-series coachwork which proved popular in Britain from September 1980 onward, costing just under £17,000 compared to £19,329 for the only other 1981 6-series choice in the UK – the 635 CSi stayed in production for Europe and the USA, while 630CS was dropped in July 1979.

In June 1982 the 628CSi and 635Ci were thoroughly revised with suspension modifications (derived from 5-series) and a 3430cc engine of unchanged power becoming standard for the 635 – which, as a result, became a smoother running car.

Production year	BMW 628 CSi	BMW 630 CS	BMW 633 CSi	BMW 635 CSi
1976	–	2,072	2,862	–
1977	–	2,518	3,263	–
1978		924	3,387	1,286
1979	286	249	2,439	3,775
1980	1,018	–	2,496	3,114
1981	All coupes together: 5,652 (1980: 6,628. 1979: 6,729. 1978: 5,597)			

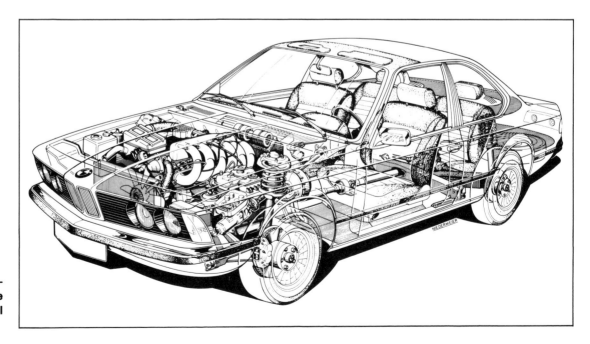

Cutaway of a fuel-injected 6-series Coupe showing conventional BMW construction.

	BMW 628 CSi 1979 on	BMW 630CS 1976-1979	BMW 633 CSi 1976 on USA 633 CSi 1978 on	BMW 635 CSi 1979 on
Motor				
Cylinders	6 inline, iron block tilted 30° right. Alloy head 80x86mm 2788cc	6 in-line, iron block tilted 30° right. Alloy head 89x80mm 2985cc	6 inline, block tilted 30° to right. Alloy head 89x86mm 3210cc	6 inline, block tilted 30° to right. Alloy head 93.4x84mm 3453cc
Bore x stroke				
Capacity				
Power (bhp)	184 @ 5800rpm	185 @ 5800rpm	200 @ 5500rpm USA 1978 yr: 177 (SAE) @ 5500rpm USA to 1981: 176 (SAE) @ 5200rpm USA 1982 yr: 181 (SAE) @ 6000rpm	218 @ 5200rpm
Torque	24.5mkg @ 4200rpm	26.0mkg @ 3500rpm	28.5mkg @ 4300rpm USA 1978 yr: 27.0mkg @ 4000rpm USA to 1981: 26.0mkg @ 4200rpm USA 1982 yr: 26.9mkg @ 4000rpm	31.0mkg @ 4000rpm
Compression	9.3:1	9:1	9:1 (USA '78, 8.4:1.USA to '81, 8:1. USA '82, 8.8:1)	9.3:1
Carburation or fuel-injection	Electronic petrol-injection with auto-choke. Bosch L-Jetronic	1, downdraught, progressive choke Solex 4A1 carburettor with auto-choke	Electronic petrol-injection, Bosch L-Jetronic (USA +Lambda sensor & Motronic)	Electronic petrol-injection, Bosch L-Jetronic+Motronic
Valves	V-pattern OHV with duplex chain-driven SOHC 7	V-pattern OHV with duplex chain-driven SOHC 7	V-pattern OHV with duplex chain-driven SOHC 7	
Crankshaft bearings	Pump, 12 litres water	Pump, 12 litres water	Pump, 12 litres of water	
Cooling	Pressurised, 6 litres oil	Pressurised, 6 litres oil	Pressurised, 6.0 litres of oil	
Lubrication	12v 66ah	12v 66ah	12v 66ah (USA: 55ah)	
Battery	Alternator, 770 Watts	Alternator, 770 Watts	Alternator, 65 Ampere, 910 Watts	
Generator	Breakerless, transistor coil	Contact breaker & coil	Breakerless transistor + coil (USA+Motronic digital)	
Ignition				
Transmission	Rear wheel drive, split propshaft	As 628	Rear wheel drive, split propshaft Single, dry plate	
Clutch	Diaphragm spring with single dry plate & self centre release bearing	Single, dry plate		
Gearchange	Floor, central lever	Floor, central lever	Floor, central lever	
Gearbox	4-speed Getrag 262/9 with Borg Warner synchro 1st-4th		Originally 633 CSI for Europe & America offered same 4-speed as for 628/630. For 1982 model year USA 633 & 635 CSi share 5-speed manual as standard but 635 CSI has closer ratios: 1st,3.717; 2nd,2.403; 3rd,1.766; 4th,1.263; 5th,1.00 USA 633: 1st,3.822; 2nd,2.202; 3rd,1.398; 4th,1.00; 5th,0.813 European 633 continues to offer original ZF auto & Getrag 4-speed	
Synchromesh				
Ratios	1st, 3.855; 2nd, 2.203; 3rd, 1.402; 4th, 1.00 Optional: ZF 3 HP 22 with Fichtel & Sachs torque convertor & 3-speed planetary gearbox: 1st, 2.478; 2nd, 1.478; 3rd, 1.0. Torque multiplication factor, 2.0			
Final drive	3.45 (optional 25% LSD)	3.45	3.25 (25% LSD optional)	3.07 (optional 25% LSD)
Bodywork	Unitary construction, all-steel (630 built originally at Karmann, Osnabruck)		Unitary construction, all-steel. 635 makes use of plastics for front & rear spoilers	
Front suspension	Offset geometry MacPherson struts, coil springs & supplementary rubber springs. Anti-roll bar	MacPherson struts, coil springs, rubber supplementary springs. Anti-roll bar	Offset geometry MacPherson struts with coil and supplementary springs, tubular anti-roll bar. 635 has hydraulic supplementary damper to reduce roll tendency	
Rear suspension	Trailing arms, telescopic dampers, supplementary springs, coil springs, rubber-bushed.	Trailing arms, telescopic dampers rubber additional springs, coil springs.	Trailing arms, coil springs, telescopic dampers, rubber mounts & supplementary springs. Anti-dive & anti-roll bar.	
Steering	ZF recirculating ball, power-assisted, 16.9:1 3.5 turns lock-to-lock	ZF-Gemmer worm & roller, power-assisted, 16.9:1 3.5 turns lock-to-lock	ZF recirculating ball, power-assisted, 16.9:1 with 3.5 turns lock-to-lock	
Footbrake	Twin circuit hydraulic with secondary failsafe. Power-assisted Front discs 280mm. Rear 272mm. All ventilated		Twin circuit, hydraulic, with secondary failsafe circuit & power assistance Front discs 280mm. Rear discs 272mm. All ventilated.	
General Data				
Wheel base	2626mm	2626mm	2626mm	2626mm
Track (front/rear)	1422/1487mm	1422/1487mm	1422/1487mm	1422/1487mm
Length, width & height	4755/1725/1365mm	4755/1725/1365mm	4755/1725/1365mm USA 1982 yr: 4922/1725/1364mm	4755/1725/1365mm
Rims	6Jx14 alloy	6Jx14 alloy	6Jx14 alloy	6½Jx14 BBS Mahle alloy
Tyres	195/70 VR 14	195/70 VR 14	USA 1982 yr: As for 635 CSi 195/70 VR 14	195/70 VR 14
Turning circle (left/right)	11.1/11.2 metres	11.1/11.2 metres	11.1/11.2 metres	11.1/11.2 metres
Vehicle weight (auto + 20kg)	1450kg	1475kg	1495kg (USA'81:1.560kg) (USA'82:1955kg)	1520kg
Max permissible weight	1830kg	1830kg	134mph	1860kg
Top speed	131mph	131mph	8.5 sec/ (USA'82:0.50mph, 6.35 sec.)	138mph
0-62mph	9.3 sec.	9.0 sec.		8 sec.
Litres/100km (City)	17.7 (15.96mpg)	17.0 (16.6mpg)	17.0 (16.6mpg)	17.0 (16.6mpg)
Fuel tank (rear)	70 litres (15.4 galls)	70 litres (15.4 galls)	70 litres/15.5 Imp galls/ 16.4 US galls	70 litres (15.5 Imp galls/ 16.4 US galls)

Top: BMW styling and initially Karmann built, as was the preceding Coupe, the 6-series got off to a troubled start on the standard of body construction. The 6-series has always been an elegant and expensive machine, further evidence of BMW's willingness to venture into Mercedes territory, but it has been a hard car to define for the marketing men in image terms. The non-spoilered body shown here was available on 630 CS and 633 CSi from 1976 onward.

Middle: Side view of the 138mph BMW 635 CSi (introduced in July 1978 for Europe and sold in Britain from October of that year) shows front and rear spoilers clearly. On the road their effect, and that of firmer suspension, brought some glowing road test reports following the rather disappointing reviews of previous 6-series models.

Tail view of the four-seater BMW 635 CSi emphasises wider Mahle wheels (6½ inch rim). Michelin TRX wheel and tyre combination was a worthwhile option later in the UK model's life. *Autocar* tested the 635 CSi at 140mph (9mph faster than 633 CSi) and measured its 0-60mph sprinting capabilities as 8.5 seconds, coupled to overall mpg of 17.5. From Autumn 1980 European production 635 CSi models gained the digital computerised fuel-injection management system and suspension/engine modifications in June 1982.

The fuel-injected 628 CSi of 1980 proved popular and capable of some 130mph. The model was slightly revised in the Summer of 1982, along with the 635, and continues in the European market. In America the 633 CSi lives on sharing much of its running gear with the 733i in emission-controlled form.

The July 1982 changes to the 635 CSi should really have made it a '634' as a smaller bore 3.4-litre engine, with water passages between the bores, was introduced as well as 5-series features like the 13° included angle for the semi-trailing arm rear suspension. Power remained unaltered at an official 218bhp, but fuel consumption was greatly improved with the further use of digital electronics and weight reductions, plus some detail aerodynamic modifications.

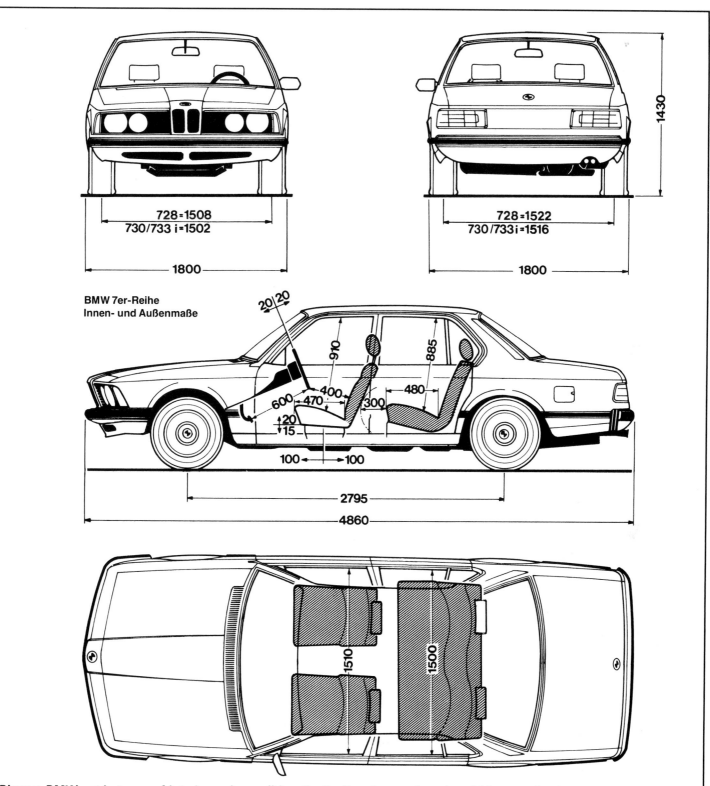

728 = 1508
730/733 i = 1502

1800

728 = 1522
730/733 i = 1516

1800

1430

BMW 7er-Reihe
Innen- und Außenmaße

20 20

910

885

400

480

600 470 300

20
15

100 ◄──►100

2795

4860

1510

1500

Biggest BMW yet in terms of interior and overall length, the 7-series was introduced 18 years after bankruptcy shareholders' meetings had threatened to end everything for BMW as an independent concern.

BMW 7-series (from 1977)

To succeed the previous big BMW saloons, the factory offered the very impressive 7-series model line, initially available with three six-cylinder engine options including the carburated 728 and 730, and topped by the fuel-injected 3210cc 733i. Much interest was aroused in Germany by 728, which followed the general works policy of beginning the range with a model of relatively modest cost compared to the enormous surcharges for the minimal performance increases offered by the 730 and the 733i although the latter models did offer more prestige ...

The main assets of 7-series were seen as the splendidly quiet running, responsive and eagerly revving engines. Overall these cars were good enough to stand comparison with the best in the world, but had to face the ultimate test of competing successfully against Mercedes. In Germany, initially at least, Werner Oswald's feeling was that they were the first BMWs in 25 years to stand up to such comparison. In Germany prices started at a little over £8000 and escalated to a little over £10,700 for the 733i at the time of introduction.

In Britain there was considerable criticism of the handling and noise levels of the original models. Answering this, and similar German comment, the factory reworked the car substantially under the skin with lighter weight and improved suspension. In European terms a new landmark was the automatic 745i Turbo (July 1979), but this 252bhp model was not made in RHD or marketed in the UK. In November 1979 the British market received the fuel-injected 7-series (728i) and the 732i with the Motronic digital engine management system, which went into German production for 735i by Autumn 1980. By September the following year Britain was receiving the 735i in RHD form with the 5-series-derived Service Interval Indicator and positive check system.

Production year	728/i	730	732i	733i	735i	745i (turbo)
1977	7,660	4,965	–	7,331	–	–
1978	14,290	8,274	–	11,525	–	–
1979	15,435	3,905	2,353	8,485	3,696	–
1980	14,230	–	9,952	97	6,984	2,175
1981	11,749	–	8,760	*6,828		2,504

*figure is for 733i & 735i

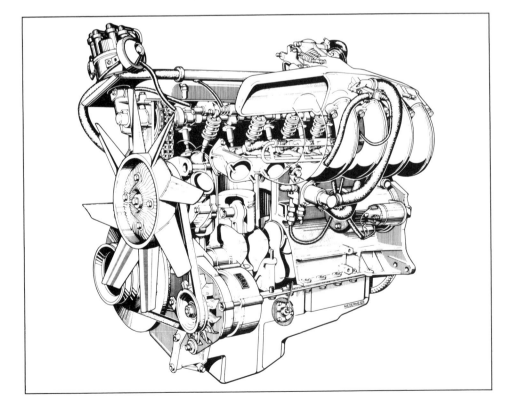

The big injected six as used in 733i, when it developed just under 200bhp. This 89 by 86mm engine (3210cc) quietly succeeded the 89mm by 88.4mm nearly square unit (3295cc) during the change from 3.3 L to 3.3 Li of 1976 in the previous big BMW series. Apparently the engine was uncomfortable at this longer stroke. Certainly the racing versions of the six rarely went over 80mm stroke, gaining capacity from 90mm plus bores that were to be found in the later 735i, M535i, 635i designs. The 3210cc motor is also at the heart of 745i turbo.

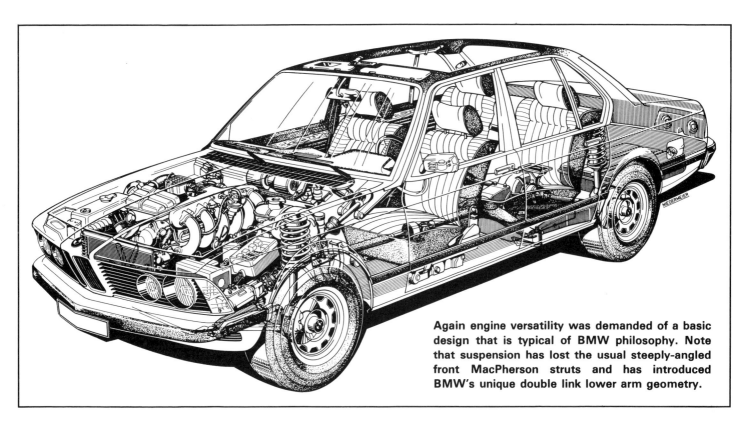

Again engine versatility was demanded of a basic design that is typical of BMW philosophy. Note that suspension has lost the usual steeply-angled front MacPherson struts and has introduced BMW's unique double link lower arm geometry.

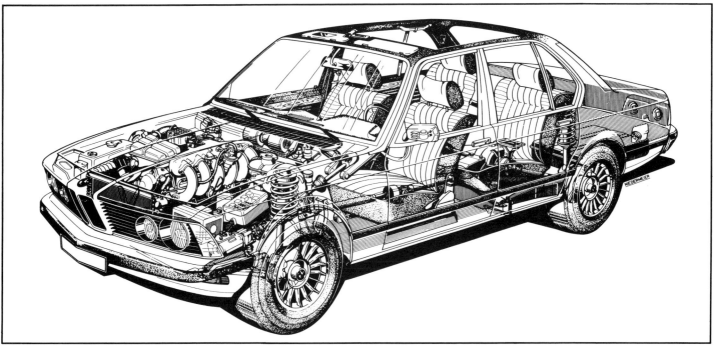

Although the prestige 7-series has barely changed externally, this cutaway of the July 1979-revised 735i tells the story of constant revisions beneath the skin of BMW's biggest model. As of July 1979 the 7-series became lighter, better suspended and offered only with fuel injection. The cutaway also reveals how BMW have adhered to the basic principles of a front mounted overhead camshaft engine driving the rear wheels. Semi-trailing irs and MacPherson strut front suspension are recurrent themes too.

	BMW 728 1977-79 BMW 728i 1979 on	BMW 730 1977-79	BMW 733i 1977-79 USA BMW 733i 1978 on	
Motor				
Cylinders	6 inline, iron block tilted 30° right. Alloy cylinder head	6 inline, iron block tilted 30° right. Alloy cylinder head	6 inline, iron block tilted 30° right. Alloy cylinder head	
Bore x stroke	86x80mm	89x80mm	89x86mm	
Capacity	2788cc	2985cc	3210cc	
Power (bhp)	170 @ 5800rpm	184 @ 5800rpm	197 @ 5500rpm USA '82:181 @ 6000rpm	
Torque	23.8mkg @ 4000rpm	26mkg @ 3500rpm	28.5mkg @ 3500rpm USA '82:27mkg @ 4000rpm	
Compression	9:1	9:1	9:1 USA '82:8.8:1	
Carburation or fuel-injection	1, downdraught progressive Solex 4A1 Automatic choke	1, downdraught progressive Solex 4A1 Automatic choke	Electronic petrol-injection: Bosch L-Jetronic, auto-choke USA '82:As above plus Motronic, 3-way catalyst & Lambda sensor	
Valves	V-pattern OHV and duplex chain-driven SOHC			
Crankshaft bearings	7			
Cooling	Pump, 12 litres of water			
Lubrication	Pressurised, 6 litres of oil			
Battery	12v 55ah	12v 55ah	12v 65ah USA '82:12v 66ah	
Generator	Alternator, 770 Watt	Alternator, 770 Watt	Alternator, 910 Watt	
Ignition	Contact breakers & coil	Contact breakers & coil	Breakerless, transistorised, coil	
Transmission	Rear wheel drive, split propshaft			
Clutch	Single dry plate			
Gearchange	Floor, central lever			
Gearbox	728/730/733i offered with Getrag 262/9 4-speed or automatic 3-speed USA '82 733i offered with choice of Getrag 265/6.10 5-speed or ZF 3 HP 22 3-speed automatic			
Synchromesh	1st-4th or 1st-5th			
Ratios	4-speed: 1st, 3.855; 2nd, 2.203; 3rd, 1.402; 4th, 1.00; 5-speed:1st, 3.822; 2nd, 2.202; 3rd, 1.398; 4th, 1.00; 5th, 0.813 (USA 733i) Automatic: 1st, 2.478; 2nd, 1.478; 3rd, 1.00 Torque multiplication factor, 2.0. Hydraulic torque convertor, planetary gears.			
Final drive (optional LSD)	3.64	3.45	3.45 (USA '82:3.25)	
Bodywork	Unitary construction, all-steel			
Front suspension	Double joint, offset geometry MacPherson struts with coil springs, anti-dive and anti-roll bar. Detail '79 changes, including Teflon coating damper internals & urethane mounts (USA 733i '80 year onward)			
Rear suspension	Trailing arms, telescopic dampers, coil springs with anti-dive braking compensation, rubber mounts			
Steering	ZF recirculating ball with RPM-influenced power assistance, 15.7:1 ratio. 3.8 turns lock-to-lock.			
Footbrake	Twin circuit hydraulic with secondary failsafe circuit, servo assisted. Common servo brakes/steering. Rear wheel handbrake operating 7.8in drum at rear wheels Ventilated front discs 280mm. Solid rear discs 280mm			
General data				
Wheelbase	2795mm	2795mm	2795mm	
Track (front/rear)	1508/1522mm	1502/1516mm	1502/1516mm (also for USA '82)	
Length, width & height	4860/1800/1430mm	4860/1800/1430mm	4860/1800/1430mm (USA:5014/1801/1430mm)	
Rims	6Jx14 (steel)	6½Jx14 (steel)	6½Jx14 (steel) (USA:as above but alloy)	
Tyres	195/70 HR 14	205/70 HR 14	205/70 VR 14	
Turning circle (left/right)	11.3/11.4 metres	11.3/11.4 metres	11.3/11.4 metres	
Vehicle weight (+20kg, auto)	1550kg	1600kg	1630kg USA'79:1670kg	
Max permissible weight	2000kg	2050kg	2070kg USA'82:2095kg	
Top speed	122mph	125mph	128mph	
0-62mph	10 sec.	9.5 sec.	9 sec. USA'82,0-50mph:6.7 sec.	
Litres/100km	16.5 (17.1mpg)	17.5 (16.1mpg)	17.5 (16.1mpg)	
Fuel tank (rear)	85 litres (18.7 galls)	85 litres (18.7 galls)	85 litres (18.7 galls) 22.6 US galls	

	BMW 732i 1979 on	BMW 735i 1979 on	BMW 745i 1979 on	
Motor				
Cylinders	6 inline, iron block, 30° to right. Alloy cylinder head	6 inline, iron block, 30° to right. Alloy cylinder head	6 inline, iron block, 30° to right. Alloy cylinder head	
Bore x stroke	89 x 86mm	93.4 x 84mm	89 x 86mm	
Capacity	3210cc	3453cc	3210cc	
Power (bhp)	197 @ 5500rpm	218 @ 5200rpm	252 @ 5200rpm	
Torque	29.1mkg @ 4300rpm	31.6mkg @ 4000rpm	38.7mkg @ 2600rpm	
Compression	9.3:1	9.3:1	7:1	
Induction	Electronic petrol-injection. Bosch L-Jetronic with Motronic computer	Electronic petrol-injection. Bosch L-Jetronic with Motronic computer from '81 model year.	Electronic petrol-injection Bosch L-Jetronic with fuel cut-off below 1200rpm over-run & over 6300rpm. KKK single vane K27 turbocharger. Max boost, 0.6 bar	
Valves	V-pattern OHV with duplex chain-drive SOHC			
Crankshaft bearings	7 (12 counterweights)			
Cooling	Water pump & 12 litres of water (+ intercooler, 745i)			
Lubrication	Pressurised by Eaton pump, 6 litres of oil, full-flow filter			
Battery	12v 66ah			
Generator	Alternator, Bosch K1-14 V, 65 Amperes (14 V/80 Amperes 745i)			
Ignition	Digital electronic (Motronic) with microprocessor control	Originally breakerless coil, then as 732i for '81 model year	Transistorised, coil induction sensor + dwell angle control	
Transmission	Rear wheel drive, split propshaft. All UK '82 model year with 5-speed gearbox; 735i always with 5-speed overdrive or 3-speed automatic option. 745i, ZF automatic only.			
Clutch	Fichtel & Sachs diaphragm spring MK 240 K, self-centre release bearing. Single dry plate		Hydraulic Fichtel & Sachs torque convertor	
Ratios	**4-speed** (Getrag 262/9) 1st, 3.855:1 2nd, 2.203 3rd, 1.402 4th, 1.00	**5-speed** (Getrag 265/6.10) 1st, 3.822 2nd, 2.202 3rd, 1.398 4th, 1.00 5th, 0.812	**3-speed** Auto 1st, 2.478 2nd, 1.478 3rd, 1.00 Torque multiplication factor:2.06	
Final drive	3.45	3.25	3.07	
(Optional)	Multi-plate ZF Limited slip differential; 25% pre-tension			
Bodywork	Unitary construction, all-steel, 4 doors			
Front suspension	MacPherson struts, eccentric coil springs, double pivot linkage with offset geometry. Tubular anti-roll bar, anti-dive compensation, supplement springs and hydraulic supplementary damper.			
Rear suspension	Semi trailing arms, telescopic dampers, coil springs and supplementary springs, rubber isolated; anti-dive brake compensation. 745i has hydropneumatic self-levelling & rear anti-roll bar, also no cost Sports package			
Steering	ZF recirculating ball steering with RPM-controlled power assistance integral with brake servo pump; Tyre 8055. Overall ratio, 15.7:1. Lock-to-lock, 3.8 turns.			
Footbrake	Twin circuit hydraulic with integral pump (steering/brakes) power assistance diagonal split, drum handbrake acting mechanically on rear wheels Vented front discs 280mm x 22mm Solid rear discs, 280mm x 10mm		Twin circuit hydraulic with ABS anti-lock. Diagonal split, drum handbrake. Vented front discs 280mm x 25mm Solid rear discs 280mm x 12mm	
General data				
Wheelbase	2795mm			
Track (front/rear)	1502/1516mm			
Length, width, height	4860/1800/1430mm			
Rims	6½J x 14 H2-B (steel) (alloys, optional)	6½J x 14 H2-B (alloy) 1981 TRX wheel & tyre option	As 735i Optional: 165 TR 390 alloy for TRX tyres	
Tyres	205/70 HR 14	205/70 VR 14	205/70 VR 14 or TRX 220 55 VR 390	
Turning circle	11.6 metres	11.6 metres	11.6 metres	
Vehicle weight	1530kg	1530kg	1610kg	
Max permissible weight	2000kg	2000kg	2070kg	
Top speed	127mph	132mph	138mph	
0-62mph	8.7 sec	8.0 sec	7.8 sec (18.6 sec to 100mph)	
Litres/100km (City:DIN 70030)	18.7 (15.1mpg)	20.0 (14.1mpg)	20.5 (13.8mpg)	
Fuel tank	85 litres/22.4 galls	85 litres/22.4 galls	100 litres/22 galls	

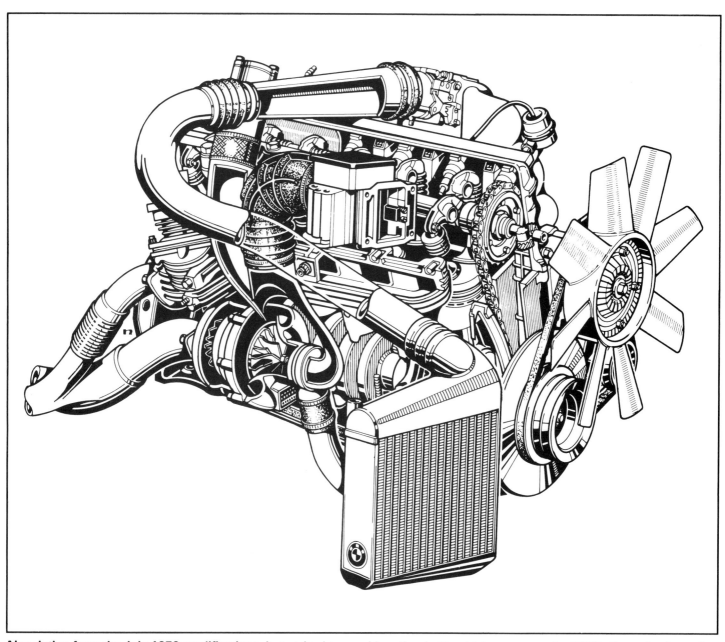

Also dating from the July 1979 modifications, but revised to provide rather better driving manners by 1982, the turbocharged 745i engine was actually the 3210cc straight-six equipped with KKK turbo and air intercooler. The 745i has remained in 252bhp LHD trim throughout its limited production life.

Engine bay of 197bhp 733i clearly shows Bosch L-Jetronic injection induction pipes and accessible fuses. This engine option has not been available in Britain since November 1979, being replaced by 735i at the top of the line, though some older 7-series remained in stock for 1980 UK sale.

Logical layout has been a strong point of BMW since the early seventies. Their early use of the single viewing pane over instrumentation (which is itself almost sparse, but beautifully legible) has been widely imitated, as has the curvature to facia panels to bring controls within easy reach, and the use of aircraft style instrument lighting with non-reflective orange glow. Note also the test panel to the left of the steering wheel, a feature introduced on 6-series a year previously. Although a top model in the BMW range at the time this picture was taken, the accommodation is based on logical comfort for long fast trips, rather than plush showroom appeal.

Opposite page: two views of the shape that launched the 728, 730 and 733i in 1977. Externally the top BMW has changed little over the years, but underskin improvements have been substantial to handling and engines, including serious efforts to improve fuel consumption, including the over-run fuel cut off system that has been a feature of later injected 7-series. The 733i returned 122mph in *Autocar* tests, allied to nearly 19½mpg and vigorous, sub-9 second, acceleration from rest to 60mph.

178

BMW M1 (prototype 1977-78 and production 1979-80)

For motorsport use and reasons of prestige BMW set themselves the task of building a high performance mid-engined two-seater sports car. Work started in 1977 under the internal code E26, externally M1 ("M1" for Motorsport, the BMW department responsible). The first 'runners' were mobile in the Spring of 1977 based on Giorgio Giugiaro's Ital Design for the body with a chassis and ancillaries from Lamborghini and BMW engine and transmission.

The contract with Lamborghini had to be cancelled in April 1978 owing to the Italian Supercar concern's increasing financial difficulties. They simply couldn't afford to put the M1 into production but BMW, and particularly Motorsport chief Jochen Neerpasch, were committed. Baur were called to the rescue to make the necessary 400 cars for racing homologation. This proved a somewhat protracted business and to get over the inevitable hiatus BMW Motorsport organised – together with the Formula One Constructors Association – the most expensive and fastest one-make racing series ever promoted which supported GPs across Europe in 1979/80. These near 200mph/470bhp racing M1s gave

The original BMW M1 in factory racing colours poses in Munich. Racers used this basic shape augmented by large wings, but on the road the 160mph M1 was a model of exciting stability, capable of reaching 60mph from rest in 5 seconds with traffic docility and excellent handling.

	BMW M1* 1979-80	BMW M535i* 1979-81
Motor		
Cylinders	6 in-line, vertically mounted, iron block, unique 4-valve per cylinder, DOHC alloy head	6 inline, iron block tilted 30° to right. Alloy head engine as per 635/735 series, unmodified, save to fit
Bore x stroke	93.4x84mm	93.4x84mm
Capacity	3453cc	3453cc
Power (bhp)	277 @ 6500rpm	218 @ 5200rpm
Torque	33.6mkg @ 5000rpm	31.6mkg @ 4000rpm
Compression	9:1	9.3:1
Fuel-injection	Mechanical petrol-injection Kugelfischer-Bosch, 46mm throttles (6)	Electronic petrol-injection Bosch L-Jetronic. Automatic cold start choke
Valves	24 valves activated via double overhead camshafts driven by duplex roller chain	V-pattern 12-valve OHV with single overhead camshaft driven by duplex chain
Crankshaft bearings	7	7
Cooling	Water cooling, 2 electric fans & front radiator	Pump, 12 litres of water, viscous fan coupling & front radiator
Lubrication	High pressure, dry sump with 8 litres of oil	Pressurised by Eaton pump, full-flow filter, 6 litres oil
Battery	12v 55ah	12v 55 or 66ah
Generator	Alternator, 910 Watt (65 Amp)	Alternator, 910 Watt (65 Amp)
Ignition	Breakerless, digital electronic Magneti-Marelli flywheel triggered	Breakerless, transistorised
Transmission	North-South mid-engine, inline ZF 5-speed transaxle	Front engine, split propshaft rear drive, 5-speed Sport box
Clutch	Fichtel & Sachs, 2-dry plates; hydraulic action	Fichtel & Sachs single dry plate
Gearchange	Centre, floor with linkage back to transaxle	Floor, central lever
Ratios	1st, 2.42 2nd, 1.61 3rd, 1.14 4th, 0.846 5th, 0.704	1st, 3.717 2nd, 2.403 3rd, 1.766 4th, 1.263 5th, 1.00
Final drive	4.22 (40% limited slip differential)	3.25 or 3.07
Bodywork	Steel, mixed type chassis construction with glassfibre Giugiaro-styled 2-door, 2-seat body; slatted back window	Unitary construction 5-series with 4 doors & sports seating (front). Plastic spoilers front & deformable rear spoiler.
Front suspension	Unequal length A-arms, light alloy hub carriers. Bilstein dampers with concentric coils & threaded height adjustment 23mm front roll bar	MacPherson struts with coil springs, supplementary springs & gas-pressurised damper & anti-roll, anti-dive
Rear suspension	Unequal length A-arms, light alloy hub carriers with Bilstein coil spring/damper units, adjustable for height. 19mm rear anti-roll bar	Semi-trailing arms, gas-telescopic dampers, coil springs, rubber supplementary springs and rear anti-roll bar
Steering	Rack & pinion, unassisted	Power assisted ZF recirculating ball, as for 528i
Footbrake	4-wheel ventilated discs with twin circuit hydraulic operation. Power-assisted, rear pressure limiter. 4 piston front calipers	4-wheel discs, front vented with diagonally split twin circuits, power-assisted hydraulics + wear and over-boost sensors. 4 piston front calipers
Brake sizes	Front 300mmx32mm discs Rear 297mmx26mm discs	Front 280mm discs Rear 272mm discs
General data		
Wheelbase	2560mm	2636mm
Track (front/rear)	1550/1576mm	1422/1470mm
Length, width & height	4360/1824/1140mm	4620/1690/1425mm
Rims	Unique, alloy, 8 in x 16 in (R) 7 in x 16 in (F)	6½J x 14 BBS Mahle alloys
Tyres	203/55 VR-16 (F): 225/50 VR-16 (R)	195/70 VR 14
Turning circle	13.0 metres	11.2 metres
Vehicle weight	1300kg	1430kg
Top speed	162mph	139mph
0-62mph	5.6 sec	7.5 sec
Litres/100km (city)	19.6 (14.4mpg)	19.3 (14.6mpg)
Fuel tank	2 x 58 litres (25.5 galls)	70 litres (15.4 galls)

*It should be noted that BMW Motorsport GmbH is a separate company within BMW. From time to time they made specials for their own use, eg: 3-litre engine in 5-series then 3.3 and 3.5-litre which led to production of their ideas. The only vehicles listed here are those made in genuine series and prefixed by the ''M'' (for Motorsport) symbol.

title wins as "Procar Champion" to double World Champion Niki Lauda and 1981 World Champion Nelson Piquet.

Although this form of racing effectively filled in the gap before enough cars could be made by Baur for international homologation, by the time the 400 were made Neerpasch had left BMW and Motorsport was headed by Dieter Stappert. The young Austrian sensibly deflected the company course to completing their 1½-litre turbo engine for Formula One GP racing instead of selling it to Talbot.

Thus the M1 entered the eighties with an uncertain future. Series production ended in December 1980 though Baur did make a few more to special order, and BMW backed even more sophisticated versions for Group C racing. A total of 450 were made.

Originally BMW told Werner Oswald that there would be three versions: the first with a normal 3½-litre injected engine was never built. The 227bhp roadgoing 24 valve motor of 3453cc was used for road cars, mounted North-South in front of the rear axle with its five speed ZF transaxle behind. Original pricing was simply "over 100,000 Dm" – in the middle of 1980 such cars were selling for over £20,000 in Britain. The third engine option for competition was originally going to be the double turbo 3.2-litre unit (as in CSL of 1976) – which should have provided at least 800bhp. Over a 1000 horsepower was talked of and this was not unreasonable, though reliability was another question! In fact the twin turbo motor was not used by the works: Schnitzer of Freilassing used much of the technology and some of the parts BMW had already prepared (enough to make ten such racing motors in Munich, prior to the F1 decision).

The further sophisticated, and considerably lighter Ground Effect developments by March for the American racing scene were powered by normally aspirated 3½-litre engines with 24 valve head.

In Pro-Car racing form, equivalent to Group 4, the M1s sported large rear aerofoils and 480bhp racing sixes. The most expensive one-make racing series of all time ran from 1980-81, taking in exotic GP venues like this one: Monaco.

Inside the roadgoing M1 a large number of production parts from other BMWs appeared, but the cockpit still had character and a clear instrument layout, including the 280km/h (174mph) speedometer!

The M1 road car had the tremendously flexible and powerful four valve per cylinder version of the 3.5-litre engine. Developed by Paul Rosche's team at BMW Motorsport this unit provided 160mph and stunning acceleration that has yet to be equalled by another production BMW.

Into the eighties as a prospering independent

Bayerischen Motoren Werke engineered their way into the eighties with a growing reputation for innovation as well as public approbation of BMW's solid six-cylinder production engines for all four model ranges. In general the growing reputation for exploring new avenues came from their work on the company's traditional *forte*: engines. By 1982 the 1979 alliance with Daimler and Steyr in Austria was beginning to produce the first BMW-Steyr diesel engines with Ford an already committed customer and BMW themselves looking confidently toward the arrival of the M60-based (that is the 3-series small six, for want of a better instant definition) turbocharged diesels for their own use. Also available in the 1982 model year was the Eta engine for the American market. Installed in the 525e this 2693cc motor provided only 121bhp (SAE), but was designed to meet all the emission and environmental challenges posed by the American market, making greater use of a second stage in the Motronic engine electronics management system. Features included fuel cut-off on over-run above 960rpm for the Bosch L-Jetronic system and exceptional mpg returns.

By the eighties BMW were a lot more open about the research projects they were engaged in as well. Looks into their aerodynamic future were allowed. A wind tunnel was not operational within the company until 1980: before that they had to use whatever facilities could be rented from other manufacturers so the first truly aerodynamic production BMWs were the Summer 1981 5-series. BMW would also show – and in some cases let selected journalists drive cars equipped with development engines, like the diesels (which received very favourable previews) or the projected cylinder cut-out engines for greater economy on a light throttle opening. The majority of this work was the result of the rewarding labour put in at BMW's Research and Development centre. Located at Ismaning on the outskirts of Munich, the site also houses the modern wind tunnel and a useful test track facility.

Business – more production and takeovers

Although we have referred to BMW's growing reputation for engineering innovation it was a paradox of the company's 1982 position that the models offered to the public faithfully reflected the business management style established by Eberhard von Kuenheim and the background Quandt majority shareholding: solidly conservative. However, a look at the record since Werner Oswald's original work was completed shows a picture of steady progress. In 1979 the company could report, "BMW AG once again succeeded in improving the preceding year's results in all of our business activities: production increased by 5% to a total of 337,000 units, thus ensuring that all of our production facilities were used to the full." That production broke down to 162,000 domestic sales (+3%) and 173,000 export (+5%) with America, Great Britain and the Far East as important major customers. Britain took a particularly high proportion of the expensive six-cylinder models.

In spite of production restrictions at the Berlin motorcycle factory (owing to a modernisation programme) *BMW Motorrad GmbH* sold 33,000 examples of R45, R65 and R100, plus a few older stock models– a third more bikes than they sold in 1978. Because of intense Japanese competition the motorcycle market was regarded as the toughest, reflected in German home sales of 8,758 and exports of 18,581 in 1979.

BMW could then report construction of the engine factory, owned 50% by the Bavarians and 50% by Steyr-Daimler-Puch, "was continued according to plan," and that they had acquired the import and distribution organisation for BMW cars in Britain from TKM. The same pattern of acquisition from private enterprises has also been followed in Japan (1981) and Australia (1980) in recent years, following the precedent of America and the main European export markets.

At the close of 1979 BMW could report a record turnover of 6,560 million Dm in Germany (+10.1% over 1978) and a near 13% improvement in worldwide turnover too, with the rider: "profits have also improved accordingly."

All this was achieved by a workforce that was steadily growing. In 1978 they had 35,171 employees in Germany: the following year it was 36,777 with nearly 42,000 employed worldwide.

For 1980 the economic conditions could hardly have been worse around the world, but BMW responded by exporting more while the home market took less. Total production from 37,246 employees in Germany (43,241 Worldwide) was slightly up at 339,232 units. The home market took over 13 per cent less (140,772) while exports were a strong 58 per cent of production at 198,460 cars (+14.8%). The best part of 1000 new jobs had been created in the overall organisation at a time when redundancies were the watchword of the motor industry. Motorcycles continued a sales expansion in Germany and overseas with 29,263 made and nearly 10,000 of those going to the German home market, showing that European manufacturers *can* face up to the Japanese, *if* they select the right area of the market and ensure the product has a discernible customer advantage.

Recent production landmarks include over 700,000 of the old 5-series from October 1972 to April 1981 and the manufacture of half a million 3-series cars in 40 months of production. In fact the 3-series showed signs of hitting the million mark before being phased out in favour of a more aerodynamic model in the Autumn of 1982.

Motorsport

In the field of motorsport, after their clearcut policy of supporting saloon car racing in the sixties and seventies,

BMW appeared to lose their way on the international front in the early eighties. The end of Jochen Neerpasch's reign at BMW Motorsport caused a lot of this, for Jochen had dictated a policy of racing sports cars at the highest levels (the M1) whilst selling the BMW 1.5-litre, four-cylinder turbo engine to Talbot.

When Neerpasch left, to run the Talbot F1 effort, former *Powerslide* editor, Dieter Stappert, took over the sporting reins at the Preussenstrasse, Munich (tucked in behind the BMW HQ and the 3-series factories) and he passionately and successfully argued with the directors that BMW should keep their own Formula 1 engine instead of selling it to Talbot. The Neerpasch policy was reversed and the 1.5-litre turbo engine—a development based partially on existing BMW technology gathered in America with McLaren (320i-turbo) and in European Formula 2 Championship racing—was further developed by a team headed by Paul Rosche. Following a deal with the Brabham team in England the engine was first seen in public (rated at 577bhp at 9,500rpm) powering Nelson Piquet's Brabham in practice for the British GP. The date was July 17, 1981, and the engine was quick enough to provide third fastest time behind the Renaults— but not as fast as it had been running earlier, so it was not raced until the following year. World Champion (1981) Piquet retained links with BMW throughout 1980-81, driving the M1 successfully in association with Hans Stuck but the F1 engine was not used again for World Championship GPs until 1982, when Brabham were again the contracted recipients. The first Brabham-BMW F1 victory came from Piquet at the June 12, 1982, Canadian GP in Montreal.

On other motorsport fronts BMW continued into the eighties with the supply of Formula 2 engines to March, having first won the European title with the Bicester-based concern in 1973, and last won that title powering Corrado Fabi's 1982 March. Over 500 of the 310+bhp 2-litre engines had been supplied by 1981 under the coding M12. In sports car racing there were a number of developments with March, but the impetus went out of these when BMW in Munich found themselves unable to support the fuel consumption proposals emanating from Paris for international long distance sports car events. Prior to these protracted and muddled decisions being issued, the BMW 3½-litre, 24-valve engine had looked a good prospect in specially designed March monocoque chassis such as the M1C (for Group C, the homologated sporting category they were built for).

Management recognition

Perhaps the most adequate tribute paid to the company, from those who should know, came when Eberhard von Kuenheim won the 1981 title "Manager of the Year" awarded by a panel of 20 leading German journalists specialising in economics.

It was a powerful endorsement of a company that, 22 years earlier, looked like becoming a hopeless bankrupt, or a division of Mercedes-Benz!

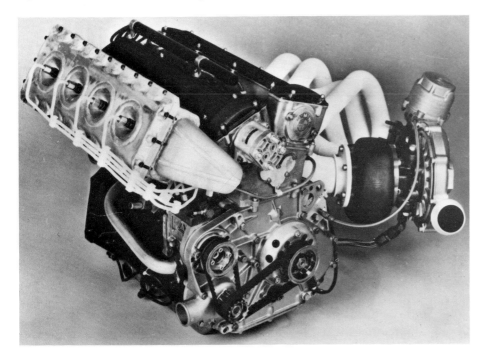

The new 3-series for 1983 still bears a striking resemblance to the original model despite its new body. All versions of the new model will have improved performance and better fuel economy. In the future the new 3-series will bring the option of four-doors – opening to a new sector of the market.

The four-cylinder BMW Grand Prix engine used a wide range of BMW parts and experience in its development, including the 1500 iron block (lightened externally) and much of the Formula 2 four valve per cylinder technology in its gear-driven-DOHC cylinder head. Power was always quoted below 600bhp in racing trim, but by the Summer of 1982 there were reports of up to 650bhp being available for rapid practice laps. The engine made its Brabham debut in the British GP at Silverstone in 1981, and won its first GP the following year in Canada.

185

BMW and the USA

Today and yesterday

"Unrestrained joy, unstinting praise. Turn your hymnals to 2002. David E. Davis, Jr. blows his mind on the latest from BMW." That was the wholehearted welcome *Car & Driver* accorded the BMW 2002 when it arrived in the USA, and that kind of enthusiasm has survived to the present day, despite the penalties of extra weight and lower engine power that BMW, along with every other motor manufacturer, has had to face in the land where legislation on emission and auto safety is king.

The 2002 was something of a turning point when it arrived in the USA in 1968. It had been designed specifically for the US market, mating the 02 series body with the 1990cc engine designed for BMW's larger cars, but within months it also went on sale in Europe too. Before the 2002 there were American BMWs, but after it increasing legislation forced BMW to supply unique products to the USA, a process that is continued today with just one type from each of the four model ranges being offered in US "Federal" trim.

Although BMWs had been imported into the States for many years, the man who really got everything pointing in the direction of organised sales and dealer outlets was Maximilian E. Hoffman, an American-domiciled Austrian who had also imported Mercedes before taking on BMW in 1950. By 1973, with the largely enthusiastic support of the press and public, Hoffman was selling nearly 13,700 BMWs a year (about the number BMW sold in Britain in 1980: in 1981 the UK took an amazing 17,006 units!) but that was to be the peak of private enterprise. BMW North America was created—after a legal battle with Hoffman—to take over the importation and sales during 1974. It only took until 1977 for them to be knocking on the door of 30,000 US sales. In the eighties the USA remains BMW's largest export market,

but one that requires quite a lot of expensive tailoring in order to legally sell their cars.

For cars imported into the USA the first year that emission laws started to bite was 1968. That was part of the reason that the single carburettor 2002 became a more attractive proposition in the USA than elsewhere, a kind of prompt to BMW to do something they would probably (given their penchant for using just about every engine in every model) have done anyway. Yet, when that 100bhp combination hit America it became a legend amonst enthusiasts, lasting as the best-selling model until 1977, when the 320i made a somewhat belated appearance. The 2002 was imported from the sixties until the 1974 model season in mildly modified form. Then a special version had to be created to comply with safety and emission requirements. This Federal 2002 had a rating of 98bhp (SAE) and weighed 2460lb instead of the European's 2185lb, thanks to extra safety equipment like the cumbersome bumpers. Officially the result was a top speed of 104mph and 0-60mph in 12.3s instead of the European's near 110mph maximum and a 0-60mph time of 11 seconds or less. For one model year (1974) the Americans were allowed 2002 Tii, which was a sensation, but then it was back to the Federal 2002 as the only option until the close of 1976.

From 1977 onward a '320i' had been offered. It started as a 2-litre fuel-injection model, with 110bhp (SAE) for all states but California, their more stringent laws lopping another 5bhp from the total. As the 3-series was already a heavier car than 02, performance was not scintillating but the public have kept faith, even to today's 1.8-litre '320i'.

Other unique BMWs for the USA included the "Bavaria" successor to 2500 and 2800 which was imported in almost original form, as was the 2800 CS. The Bavaria was an especially packaged 2800 for the American market, the badge so popular that you will see it today on some *'Muncheners'* own cars that have no relation to that 1971 offering! It was with the 1972 season, and the advent of 3-litre sixes, that European and American specification started to sharply differ. The first step was a lower CR than offered in Europe and the ability to run on regular fuel. The USA 3-litre was rated at 170bhp, instead of 180bhp and used a numerically raised final drive. The Bavaria package wrapped around the 3-litre carburated engine and then an injected successor continued until 1975, when the model was still reckoned to be capable of 120mph on 176bhp in place of the European 200 horsepower. Incidentally it is interesting to note that the three-sphere combustion chambers of the six-cylinder engines inspired a short emission renaissance in 2002 power levels when such chambers were used within the four-cylinder for the 1973 model year, which made the 98bhp power rating a more equivalent figure to that of the European 100bhp motors.

For 1975 the 3-litre CS Coupe had to be dropped in America owing to the US safety tests involving dropping an inverted car "on its head." As the Coupe passed from the US scene BMW decided on a different tack and, for the 1975 model year they wrapped up their 1972-introduced 5-series for the Atlantic crossing. This was an attempt to specify a car exactly to American requirements, amounting to a 528 (then only a recent European introduction in 165bhp carburated trim) and a fuel-injection 3-litre engine with thermal reaction and exhaust gas recirculation emission control devices, which provided 176bhp, as for later Bavarias. The increased weight of safety equipment that American versions carried meant that the 530i was in the same performance league as the European 528i, though the tougher Californian regulations meant an even heavier appetite for fuel and less performance.

From 1978 onward the USA was served with a BMW Coupe once more: the 1978 model introduced with 177bhp from 3210cc (633 CSi) enough to provide 0-60mph in 8½ seconds and 125mph according to the manufacturers, despite the enormous 3,500 plus pounds kerb weight it was forced to carry.

The 7-series also arrived in the USA from 1978 onward, utilising the same 3210cc/177bhp Bosch L-Jetronic injection layout.

BMW 320i USA (1982 model year)
BMW 528e USA (1982 model year)
BMW 733i USA (1982 model year)
BMW 633 CSi USA (1982 model year)

The current Federal range of BMWs is aggressively merchandised and occasionally deceptive in nomenclature.

The 320i is the most confusing, packaging a number of different 3-series features into a shell that has the quadruple headlamp look of the current six-cylinder models. However, underneath the hood is a beautifully presented four-cylinder, born of a tradition that started in the early sixties 1500, but brought into US trim with Bosch K-Jetronic injection, a three-way catalyst with Lambda sensor and no need for any other emission control hardware.

Marketed as "The BMW 320i, the car that has inspired a generation of imitators," this 320 is actually a 1766cc device. It is a significant six inches longer, thanks to US bumpers front and rear that are mounted on hydraulic shock absorbers, and is therefore rather heavier than its European sisters.

Inside, the car looks very similar to the European models, though a sharp eye on the instrumentation shows a speedometer reading to just 80mph, with the overall 55mph limit marked in red. Unlike the bigger six-cylinder models there is no dashboard reminder that these models for the USA run on 91 RON unleaded fuel. Standard equipment is based on the overdrive 5-speed gearbox with a three speed automatic as an option. With the manual gearbox acceleration from rest to 60mph is said to occupy 8.1 seconds ...

Since the Americans taught us the option game, it's not surprising to see that BMW took it back to its inventors with a vengeance. Tilt and slide sunroof, air-conditioning, a selection of sound equipment and multi-spoke alloy roadwheels were all offered as options. There was also a complete sporting S-package that provided better handling through a thicker front anti-roll bar and the addition of a rear anti-sway bar. Also included was a limited slip differential, alloy wheels along 635 CSi optional lines (but 5½in by 13), a larger front spoiler, Recaro sports seating, three spoke sports steering wheel and so on.

320i. Despite its four headlamps the USA version of the 320 has a four-cylinder engine — not the six which Europeans would expect. Also, the '320' tag is misleading as the engine is of 1766cc. Nevertheless, the 320i is still very much a performance car.

528e. The 'e' is for 'eta' — a unique package of 2.7-litre six-cylinder engine and "tall" gearing to provide this model with performance, refinement and economy.

633 CSi (top) and 733i. These are the only 'big' BMWs available in the USA – both sport the 3210cc sohc six-cylinder engine and identical gearing and are very fully equipped.

Brief specification: 320i

Engine: Four-cylinder inline SOHC with alloy cylinder head and five bearing crankshaft. Bore and stroke, 89x71mm for 1766cc. Bosch fuel-injection, 8.8:1 CR and transistorised ignition. 101 SAE net bhp at 5800rpm; 100lb.ft torque (SAE) at 4500rpm. 65 Ampere, 910 Watt alternator.

Transmission: Standard five speed manual with hydraulic single plate clutch and ratios of: 1st, 3.68; 2nd, 2.002; 3rd, 1.33; 4th, direct (1.0); 5th, 0.806. Final drive, 3.91. Automatic fluid clutch with torque converter option and oil cooler, ratios of: 1st, 2.73; 2nd, 1.56; 3rd, direct (1.0). Final drive, 3.64.

Chassis: MacPherson strut front suspension with anti-roll bar and rear semi-trailing arm with helical springs mounted over shock absorbers with Teflon-coated pistons. Rack and pinion steering, 21.1:1 overall ratio. Steel 5½Jx13 H2 steel wheels with 185/70 radials.

Brakes: Servo-assisted twin circuit braking system with rear pressure regulator and 10.04in diameter front disc, 9.84in rear drums.

The Eta arrives

As before the 5-series model for the USA contained something different for 1982. Using the Greek letter, Eta, BMW aimed for an inline six-cylinder engine (this one of a unique 2.7-litres) to provide "a considerable decrease in fuel consumption and a far lower noise level while the standard of performance remains the same." Design features included "considerably increased compression ratio," (which was 9:1) and an accent on lowering power losses through a lower rpm scale mated to revised 'long' transmission ratios. Engine torque at low and medium speeds was therefore the prime consideration. BMW felt that the finished result was good for a 15% reduction in petrol consumption. Electronics, including the Digital Motor Electronics system with fuel over-run cut off, and a computer modified to take account of the Lambda sensor readings allowed even this comparatively big six to go to America with only the 3-way catalyst and Lambda sensor as emission control devices.

Again the interior was similar to that of European BMWs, but the instrumentation reflected the Eta motor's lower rpm abilities, redlined at 4900rpm with a caution from 4700rpm. There was an unleaded fuel reminder and the European service Interval Indicator of the new 5-series was a notable absentee, as were the larger outer headlamps of Europe.

A high level of equipment was standard, including four speaker radio/cassette player, alloy wheels and electric operation of both sunroof and side glass. Cruise control was also standard. For Americans the 528 grew to 188.4ins overall length instead of 181.9ins of the new 528i. The chassis equipment followed European lines with four wheel disc braking and the modification of front and rear suspension found in 528i. Acceleration of the manual version was quoted at 6.6s for the 0-60mph sprint.

Brief specification: 528e

Engine: In-line six-cylinder SOHC with toothed belt drive, alloy cylinder head and seven bearing crankshaft. Bore and stroke, 84x81mm for 2693cc. Bosch L-Jetronic fuel-injection, Digital Motor Electronic, transistorised ignition. 121bhp (SAE net) @ 4250rpm: 170lb.ft torque @ 3250rpm (SAE). 64 Ampere, 910 Watt alternator.

Transmission: Standard five-speed manual with hydraulic single plate clutch and ratios of: 1st, 3.822; 2nd, 2.202; 3rd, 1.398; 4th, direct (1.0); 5th, 0.813. Final drive: 2.93:1. Automatic three-speed with fluid clutch and torque converter (optional) with ratios of: 1st, 2.478; 2nd, 1.478; 3rd, direct (1.0). Final drive, as manual.

Chassis: MacPherson strut front with double pivot and positive kingpin offset, anti-roll bar, eccentric coil springs and urethane bump stops. Semi-trailing arm rear suspension with rear anti-roll bar and helical coil springs, plus 528i linkages. Road speed sensitive power steering with 16.2:1 overall ratio. Alloy 6.5in rim by 14in diam alloy wheels with 195/70 radials.

Brakes: Twin circuit, servo-assisted with pressure regulating device at rear and brake lining wear sensor.

Four wheel disc brakes of 11.8in diameter with ventilation slots at front only and mechanical drum handbrake for rear.

The big sixes

From 1978 onward the 3210cc version of the classic BMW chain-driven SOHC six was the power train behind 733i and 633 CSi, the only big BMWs offered to the USA. Despite an identical 181bhp and the same ratios of gearbox (manual or automatic) and final drive, the two big BMWs nevertheless maintained a slight performance differential; the Coupe's gross vehicle weight of 4300lb providing 0-50mph in 6.35 seconds in manual trim and the 733i performing the same trick in 6.7 seconds. Both these cars look rather odd to European eyes at first glance inside with their mandatory 80 and 85mph speedometers.

Length of the 633 CSi for the USA went up to 193.8in compared to 187.2in of European 6-series, while the 733i measured 197.4in instead of 191.5in. Both models coped with emissions via the digital electronics system, 3-way catalyst and Lambda sensor.

Standard 6-series equipment included cruise control, but only with the automatic option, while it was available for both gearboxes on 733i. Generally the 7-series went to America slightly better equipped, but both models had built-in air-conditioning, alloy wheels and central locking, the 7-series offering a slight bonus with the clever computer as standard. In both cases the only real options were automatic transmission and a limited slip differential.

Brief specification: 633 CSi & 733i

Engine: In-line six-cylinder with chain-driven SOHC and alloy cylinder head plus seven bearing crankshaft. Bore and stroke, 89x86mm for a capacity of 3210cc. Bosch L-Jetronic fuel-injection. Digital Motor Electronics, transistorised ignition. 181bhp (SAE net) at 6000rpm: 195lb.ft torque at 4000rpm. 65 Ampere, 910 Watt alternator.

Transmission: Standard five-speed manual overdrive with hydraulic single plate clutch, torsional dampers and automatic adjustment.

Ratios: 1st, 3.822:1; 2nd, 2.202; 3rd, 1.398; 4th, direct (1.0); 5th, 0.813. Final drive, 3.25:1. Automatic three-speed with fluid clutch and torque converter (optional) ratios: 1st, 2.478; 2nd, 1.478; 3rd, direct (1.0). Final drive, as manual.

Chassis: Aside from 5-series original derivation for 6-series, principles remained common of MacPherson strut front semi-trailing arm rear, but 633 lacked 733's double front pivot layout and small positive kingpin offset. Similarly both had speed-related power steering but the 6-series had 16:9:1 ratio and the 7-series 17:6:1. Alloy 6½in rims, 14in diameter, wheels carry 195/70 radials (633) and 205/70 (733i).

Brakes: Both had twin circuit systems with pressure regulators but 7-series had an hydraulic booster with integrated pump and pressure booster for the same vented, four piston front discs (11.0in diameter) as 633 CSi, but at the back 6-series had vented 10.7in units, while 733i had floating caliper automatic adjustment, 11in diameter, solid rear discs.